# Married Men Coming Out

The Ultimate Guide to Becoming
the Man You Were Born to Be

David Christel

David Christel

www.TheEssentialWord.com
info@TheEssentialWord.com

Married Men's Coming Out blog:
www.theessentialword.com/#!coming-out-as-a-married-man/c1hpu/3

*Married Men Coming Out*
*The Ultimate Guide to Becoming the Man You Were Born to Be*

© Copyright 2012, David Christel. All rights reserved.

Cover design: David Christel
Cover Photo: Chromatica, iStockPhoto, File #8108166

Back cover photo "multi-colored smoke": Onur Ersin, Dreamstime, File #11806439
Back Cover "GAY": Serdar Tibet, Dreamstime, File #16481335

Interior book design: David Christel

No part of this book may be reproduced or transmitted in any form or by any means, electronic or mechanical, including photocopying, recording, or by any information storage and retrieval system, without permission from the author, except for the inclusion of brief quotations in review.

Printed in the United States of America

Kindle Direct Publishing

ISBN: 978-0-578-40057-0

Library of Congress Control Number on File.

\*\*\* The names of individuals mentioned in stories and examples
have been changed to protect their privacy. \*\*\*

# Married Men Coming Out

# What Others are Saying about *Married Men Coming Out*

"Having gone through coming out while in an opposite sex marriage twice, I wish I'd had this resource available so that I may not have made the same mistake twice, hurting many people along the way. David Christel has done his research well and covers most potential scenarios with great clarity. Utilizing excellent anecdotal information, this book is written mostly for gay men who are married to women, but can be very helpful for wives or families who are willing to have open dialogue about their situations. *Married Men Coming Out* is not something that can be read only once, but it is a practical reference manual that can be used throughout the process of coming out and dealing with marriage and family issues through the journey."

~ John J. Smid
Formerly married gay man
Former Exodus International Board member
Former Director for Love In Action for 22 years

"David Christel's personal stories from a diverse range of gay men in heterosexual marriages and his discussion of constructive ways for gay married men to work through the excruciatingly hard task of coming out to themselves and others is right on, fitting all that I have observed and researched over the past thirty years. Christel presents not only the extraordinary diversity of individual experiences, but also the multiple audiences to whom gay married men need to come out, ranging from immediate families and outside contacts to the gay community. Especially noteworthy is his sensitive counsel about constructive ways to disclose to one's wife and to try to resolve post-disclosure relationship and family issues together."

~ Amity P. Buxton, PhD
Author, *The Other Side of the Closet:
The Coming Out Crisis for Straight Spouses and Families* and
*Unseen-Unheard: Straight Spouses from Trauma to Transformation*
Founder, Straight Spouse Network

"Thank you for the opportunity to read *Married Men Coming Out*! I thoroughly enjoyed it and believe it will be a valuable resource for many men who, like me, have lived or are still living the story. As a practical guide presented in a straightforward manner, MMCO offers support and direction without getting mired in the valuable, but theoretical, thickets while, at the same time, encouraging men to explore those thickets as they get their feet on the ground. The personal stories serve to reinforce the book's underlying premise that many men have succeeded in coming out of heterosexual marriages with their psyches, their personalities, and — in many instances — their friendships and relationships altered, but intact. The thematic balance between the difficulties and the rewards rang true for my journey and those I observed in the lives of a number of men in the ManKind Project."

~ Robert G. Powell
Former Chairman
Charter Lifetime Member
ManKind Project USA

"At last! A book that sheds light on the predicament of gay men whose journey of self-acceptance takes place within their heterosexual marriage. *Married Men Coming Out!* explores the struggle and resulting journey, which can lead to the serenity of knowing one's inner and outer lives coincide. David Christel's work draws on the experiences of those who have walked this path, who have experienced pain, but who now possess the possibility of authenticity that becoming true to oneself implies."

~ Mark Tedesco
Author, *That Undeniable Longing: My Road to and from the Priesthood*

"My personal experience of being married sixteen years with two children, coming out, and eventually telling my story in my autobiography has brought me in contact with hundreds of people in similar situations seeking support and answers. I have no doubt that those beginning this process or in the midst of it will benefit greatly from Mr. Christel's book as they work through the layers and potential consequences of truth telling and living authentically."

~ Anthony Venn-Brown
Founder and CEO of
Ambassadors & Bridge Builders International
Author, *A Life of Unlearning*
Twice voted one of The 25 Most Influential
Gay and Lesbian Australians

"David does a great job at helping you face your fears, and above all, knowing that many others have walked in your steps and that you are truly not alone. We all make mistakes, and this book helped me realize how very unique we are, yet very similar. Time and again, I caught myself saying, "I did that, too!" Depending on your relationship with your (ex) wife, you may recommend she, too, read the book. It will help her to have a better understanding of your journey."

~ Former Rep. Mike Fleck
Pennsylvania

"More than a comprehensive resource, David Christel's book is comparable to a life coach helping gay men in heterosexual marriages navigate the challenging process of coming out and exploring the possibilities of living a life true to who they were born to be. The author leaves no stone unturned as he provides deep insights from personal experience, psychology, sociology and history, providing a step-by-step manual that outlines a healthy path forward amidst potential pitfalls. Ultimately, the reader is gently guided toward connecting with his true identity, history, and community. *Married Men Coming Out* will make a huge difference for many!"

~ Rev. Frank Schaefer
Pastor, social justice activist
Author, *Defrocked: How A Father's Act of Love Shook the United Methodist Church*

"For years, I've written books and articles about the other side of this closet, the plight of the straight wives. David Christel's excellent book balances that equation, sensitively presenting complex issues, motivations, fears, and successes of gay married men coming out — while causing the least amount of pain possible for everyone involved. It's a superb handbook for closeted gay men seeking authenticity."

~ Carol Grever
Author, *My Husband is Gay* and
*When Your Spouse Comes Out*
www.straightspouseconnection.com

"Every married man's experience of coming out is different. It can be frightening or heartwarming, confusing or enlightening, repressive or liberating. In fact, it can be all of these at the same time. In *Married Men Coming Out*, David Christel has distilled the wide range of emotions and experiences one might expect when coming out. In its pages will be found nuggets of information and suggestions about how a married man going through the coming out experience can deal with these issues. As one who was formerly married myself, I know that I would be turning to its pages time and again for guidance."

~ Jim Kolbe
Former Member of Congress

"Having traversed this road less traveled, I only wish I'd had this type of resource in my hands when I came out in 1999 after being married for 13 years to a wonderful woman, and fathering two beautiful daughters. They say it gets easier, and it does, but not without the right type of guidance and support. Christel has outlined the most common challenges and provided solid steps for navigating each step of the coming out process. I am very excited to have this book at my disposal to recommend to my coming out clients. If you're questioning if you can take this journey out of the closet, trust that you can in your own way, in your own time, and use *Married Men Coming Out* as a positive tool for helping you come into your truth."

~ Rick Clemons, Motivational Speaker, Coming Out Coach
Author, *Frankly My Dear I'm Gay:
A Late Bloomers Guide to Coming Out*

"Not many days pass in any given week or month that I don't hear from some man or some woman somewhere in the world who is facing the daunting task of coming out, and is trying to figure out how in the world to do it. Coming out certainly is something that changes a same-sex loving person's life forever, but it's especially challenging and life-altering for people who are or who have been married, because the decision to finally do it affects so many people on so many levels. I know in my own case that when I got married the first time, it was in a sincere attempt to change my innate orientation, which was something that I had been aware of for practically my whole life. But I realized early on that my basic wiring was never going to be re-routed, in spite of two (eventual) marriages, and fathering four children. Married people who come out are officially parting with the illusion, once and for all, that somehow their sexual/romantic orientation can or ever will be changed, and are embracing the whole truth and nothing but the truth for the first time in their life.

"Coming out doesn't necessarily make one's life easier, but it definitely makes it better, and *Married Men Coming Out* opens up a path to that which is much better…namely, living an authentic life. David Christel's book is a labor of love that provides a step-by-step 'how-to' for people who are in this situation, and, to my knowledge, is the only such work of its kind. Nothing is more helpful than good advice from someone who has been there and done that, and this is a true self-help book if ever there was one.

"I applaud Mr. Christel for taking on the enormous task of helping out his brothers and sisters in this way. Those of us who have already travelled this road, and understand the unique situation in which married gay people find themselves, salute you!"

~ Jim Swilley
Bishop of Now Ministries
Founder of Church In The Now
Founder of METRON Community
www.churchinthenow.org/#

# Married Men Coming Out

**Other books by David Christel —**

Convergence of Being –
Awakening to the Interconnection of You, Me, and We

Now What?
One Man's Search for a Father

Stimulus Addicted –
America Adrenalizing Out of Control

**Books in the Pipeline —**

The Black Sheep Imperative –
Understanding the Black Sheep in Families
and How They Save Us from Ourselves

Clarissa's Flight
*A children's novel*

A Life of 2 x 4's to the Head –
Wake-up Calls and What to Do About Them

# Married Men Coming Out

## The Ultimate Guide to Becoming the Man You Were Born to Be

David Christel

# Dedication

This book would not have been possible without the courageous men who attended the Married Men's Coming Out Group. They dared to defy socio-cultural and religious conventions to be the men the Divine intended.

To them and all who were and are currently involved in their journey home to authentic selfhood, I dedicate this book. In my eyes and heart, you are heroes, pioneers, models, and educators. The truth has set you free.

# Contents

List of Illustrations .................................................................................. vii
Foreword ................................................................................................. ix
Acknowledgments ................................................................................... xi
Introduction ......................................................................................... xiii
**Chapter 1:** Coming to Terms with Being Gay ......................................... 1
    Finally Admitting You're Gay ... At Least to Yourself ...................... 3
    What Have You Just Done?! ............................................................ 7
    Discovering Your Gay Roots ............................................................ 8
    Getting to Know You ..................................................................... 12
**Chapter 2:** Communication ................................................................ 17
    Communicating with Self .............................................................. 20
    Communicating with Your Family ................................................ 21
**Chapter 3:** The Next Step: Coming Out to Your Immediate Family ...... 29
    Coming Out to Your Spouse ......................................................... 32
    Coming Out to Your Children ...................................................... 47
    Coming Out to Siblings, Parents, and Other Relatives .................. 57
    The Emotional Effects of Coming Out for You ............................ 62
**Chapter 4:** Coming Out to Others ...................................................... 65
    Coming Out to Friends, Co-workers, and Other Important People .... 66
    Being "Outed" by Your Spouse ..................................................... 76
    Going Public ................................................................................. 79
**Chapter 5:** Issues within the Family ................................................... 81
    The Specter of Separation and Divorce ......................................... 82
    Parent/Child Dynamics ................................................................. 84
    Child Custody ............................................................................... 87
    Moving Out of the House ............................................................. 90
    Wrangling with Relatives ............................................................... 92
    Marriage ........................................................................................ 92
**Chapter 6:** Identity: The Path of Self-Acceptance ............................... 97
    Oh, to be "Normal" .................................................................... 100
    Self-Reflection = Clarification = Identity .................................... 101

Nurturing #1 .................................................................................. 105
　　Highs and Lows............................................................................. 107
Chapter 7: Loss ...................................................................................... 109
　　Secondary Types of Loss ............................................................. 117
　　Coming Out to Friends, Colleagues, and Clients ..................... 121
　　Losing Home, Job, Career, Lifestyle, Money, Inheritance,
　　　　and Position in Life ............................................................... 125
　　Loss through the Suicide of a Love One................................... 128
Chapter 8: Relationships ...................................................................... 131
　　Relationships: Do You Wanna Dance Under the Moonlight?... 136
　　Chariots of Fire............................................................................ 142
　　Dating Roulette ............................................................................ 149
　　Addicted to Love .......................................................................... 155
Chapter 9: Coming Out in the Gay Community ............................... 165
　　Beyond Baptism............................................................................ 166
　　Homophobia within the Ranks................................................... 170
　　What to do if.… ............................................................................ 173
Chapter 10: The Future ........................................................................ 175
　　On Being a Pioneer...................................................................... 177
　　On Being a Role Model ............................................................... 179
　　On Being an Educator ................................................................. 182
　　Becoming a Part of the Global Community............................. 185
Resources................................................................................................. 187
Appendix A: Gender Identification Options..................................... 197
Appendix B: Archetypes ....................................................................... 199
Appendix C: List of Gay Archetypes................................................... 205
About the Author .................................................................................. 207

# List of Illustrations

Page 9:

    Alsenas, Linas, *Gay America; Struggle for Equality*, Amulet Books, 2008.

    Nickels, Thom, *Out in History*, STARbooks Press, 2010.

    Aldrich, Robert, *Gay Life and Culture: A World History*, Universe, 2006.

    Marcus, Eric, *Making Gay History: The Half-Century Fight for Lesbian and Gay Equal Rights*, Harper Paperbacks, 2002.

    Book cover from *HOMOSEXUALITY AND CIVILIZATION* by Louis Crompton appears courtesy of Harvard University Press, Copyright (c) 2003 by President and Fellows of Harvard College.

Page 93: Pay Payne, http://patpaynecreatrix.com/

Page 207: Me, the author.

# Foreword

*Former Representative Mike Fleck served 4 terms in the Pennsylvania General Assembly. In December 2012, he came out and at that time was the only sitting republican legislator in the United States. A former Boy Scout Executive, he was married for 10 years.*

On December 1, 2012, I came out publicly. Within hours, my story went viral, bouncing from coast to coast and even abroad. The secret I thought I would carry to my grave was now front page news. By the end of the day, I had over 1,000 e-mails, most of which were from gay men who were, like me, formerly married, or in the process of accepting their sexuality and struggling with the next steps.

Though I was already out to family, friends and my staff, I didn't think coming out publicly would be as liberating as it was, but I was wrong.

Today, I can walk around a free man, no longer faced with the daily fear of not being true to myself. It is a journey — though a very long, hard, and often painful one — that begins with the first step. The fact that you're reading this means you've more than likely started down that same path. No two journeys are alike, but the similarities are uncanny. The one thing you will now need more than ever is support — a good friend, a safe environment and, hopefully, a good therapist. Our journey is not only about acceptance of ourselves, but one of forgiveness, so that we can move on to bigger, better, and fuller lives as the men we are meant to be.

Growing up on Fleck Road in rural Huntingdon County, Pennsylvania, I never thought of myself as gay. Different than the other boys, yes. But gay, no. There were no openly gay people in my neck of the woods and the ones I saw on TV and the news were nothing I could relate to.

Coming to terms with one's sexuality is truly a process that few can possibly understand. Having walked in your shoes, I get it. If you're like me, it's taken you a very long time to get to this point. I, too, got married for many reasons: she was my best friend, I was in love, I wanted a family, the white picket fence. All I had to do was get married and that little gnat humming in my ear would simply go away for good. After all, that's what everyone tells us, right? Just get married.

Now, after all these years, you're coming to terms with who you truly are and it's freaking scary. You feel alone, embarrassed, and full of regret.

First of all, knock it off. Forgive yourself, you're only human. You will survive, but you have to focus on the future and not the past — it's way too easy to get bogged down by our past mistakes.

Hopefully, you have a good therapist; if not, work with one. Find a support group: the sooner you realize you are not alone, the better. Even so, we are men and we think we can fix it. Therefore, many of you will try to go it alone. I know I did. Be aware that this only prolongs the process and could very well destroy you. It's way too easy to numb the pain with alcohol (or insert the vice of your choice), but once you sober up, you realize nothing has changed. Thankfully, I survived and you will, too. Coming out is likely the most difficult decision you will ever face, but rest assured: It does in fact get better.

During my deepest and darkest hours, I searched high and low for a book that I could relate to. Unfortunately, there are few resources out there. That is until now. David Christel's guide is a must read, long overdue, and packed full of helpful tools that will guide you down this scary, yet exciting path in becoming whole again. Life is a journey and it's way too short to not be living as your true self.

At forty years of age, I'm happier than I've ever been and I look forward to each and every day. I know you will benefit from David's years of research and his own personal awareness of what we as gay men face in the world today.

Mike Fleck<br>
February, 2014

# Acknowledgments

First and foremost, I'd like to thank Kurt Buis, PhD who first asked if I'd be interested in facilitating the Married Men's Coming Out Group — just for a year, which seemed a long commitment to me at the time. Six years and over 300 sessions later, who knew?

Secondly, I'd like to thank my own therapist extraordinaire, Chris Mercier. He helped me through personal issues that I could then parlay into becoming an effective listener and facilitator — not to mention the self-exploration I did that helped me resolve some deep-seated pain and misunderstandings about my own life. He was a superb example of conduct, nurturance, intelligence, and heart.

Alan Brown, another therapist with whom I worked, was compelling in his message to me: to take care of myself first. I was so gung ho about facilitating the Men's Group at first that I easily got sucked into its emotional vortex. Alan helped me realize I needed to stay detached while involved.

The 70-some men who came through the Men's Group consistently pushed my personal envelop to see, hear, and feel between the lines. Because of them, I became quite expert at sub-text and body language. They provided an extraordinary tapestry of humankind through which I was better able to understand their individual and group needs, as well as the psychology behind their journeys. And in equal measure, they gave me phenomenal feedback and support, which I will never forget. To each of them, I send all my love and deepest gratitude.

To Rep. Mike Fleck for stepping out on yet another limb: writing his first book foreword. You've done us all proud as a model of courage, a resilient pioneer, and as a forward-looking educator. Upward and onward!

Finally, to my life partner, another married man who has made the journey from two marriages to being a fully-expressed gay man. It was my joy to support him in his journey (he didn't know it, but I just happened to be facilitating the Married Men's Coming Out Group at the time, so he was under my microscope). To him I say, "Now is the grandest of times!"

# Introduction

*Married Men Coming Out* is about the evolution of personal identity when a man who has previously been identified as heterosexual and married finally comes to terms with his true sexuality and chooses to accept, with conviction, who he really is: a gay man.

In our country, this can be one of the most harrowing, challenging, and growthful experiences a man can have. The journey is perceived as being mostly upstream, yet it is required if the individual making the choice is to attain any level of inner peace. It is not a choice that any man would wish upon another man. Any man who has made this transition, though, would be there to support an individual who is tired of living a double life straddling two worlds, each with their ugliness and beauty, and feeling as though they don't fit anywhere.

Different cultures have different attitudes concerning sex and individual identity. In many cultures, homosexuality is taboo, a sin, punishable by death. In some religions, the outcome is eternal damnation. In other cultures, homosexuality is celebrated, considered an important and integral component of cultural and community interaction.

The purpose of this book is not to provide reasons for or against homosexuality. It is a guidebook for those who, having lived a heterosexual lifestyle, realize that they've made an error by denying and suppressing their true identity — being attracted to members of their own sex — and now realize that being married and even having children, they can no longer live a double life. They need to be who and what they truly are: gay.

None of the men in this book ever intended to be a hero or leader or even a role model, but how else could they be perceived: they've denied their real self for many years, they've fought with their inner demons, they've gone against the grain of cultural America and religionists, and they've achieved a level of congruity with themselves that few other people, whether hetero- or homosexual, have achieved, despite the phenomenal forces working against them. They are worthy of tremendous respect and admiration. The world should have such men!

I facilitated the Married Men's Coming Out Group for six years. Each man attended for at least 6 months arriving scared, uncertain about their future, and confused beyond belief. Each was confronted by me and group members with a single question: *"Do you know who you are?"* Through discussion, exploration, intuition, the relating of personal experience and revelation, each man wrestled with the daily issues with which they were confronted. They studied their inner terrain, working on the personality characteristics that come with growth: self-respect, self-worth, honesty, authenticity, sincerity, sensitivity, and integrity. Some of the attributes they accrued in this process were: a higher level of communication, a greater connection with self and others, compassion, unconditional positive regard for others, centeredness, respect for and from others, happiness, and inner peace.

All of this sounds wonderful and complete, but, like any process, it is a life-long study of self with new aspects of personhood to discover, new levels to explore, and deeper life meanings to be ascertained and understood. Though it has been a difficult path for each man, not one they would want to relive, each has accomplished what most people never consider or strive for: the knowledge, acceptance, and living the life that is their unique being. What greater gift can a man give himself and to others but the gift of his true identity?

Married men were and still are coming out of the woodwork to finally be who they truly are. They are no longer willing to compartmentalize their lives, their relationships, and their hearts — no matter what they are told by their religion, state and federal laws, current trends, or social media. This diverse group of over seventy men ranged in age from 21 to 70, parents and non-parents, famous and not famous, newly married or married for decades, familiar with the gay world or terrified of it. Some of the men were even expecting a baby. Whatever the individual's situation, they needed to come out, to live their life in honesty. The Married Men's Coming Out Group was formed out of this need.

At heart, this book is about authenticity, a word that's been prominent in spiritual circles for several decades now. Being a non-denominational term, authenticity is described as: "...having a genuine...authority in opposition to that which is false, fictitious, or counterfeit." All human beings want to be the opposite of false, fictitious or counterfeit, yet the vicissitudes of life are such that we work incredibly hard doing just the opposite. Hence, the need for this book is paramount as we each seek to live *authentically* and in so doing, find some level of inner peace, self-acceptance, integrity, joy, and love. Without this, the world may not evolve to reflect these essential attributes for all of mankind.

*David Christel, 2016*

"My only regret about being gay is that I repressed it for so long.
I surrendered my youth to the people I feared
when I could have been out there loving someone.
Don't make that mistake yourself.
Life's too damn short."

~ Armistead Maupin
Author of the *Tales of the City* series

## Chapter 1

# Coming to Terms with Being Gay

> "The day I married my wife —
> I had sex with a man that night.
> My life is so screwed up!
> I've got an 8-year-old son.
> What am I going to do?
> I don't want to lose him...."
>
> ~ Disclosed by Raphael
> during his intake interview for the
> Married Men's Coming Out Group

In 1995, Raphael came in for an intake interview. He wanted to become a member of the Married Men's Coming Out Group that I was facilitating in San Diego. His story was typical: he'd gone through life with the world expecting him to be a man, which was in part defined by getting married, having children, etc.

So, he got married. He and his wife had one child, who was now eight years old. But, there was another component of his life that he couldn't ignore anymore. He was in tremendous emotional pain and turmoil to the point that he was depressed, considering suicide, and he'd started drinking heavily.

I asked him what the issue was and he sheepishly stated that he was actually gay. I asked how he knew this and he told me his story. I assured him that there were many men in similar situations. He was so relieved to hear he wasn't the only one.

What surprised me about his particular story, though, was the fact that he had sex with a man on his wedding night. Knowing what his inclination was, I asked why he had married. I received the same answer I'd heard countless times: "Because that's what I was supposed to do." Everyone from family to friends to school to church to community was pressuring him, telling him who he should be and what he should do.

Over the 6-year period I'd facilitated this group, I'd listened to the anguished stories and journeys of over 70 men, my heart aching. They described how they felt like hunted animals, that the world could see through their "heterosexual" disguise, and that every day felt like it was going to be the day the shoe might drop.

They argued with God, asking why God had made them this way. Many nights were spent in tears as they fought the urge to find a man, any man. They wanted release, they wanted male companionship — ultimately, their dream was to love and be loved by another man.

One-on-one sessions with these men often involved tears; the pain and fear suppressed over a lifetime finally being given voice. Anger and regret turned faces purple-red with fury at themselves, at loved ones, at the world. Why — why did the world hate them so? What had they done to deserve this life, this hell?

Raphael was deathly afraid his family was going to find out. Originally from Mexico, he felt that all he had to look forward to was religious persecution and hellish bullying from the men in his extended family, possibly getting beat up and even receiving death threats. His greatest fear, though, concerned his son. What if he lost his son? Raphael would kill himself.

Raphael's unfortunate story truly is typical. Men in our culture are not encouraged to get in touch with what they actually desire in life. Instead they are told what is desirable, what they should want, who they should want to be, what feelings they can express, and what is acceptable no matter who they *think* they are.

Personal feelings are beside the point. As a child, you can have feelings and about what you want to be when you grow up — a policeman, fireman, doctor, priest, architect, military man — but not about your sexual identity. It's black and white: you're either a man hooked up with a woman or you're not. If you're not, then you're a disgusting thing called a fag, a queer — which is your one-way ticket to hell.

## *Finally Admitting You're Gay —*
## *At Least to Yourself*

"When you finally come out,
there's a pain that stops,
and you know it will never hurt like that again,
no matter how much you lose or how bad you die."

~ Paul Monette
*Becoming a Man: Half a Life Story*

As Lao-tzu said, "A journey of a thousand miles begins with a single step." Truly, the first step on the journey to being our authentic self is the most terrifying. We have no idea what our journey will look like, with what we'll be faced, what will be demanded of us, who will be involved, what will be lost, or even if something will be gained. Will we survive the journey? We do know one thing, though, that what will be gained is priceless. No matter how heartrending and frightening the envisioned journey, we must still take that faltering first step.

"Fags are Beasts"
"God Hates Fags"
"Homo Love is Sin"
"God is Your Enemy"
"You're Going to Hell"
"Thank God for AIDS"
"Your Doom is Coming"
"America is a Fag-enabling Nation"
"Homosexuality Makes God Throw Up"
"Homosexuals are Possessed by Demons"

~ Anti-gay placards

Despite some groups' passionate opposition to homosexuality and the intense pressure from childhood to fit within other people's comfort zones, men are still discovering at some point that they are different and that they need to finally act on their feelings.

The journey many men take to finally admit they're gay and live as a gay person can be harrowing. The family and community dictates, as well as the edicts and diatribes by various religions can create a living hell for the boy/man who realizes that he's attracted to men, he likes sex with men, and he loves men. The pain, turmoil, suffering, and self-loathing men experience can lead to mental discord, depression, and suicide. Sometimes, ostracizing, torture, and death can result at the hands of those who fear gay people. For many men, though, the only acceptable path to follow is to deny their authentic being and step to the proscribed drumbeat of the heterosexual lifestyle.

Yet married men are coming out even though the world seems to be against them. And they are surviving and thriving in spite of the opposition they experience. So, for those of you who have yet to come out, the first step is to admit that you're gay.

> "Every time you don't follow your inner guidance,
> you feel a loss of energy, loss of power,
> a sense of spiritual deadness."
>
> ~ Shakti Gawain

> "Dedicate yourself to the good you deserve and desire for yourself. Give yourself peace of mind. You deserve to be happy."
>
> ~ Mark Victor Hansen

Admitting you're gay isn't easy and you know what? Contrary to what you may believe, it's not the end of the world. Up to now, you may have created a well-rehearsed list in your head as to why you're not gay, such as:

> Gay men are effeminate wannabe girls, I'm not.
> Sex with men is just sex, a bodily function, not love.
> I only do it once in a while for release.
> I could never see myself partnered with another man.
> It's against my religion and I support that.
> It's contrary to Nature.
> Gay men are perverts and pedophiles.
> A man is incapable of loving another man.

These are just rationalizations, ways to avoid the reality of who you are. They may make perfect sense to you at the moment, but over time, inner pressures will build up to a point where those rationalizations will crumble — especially if you suddenly meet a man who takes your breath away. As Shakespeare wrote in *The Merchant of Venice*, "...at the length, truth will out." The day will come when you'll finally decide that enough is enough.

When that day comes, you will admit to yourself in your own head or say out loud in private, "I'm gay." Try looking at yourself in a mirror, right into your eyes, and state "I'm gay." There, you've said it and you're still alive, not burnt to a crisp by a thunderbolt. Now what do you do?

Having made this pronouncement, the first thing is to consider how you're *feeling*. I know, you're a guy, so checking in on your feelings isn't what you do. Do it anyway! Not dealing with your feelings is a cultural myth about men that's been promulgated for eons — men don't feel, men DO! Yet, men do have feelings that are fundamental to their being. Shutting yourself off from your feelings is like wearing sunglasses at night. You're going to miss a lot.

**Hint:** The people who tell you to cut yourself off from your feelings are people who are afraid of their own feelings.

*So, how are you feeling?* Feeling lighter, like a huge weight has been lifted from your shoulders? Feeling relief, a sense that you've done the right thing? Do you feel guilty because this shift goes against everything you know and have been taught about homosexuality? Are you feeling bad because you aren't living up to someone else's expectations of you? Feeling fearful because you know the next step is to let someone you trust know that you're gay and they might not take this news well?

What drives most of us — male/female, straight/gay — is the need to fit in, to be part of a group, to feel acceptance from others, to know that we are loved for who we are. "*...to know that we are loved for who we are.*" This is the one that sticks in one's craw. How many of us are truly our authentic selves with family, friends, acquaintances, community, etc.? How many of us dress and talk a certain way to fit in with peers and colleagues? How many people know who we really are: what's going on inside our hearts and heads, what moves us, our perceptions of the world around us, what we truly feel about any given thing, our aspirations? How many of us are just who we are no matter what other people may think? Not many.

> "The individual has always had to struggle
> to keep from being overwhelmed by the tribe.
> If you try it, you will be lonely often,
> and sometimes frightened.
> But no price is too high to pay
> for the privilege of owning yourself."
>
> ~ Friedrich Nietzsche

Fear is the number one emotional factor that drives most people. Fear is powerful and insidious. It creates confusion, invites delusion, and leads us to do things we wouldn't ordinarily do. Fear is the filter through which we'll make life decisions believing we're on the right track. Yet fear actually leads us astray, further away from being who we truly are in all respects.

Essentially, at the heart of our fear is the potential for rejection and abandonment. And what many times comes with rejection is loss of friends, family, groups, status, lifestyle — and the withholding or complete withdrawal of love. To most people's reckoning, these are all good reasons to be fearful; to not rock the boat.

- Many of us are externally based, our sense of self is dependent on being accepted by others. We'll do just about anything to ensure that we stay on the "right" side of people.

- We all want to be considered "normal," yet, at the same time, unique and an individual. So many of our perceived or developed options are based on others' judgment of our actions and decisions.

- We'll remain in destructive or unsupportive relationships rather than have our spouse think badly of us, though they may think that of us already for other reasons. We'll practically starve and almost kill ourselves in order to "keep" our spouse with us.

- Our egos are such that we'll "stand up to city hall," but not stand up to the marital relationship we're in that doesn't satisfy our needs or make us feel proud of ourselves.

- Many people have such low self-esteem that they'll labor to attain extremely high-profile positions and manipulate their relationships just to have others think well of them. But what has really been achieved? If others reject or shun them, they fall apart, get angry at "them," blame "them," and rationalize to the nth degree to ensure that they are right and everyone else is wrong.

What is this need to ensure that, at any cost, others like and accept us?

True, walking through the world by yourself can, at times, be quite a lonely journey. But don't you think that we all have moments wherein we feel like we're truly alone, that no one "gets" us, that we're the only person who feels the way we do, that our uniqueness isn't recognized or acknowledged, that our life experiences are not shared by anyone else? The fact is, you're not the only person who's admitting he's gay. As the saying goes, "[We've] come a long way, baby." Gayness is very much in the public forum now.

What it all comes down to is your private universe and who you are in it. Did the world end when you stated, "I'm gay"? No. You weren't struck by lightning, the earth didn't suddenly open up and swallow you, and a booming voice didn't come out of everywhere saying, "Do not pass GO. You're going straight to hell."

## *What Have You Just Done?!*

Okay, now that you've said "it," the question is: What have you just done? Fundamentally, you've taken your first step toward liberation, freedom from all the fear surrounding homosexuality. You're not a horrible person. You're still the same man you've always been, but now you're being honest about one aspect of yourself and your life. Of course, you may experience some regret having admitted your true sexual identity and fear may definitely creep in.

Remember the first time you ever had sex? Afterwards, you felt like everyone knew what you'd done, like there was a neon sign on your forehead flashing, "I JUST HAD SEX!" The same thing here. No one knows what you've just admitted to yourself and you're still safe in your universe.

Once again, recognize your feelings. Feeling fear? Face it. At this juncture, you're the only person who knows you're gay (unless you've been secretly seeing men). You may have still not admitted to yourself that you're gay, simply that you feel compelled/driven to have sex with men or that you truly enjoy having sex with men. For many men, this is a distinction they are willing to live with rather than admitting to themselves or to anyone else that they are gay. That's their choice.

On the other hand, you are seeking to be authentic — no more games, no more dishonesty in your marriage or relationships, no deceitfulness, no lying, no more manipulating information and people, no more hiding, no more secret gay sex. You want to be fully present and available in all your relationships.

Allow yourself to really feel the full range of your emotions. If you need to, write down what you're feeling. Be sure, though, that no one discovers what you're writing (see the story about that in Chapter 2). This is only for your eyes. Essentially, what you'll be doing is what's called journaling.

A journal is a record of your feelings, thoughts, and impressions about your life, as well as a repository of things you collect and remember from special cards to pictures, letters, and other meaningful mementoes. It'll be easier to actually write what you're feeling rather than relying on your mind to keep track as you go through this process. There's also something about seeing your thoughts on paper that brings a realness, immediacy, and depth to your experience. In the future, you can come back to what you've written and see just how far you've traveled on your journey.

**If you want to buy a journal...**
- www.oberondesign.com
- www.mindseyejournals.com/
- www.epica.com/journals/
- www.celerystreet.com/writing-journals/lined-journals/back-pocket-writing-journals
- www.ghilliesuits.com/journals.aspx
- http://thewrendesign.com/gift-idea-moleskine-journal-sets/
- http://matrboomie.com/shop/?search=journals

As you move through your emotions, try not to analyze them, just feel them. You can analyze them later. The trick here is to not avoid feeling your feelings by jumping to analysis, which is a mental process, not heart process. You might be like many men who often don't even analyze their feelings, which could open up a Pandora's Box letting out God knows what and leading to God knows where. Too frightening — better to leave things closed off. Wrong! You wouldn't be in this emotional spot if you had always acknowledged and honored your feelings in the first place. Better late than never. Believe me, whatever your over-imaginative mind can come up with, reality is never as scary.

So, take the time to feel. Eventually, you'll find life in general much easier to deal with because you haven't closed off an intrinsic part of your being. You were born with a full complement of emotions for a reason: to experience life more deeply and with greater fulfillment and richness. Anyone who tells you differently is simply afraid to access and work with their own feelings. You are a gay man — it's okay. There are many other men just like you. What you are going through is scary, but it is also liberating. Experiencing a new level of freedom is worth the challenge.

### *Discovering Your Gay Roots*

It's time for you to do some research, dispel myths about gay people, learn some history about the gay movement, and read about the stories of other gay men's journeys. Find out who's spreading dis- and misinformation about gay people and gay culture. Read books on gay history, gay fiction, see gay-themed television shows and movies, maybe even go so far as to attend a Gay Pride event. Get on the Internet and Google the word "gay" or related words. See what you discover.

Another area you'll want to get familiar with is: what's going on in the gay community and how gay people are perceived in the larger culture of our country and the world. Check out what's happening with gay marriage, gay rights, gays in the military, and gay politicos. What does the religious right think of homosexuality and upon what they base their understanding? What's changing in some churches concerning acceptance of gay people? Who's out there fighting for or against gay rights? What's the story with gay adoption and parenting? What are the current legalities concerning partnership rights and laws when it comes to estates, joint finances, custody of children, and gay rights with families/hospitals/hospices concerning death and dying issues?

By the way, the acronym LGBT stands for Lesbian, Gay, Bisexual, Transgender. That has been added to over the last couple of years. The extended acronym is LGBTQQIAA2P — Lesbian, Gay, Bisexual, Transgender, Queer, Questioning, Intersex, Asexual, Ally-heterosexual/straight, 2-Spirit, Pansexual. (For a more expanded list, see Appendix A.)

> "The white light streams down
> to be broken up
> by those human prisms
> into all the colors of the rainbow.
> Take your own color in the pattern
> and be just that."
>
> ~ Charles R. Brown

Since you've admitted to yourself that you're gay, you'll also want to review who you are. Again, nothing has really changed since you've rocked your universe with this admission. You are still you. By getting real, this is your first step toward leading a life that's more congruent with your inner being. You've spent plenty of time hiding the fact that you are gay, which is time you've not been honest or necessarily ethical according to your own standards. What does it feel like to know that you're finally coming into alignment with those standards? Are you standing taller, feeling stronger, more self-assured about who you are and what you stand for in terms of honesty and authenticity?

If you are feeling this way, are you willing to take some tentative steps into the gay community? You might find this a very scary thing to do. What if someone you know sees you there? What if they question why you're there? What will you say? How will you act? What if they tell others they saw you there? What if they tell others you're gay? How will you handle that?

These are definitely things to carefully consider. You may be ready to come out to yourself, but certainly not to the rest of the world. So, you may not want to go to a Pride event yet, go to a public theater to see a gay movie or theater production, visit an LGBT (Lesbian-Gay-Bisexual-Transgender) Community Center or event, or even consider a gay support group for married men coming out.

The important thing to determine is what *you* are or are not ready to handle. For most men in your situation, coming out publicly is something that will take time. And there's no rush. As the Wicked Witch of the West in *The Wizard of Oz* stated, "These things must be done delicately." The same with your journey — it's yours to handle as you see fit. There is no standard protocol in this process — it's strictly individual. And don't let anyone goad you into doing something for which you're not ready. They're just pushing their own agenda and obviously don't have your best interests at heart, as well intentioned as they may be.

For many married men coming out, safety, privacy, and confidentiality are primary concerns. They want to make sure that they control their coming out process. Most are not ready to publicly announce that they're gay. Being "outed" before you're ready can be majorly destructive to your world and sense of well being. Men do get fired from their jobs for being gay, even though that's illegal in most states. You manage the disclosure process in a sensitive manner by being the originator of that admission. Spouses who find out through other people, gossip mongers, or even on the news (print, broadcast, or web-based) will have a much more difficult time dealing with the information that you are gay. The same goes for your children, if you have them. The damage done by someone else leaking the news can be devastating for your loved ones.

Most married men in the coming out process will seek to be very covert and protective of themselves because coming out can have a very negative impact on one's life. They'll make sure the LGBT Community Center they contact and/or visit is far from where they live and work. Phone calls will be made so that no one can overhear conversations, calls can't be traced, and no records will exist. Gay-themed web sites and Internet tracking will be disguised and/or records of sites visited will be deleted. Phone number lists and text messages on cell phones will be quickly deleted to avoid accidental discovery. Hiding places for information will be found in one's home, office, car, storage space, garage, etc.

Many married men who have gone through this process have felt like they're an agent for the CIA, NSA, or Homeland Security. Though they feel like they have no other choice but to handle things this way, they still feel uncomfortable, dishonest, and unethical. They live for the day when they are strong enough to no longer hide who they are, their movements, and who they know.

> "I'm a supporter of gay rights.
> And not a closet supporter either.
> From the time I was a kid,
> I have never been able to understand
> attacks upon the gay community.
> There are so many qualities
> that make up a human being…
> by the time I get through with all the things
> that I really admire about people,
> what they do with their private parts
> is probably so low on the list that it is irrelevant."
>
> ~ Paul Newman

In spite of the negative component of coming out, the bigger picture is that you'll lead your life in honesty. This is huge and far outweighs the difficulties one could face from family, friends, co-workers, and the community at large. Yes, it is very possible that you will lose or be shunned by some family, friends, and co-workers. Then again, since the discussion concerning homosexuality is light years from where it was just 20 years ago, people are not quite so shocked by such a disclosure.

Will it be hard emotionally? Yes. Are you going to face uncomfortable conversations and situations? Yes. But you can get through it just as numerous other men have. And, what you imagine might happen is generally out of proportion to what you'll actually experience. That is not to say you should approach this process in a Pollyanna-ish fashion. You still need to deal with reality.

People are people and they have their expectations, dreams and illusions about you, men, and life quite intact. By your disclosure, you'll be dispelling or even shattering some of these, which could be quite upsetting for those you tell. They want their world to be on as even a keel as possible. Disclosure for them may feel like the rug is being pulled out from underneath them — their world is not as comfortable, organized, squarely compartmentalized as they thought, and/or that what they thought. And what they thought they knew about you, they don't.

What is primary here is to help the person understand that you can sympathize with what they're experiencing and that you are still the person you've always been. Really, very little has changed. (We'll go into this in greater detail in Chapters 2 and 3.) Meanwhile, you have some other work to do before you decide to begin telling people your long-held secret.

## *Getting to Know You*

Step 1 is you coming out to yourself. That's done.
Step 2 involves learning about the gay world and its many facets.
Step 3 is all about getting to know yourself.

You need to get comfortable with acknowledging yourself as a gay man. All the mental, emotional, and behavioral habits you've developed over a lifetime may need some adjustment or major overhauling with this admission. You are now moving into a chapter of your life where you won't need to hide anymore. All the habits formed around stealth, caution, and deception will need to be addressed and resolved over time.

Additionally, there are other things you need to explore about yourself that have remained obscure simply because you've been hiding from yourself. You'll want to review what it means to be a man in general, not just a gay man. How you've conducted yourself as a straight man modeling yourself after other straight men will need some reflection to determine what is an intrinsic aspect of yourself and what is fiction. By fiction, I mean those things that are familial, religious, and socio-cultural conventions based on other people's agendas, misunderstandings about human nature, dis- and misinformation, and outright ignorance.

You'll want to look at what kind of man you are in terms of ethics, morality, kindness, emotions, fear, how you dress, how you express yourself, integrity, honesty, compassion, patience, acceptance, inclusiveness, spirituality — a whole host of things that comprise the full spectrum of who you are and can be. Yup, you've got some work ahead of you, but it's vitally important work from which you will positively benefit for the rest of your life.

As you research the world of the gay community, think about what any and all of it means to you. For instance, part of the gay world includes rough & tough men in leather, studs, chaps, and boots. For some people, meeting these guys is cause for fear. For others, it's a complete turn on. What are your feelings about leather men?

On the opposite end of the spectrum are the drag queens who live for a new frock and matching accessories. You've seen news articles and movies of them, e.g., *To Wong Foo, Thanks for Everything, Julie Newmar*, *Priscilla, Queen of the Desert*, and *The Bird Cage*. Is that a group you identify with or shun? How about transgendered people? What about lesbians? Are you a top or a bottom or versatile?

What are you attracted to: b-boys, Asians, Latinos, fems, twinks, skater boys, Goth or punks, emo boys, daddies, school boys, thugs, queens, chubbies, club kids, frat types, athletes, otters, bears, bar dancers, bad boys, silver wolves, professionals and businessmen, impersonators, he/she's, lady boys, transsexuals, men in uniform, gym bunnies, muscle men, intellectuals, nerds, dumb bunnies, S&M types, fetishists, bossy bottoms, the unavailable, needy types — the list goes on. The whole gay world is opening up for you and you can pick and choose where you want to land.

One thing you need to know about the gay community is that it's made up of human beings with all the same strengths, beauty, ugliness, skills, challenges, and positive/negative characteristics that the "straight" world exhibits. People are people and you can't avoid dealing with their foibles. Racism exists within the gay community. Stereotyping exists. Sexism and ageism exist. Labeling and compartmentalizing exist. Phobias and psychoses exist. Addictions of all types exist. And homophobia exists.

You may be feeling the first blush of a new life and community to get involved with, but be aware that you're going to run into many of the same problems in this community that exist elsewhere. Taking the rose-colored glasses off as you delve into this new world will help you avoid unreasonable expectations and potentially deep disappointment and dissatisfaction.

One aspect of the gay world you'll probably find rather enticing is the bar scene. This is a major draw for most men because, as is well understood about men, they so often think with their little head. The idea of being in a place with people of your own kind can be intoxicating when mixed with hot bodies and alcohol. The freedom you'll feel to just be you is amazing. No longer do you have to worry about the bar being raided by the police and people being carted off to jail. For the most part, thugs won't be waiting to jump you when you leave the premises. And there are so many types of bars to choose from depending on what tickles your fancy.

Something I used to do when I had a new crop of men join the Married Men's Coming Out Group was take them on a bar tour either on a Friday or Saturday night. You've never seen so many excited, anxious, eyes-popping-out-of-their-heads, "I'm in love!" men at one time (well, maybe when the Dallas Cheerleaders come out on the field at half-time).

If you've not experienced the bar scene, then put that on your itinerary. It's not something you may want to do right away. For some men, they need to build up their courage before stepping through the doors of one of these clubs. For other men, they can't wait to pay a visit. For yourself, you may want to go with a gay friend or two just for comfort, someone to talk to, maybe get out on the dance floor with, and even for protection from overly forward bar bunnies or sexual predators. You never know what you'll see, how it will affect you, and how your night may end up. Just remember, "no" still means "no" in a gay bar, the same as it does in a straight bar. Bartenders and bouncers will enforce it. So, if someone won't leave you alone, bartenders and bouncers will assist you.

Finally, there's one thing we've not discussed and that's your mental/emotional health. Working with a therapist trained in gay issues could be a tremendous boon to your self-esteem and in coming to terms with all the turmoil you may be experiencing. Don't feel you need to do this alone or that you don't need help and can handle it yourself. You need to talk to someone and a therapist can provide the neutral insight and support you need through this process. You need to get out of just being in your own head. You will feel much better knowing you have someone to talk to who won't judge you and can help you wend your way through the phases of the coming out process.

> A gay man, finally deciding he could no longer hide his sexuality from his parents, went over to their house, and found his mother in the kitchen cooking dinner. He sat down at the kitchen table, let out a big sigh, and said, "Mom, I have something to tell you — I'm gay."
>
> His mother made no reply or gave any response, and the guy was about to repeat it to make sure she'd heard him, when she turned away from the pot she was stirring and said calmly, "You're gay — doesn't that mean you put other men's penises in your mouth?" The guy said nervously, "Uh, yeah, Mom, that's right."

> His mother went back to stirring the pot, then suddenly whirled around, whacked him over the head with her spoon and said, "Don't you EVER complain about my cooking again!"
>
> www.jokes4us.com/peoplejokes/comingoutoftheclosetjoke.html

You'll go over all the ins and out and ups and downs of coming out again and again in your mind, letting yourself obsess on the subject. That's okay. It's part of the process of getting comfortable and secure in your re-identification. I say "re-identification" because you've not been yourself up to this point — you've been striving to be someone you are not. Therefore, allow yourself to obsess for a bit, but also do your homework and research the world of gaydom so facts and data are also filling up your mind. You'll begin feeling much healthier and grounded for it.

What will aid you in weathering the process of coming out is ensuring that communications with every person you talk to about your coming out is handled sensitively and with consideration. That means you first need to recognize and acknowledge the feelings and the thoughts you're having and what to do about them.

# Chapter 2

# Communication

Arthur was one of the original members of the Married Men's Coming Out Group. He was still living with his wife and had a son about to graduate to high school. In group sessions, he didn't say much, just observed. Most everything he had to say was non-committal and he rarely expressed what was truly going on inside himself.

He had grown up in the South and had southern sensibilities that forbade him to act in ungentlemanly ways. One unspoken rule is that inner turmoil is to be kept to oneself and certainly never spoken of in public. Another is that one doesn't burden one's wife with that same inner turmoil, but toughs it out "as a man."

Arthur was certainly toughing it out. He had come out to his wife who didn't really understand what he was going through and had also come out to his son. Divorce was imminent and his son began to act sullen and withdrawn. He loved both his parents and didn't want to have to choose with whom he was going to live.

Arthur was aware of some things in the gay community that he didn't approve of and was afraid he might get pulled into them, things like group sex, AIDS, leather men, and drag queens. It all scared him enough for him to consider staying married. He was getting depressed and a psychiatrist had put him on Prozac to elevate his mood.

One early morning, I received a call from Arthur's wife. She was frantic. Arthur had a gun in his room and was talking about suicide. I immediately drove over to his house. Arthur's neighborhood was very quiet, unaware of the drama playing out inside his house. I rang the doorbell and Arthur's wife quickly pulled me in so the neighbors wouldn't see anything. She pointed to the room where Arthur was located, a converted garage made into a bedroom.

Arthur was sitting on the side of the bed, sagging like a sack of potatoes. I didn't see the gun anywhere and asked Arthur what was going on. He was glad to see me and immediately began describing for me his desperation.

Arthur and I talked for some time: he was despondent, unsure what to do with his life, wanting to end the emotional pain, wanting out of his marriage, wanting to not be gay, wanting a loving relationship with a man, not wanting to disappoint his son by killing himself, not feeling attractive to other men, feeling old, and feeling not "with it" enough to keep up with the gay community.

At heart, Arthur was thinking it was safer emotionally to stay in his unhappy marriage. He was afraid he'd never find a man to be in a relationship with; part of the problem being that he was in his early fifties and was attracted to younger men in their early twenties. For one thing, the young men seemed too close in age to his son, and secondly, he had trouble relating to them due to the age difference.

This was all news to me. Why hadn't he communicated all of this to the group so they could support him in dealing with it? Why was he trying to do this alone and waiting until he thought suicide was the only option left?

The good news is that several years later, Arthur had managed to move forward and divorce. His son was living with him and was pursuing his dream by going to a high school for the performing arts, and Arthur had met a man who was closer to his own age. Arthur was also off the Prozac.

A positive ending to what could have been a truly sad story. What's interesting is that Arthur had been raised and trained to go it alone, that's what it meant to be a man. His rather strict and regimented father promoted this viewpoint. He didn't want Arthur to turn into a wuss, or worse, a pansy. How many men have been brought up this way?

As my friend Steven Griffith, founder of High Performance Coaching, says, "The conversation *is* the relationship." No truer words were ever spoken. It is through what we say and how we say and convey it that we are able to create and sustain relationships. For many men, though, saying what they're actually feeling is not familiar territory.

Most men can talk about all sorts of things…just not their inner feelings. To express their intimate feelings in front of other men — other than anger, joy, disappointment, confidence, and power — means that they are weak. It means that they can't handle their situation, they don't have the wherewithal, aren't tough, don't have the strength or courage or stamina — they just aren't "real" men. Does any of this sound familiar?

Too many of us go the stoic route, even within ourselves. We shut the door on our emotions, sticking to a small range within which to express ourselves. We don't dare think about what we're feeling because all those "real men" admonitions would flare up, backhanding us into bucking up, forcing us to "take it like a man." The world is supposed to understand us, know us, and want to engage in relationships with us. And, in spite of this, we do — even though we do everything we can to push the world away, to hide our true being.

One wonders, then, how we're supposed to get along, how we're supposed to convey what we're thinking in a manner that's effective and meaningful. The abbreviated language of many men is relegated to business and sports. Everything else gets squeezed into business/sports metaphors. Meanwhile one's heart language diminishes. It's sort of like a person I know whose values are such that when seeing a beautiful vista with his wife remarks, "Yeah, yeah," because what he's mostly interested in is focusing on business. His wife, on the other hand, is all caught up with the beauty and is exclaiming over it. The totality of life is a diamond of which business is just one facet. Imagine how much we're missing, both in our external and internal lives. Imagine how much we're missing in terms of connecting with other people.

Fear of potential rejection is one of the main reasons we men don't have more heart to heart connections more often with men and women. Perhaps another reason is that we've been hurt and disappointed in the past by someone we cared for deeply, so our trust quotient is low. Some of us grew up in families where showing loving emotions just wasn't done. Whatever the reason, it's time to break old patterns. It's time to stop letting the past create our future. Just because the past is what it was doesn't mean our future needs to be a repeat of it. We're in the here and now. Each new day holds within it the opportunity for creating a new life.

## *Communicating with Self*

Let's begin with the communication you have with yourself. What's going on in your head most of the time? Are you re-hashing stuff from your day or from days/weeks/months/years ago? How do you talk to yourself? Are you admonishing, berating yourself as being stupid, slow, out of it, old-fashioned, boring, old, out of shape, uninteresting, etc.? Or are you supportive of yourself: being creative, seeing a future that holds promise, wanting to engage with other people and be involved in activities?

If you're into self-admonishment, that's a waste of time and energy. As the Wizard of Oz said to the Cowardly Lion, "You, my friend, are a victim of disorganized thinking." How do you expect anyone else to support you if you don't support yourself? Time to get over self-flagellation as you're really not helping yourself, just continuing an old pattern that consistently puts you down and eventually makes you "the victim." If you want to stay a victim, fine. Just be aware that no one dug that particular hole for you, You did it yourself. Stand up, shake yourself off, and take stock of who you really are.

Another pattern to break is the type of people with whom you surround yourself. Are they supportive, would they give you the shirt off their backs, are they there for you when you need help? What kind of conversations do you have with your friends, shallow and pointless or engaged with life and uplifting? There is plenty in the world to grouse and gossip about, but how much time do you spend discussing what is good in the world and creating a more positive future for yourself and humanity?

Healthy discussions are key to making sure you are consistently moving in an upward spiral. Sure, there are going to be the things that are upsetting, the mundane things that need attention on a daily basis, the people who get your goat, negative situations and events that occur. But they are the sum total of life's experiences from day to day. Read the newspaper every day or watch the news and it will begin to feel like the world is going to hell in a hand basket. But those are just the headlines making the "news." Go to a book store and take a gander at the tons of magazines. You just wouldn't believe the vast array of topics they cover: green magazines, the arts, wholistic living, alternative lifestyles, back to the earth, educational, etc. There's a lot going on that isn't reported that's moving in the opposite direction from the mainstream.

And there are people with whom you can connect who are incredibly interesting and vital and engaged. What kind of communications could you have with any of them? What could they introduce you to that would open up your world, help you explore and discover aspects of life you've never known about? How might you change? Perhaps you'd begin to have discussions that are more relevant to who you are and what deeply interests you in life, concepts like honesty, genuineness, authenticity, respect, depth, true feelings, vision, and values and beliefs might lead you to a higher understanding of yourself and life in general. How might your language and relationship dynamics change? Maybe you're ready to truly take full responsibility for your life and create your future on a level you've never attempted before — and I don't mean by just coming out of the closet. There's more to life than just knowing whether you're straight or gay.

The ways in which we communicate allows the rest of the world to more clearly see who we are. To hold back is to hide from yourself and others. It's true, you will get along well with some people and not so well or never with others. That's okay. Your goal is not to get all seven billion+ people on the planet to like you. Even Elvis didn't do that (I never cared for him as an entertainer and I'm not alone in that). Now is the time for more research into you. Figure out how you support yourself in your mental conversations and get out there, push the envelope, think outside the box, expand your horizons, and work on taking your communications to a new level.

## *Communicating with Your Family*

The conversations you'll need to have with your spouse, children, and relatives are very important. What you say, how you say it, and when you say it will be key in determining just how your process of coming out proceeds. That process can be anything from a walk in the park to hell on Earth.

> A friend of mine, Jason, decided after about nine years of living with his girlfriend, Suzanne, to move out. He didn't tell her why he was moving out and never said anything about the state of their relationship. They'd not had intimate relations in at least five years. Suzanne was completely confused as to what was going on with him.
>
> Ironically, Jason has always thought of himself as a "high communicator" and was always talking about how he wished other people were more honest and had greater integrity in their communications. He also viewed himself as being highly respectful and considerate of others.

One evening, the two got together at a restaurant to talk about where things were at. While Jason did the majority of the talking, most of it was not about their relationship. Then, as the two were leaving the restaurant, Jason saw some people at the bar he knew. He stopped to talk to them while Suzanne kept walking, unaware he wasn't with her. She waited by the front door wondering where he was. Starting to get annoyed, she looked around the corner into the bar and saw Jason. He motioned for her to come join him and his friends. She did and was introduced to his friends as his "EX."

Suzanne was floored and humiliated. She thought to herself, "You'd think that after being his partner for nine years and all we've been through that I'd be the first to be told — and not like this!"

It's interesting how some people choose to communicate with others. Jason, like many people, needs to take some time to learn about himself (other than finally coming out). His desire to have others be more honest in their communications follows that old adage: we teach what we need to learn. To modify it slightly: we are aggravated by the behavior of others that we ourselves are exhibiting and need to let go of. If Jason would *be* the honest communicator he claims to be, his life would be quite different. As it stands now, not only is his "ex" confused, Jason's friends are at a loss as to what is going on with him.

If you are coming out to your spouse, then one very important thing you'll want to do is put yourself in her shoes (not literally, though I know it's tempting). Seriously, imagine what she's going to feel when you tell her, what she's going to be thinking about herself, the two of you, your marriage, the children, the life and home you've created together. Most likely, her world is going to be turned upside down and inside out. She may be devastated by your admission.

As uncomfortable and painful as this first conversation is probably going to be, it has to happen in order for you to get on with your life; for your spouse and children to pick up the pieces of their shattered lives and move on. This may sound crass, but it is the reality of what you'll all be facing. Life will go on, though not quite as you had intended or envisioned.

Even though you're looking to a new and different future as a gay man, your family didn't ask for this, so the least you can do is be as forthcoming in your communications as possible. You're going to be hurting, they're going to be hurting. Acknowledgment of everyone's feelings is vitally important, as well as working to keep the communication lines open. This is going to be a challenge as the anger and resentment you may get from your spouse, children, and relatives could be intense and long lasting. Keep at it in a loving and supportive manner.

You can all continue to give each other support in spite of the circumstances, and you're the one who will need to take the initiative on this, not them. You're the one creating change when others weren't asking for it, so you need to take the lead to ensure everyone will make it through this situation as best as possible. In short, you need to be the designated driver.

As your discussions progress, you'll very likely be seen as the bad guy. To help everyone stay away from this designation, especially your spouse, you'll both need to take a hard look at just how your relationship has functioned over the years of your marriage. When you discuss how long you've known you are gay, there are some things you may not want to explain right away (like Raphael having sex with a man on his wedding night: beginning of Ch. 1) — not a great way to launch this particular discussion, especially since you want to cover this issue as calmly as possible.

Don't be afraid to really discuss what you've been feeling since knowing you were different and then determining that you're gay. Talk about why you got married, your feelings for your wife then and now, what it's been like hiding this knowledge, why you're coming out now, and what you're looking for concerning your future.

The idea is to be as realistic as possible: where your marriage was and the feelings you both have had during the length of the marriage. Don't get stuck arguing about minutia and who did what to who, but do go over the good, the bad, and the ugly. The point is not to have one person come out the winner, but to come to an understanding that you didn't have a perfect marriage. Talk about how your partnership worked dynamically, what didn't work and what did work.

I'll stress again the idea of individual therapy and couple's therapy. (1) There is no need to go it alone through this process, (2) you'll need someone who doesn't know the particulars of your relationship and life to provide neutral feedback, and (3) you'll need someone who isn't involved in the situation to help you sift through and make sense of all the feelings both of you'll be going through. Please do not attempt to DIY this process. This is neither the place nor time.

Whatever blocks you may have against therapy, it's time to break them down. If you insist on doing it yourself, consider that the real reason for doing so is to avoid dealing with the deeper issues tied to the situation. Don't do what Jason is doing to himself, his girlfriend, and his friends.

There is one idea you may be accused of: you're going through "manopause." You read correctly — manopause. For millennia, men have gone through what has been described as a "mid-life crisis," an interestingly appropriate characterization for when a man looks at his life and decides to recapture the vigor and ideals of his youth. What this usually entails is a divorce, marrying a much younger woman, changing one's lifestyle to one of youthful vitality, and maybe buying a sports car.

> In 1973, Spencer was the head of the Psychology Department at a state university. He and Ariel had been married for almost 30 years and had four children. Everyone thought they had the perfect marriage, a wonderful blend of intellect and things in common, and an incredible family with smart and talented children.
>
> Spencer started wanting more and he attained a higher paying and more nationally visible position in a large metropolitan city. Though it uprooted the family, everyone seemed to be adjusting well to the move. Typical of this energetic, creative, and dynamic family.
>
> One morning, Spencer got out of bed, turned to Ariel, and announced that he wanted a divorce. Ariel was dumbfounded. In shock, she granted him the divorce. I got a call from Ariel, who was devastated. She explained that Spencer wouldn't talk to any of their kids, to her, their friends, colleagues, or their parish priest. He was completely withdrawn from the family and just wouldn't make himself available on any level. The kids were very hurt. Would I, as one of their foster kids who'd remained close to the family, come talk to him (I was 20 at the time). I declined as I thought it was entirely inappropriate.
>
> The divorce was final within a few months. Ariel was given the house to do with as she pleased. She sold it and moved the family back to their home town.
>
> Spencer, on the other hand, moved out of state and a year later re-married — a 20-year-old student from the

college where he was now teaching. He'd also bought a red Corvette. He still wouldn't talk to anyone in the family about the divorce, but we all had a pretty clear idea of what the real story was.

The irony in all of this was that he was a psychologist.

Manopause, or mid-life crisis (andropause), is defined as:

(a) a change of life for males that may be expressed in terms of a career change, divorce, or re-ordering of life. It is associated with a decline in androgen levels that occur in men during their late 40s or early 50s (*Mosby's Medical Dictionary*, 8th edition. © 2009, Elsevier);

(b) a constellation of changes that occur in older males, including libido, sexual performance, sperm quantity and quality, erectile dysfunction, frailty, muscle and bone mass, body fat, clinical hot flashes, insomnia, mood swings, irritability, weakness, lethargy, and impotence management (McGraw-Hill *Concise Dictionary of Modern Medicine*. © 2002 by The McGraw-Hill Companies, Inc.).

Additional symptoms may include: stiffness in the muscles and joints, night sweats, dry skin, hair loss, weight gain, an inability to sleep deeply, and a loss of ability to recover quickly from injuries. Does a lot of this sound familiar?

Let's face it: men go through hormonal changes during various phases of their life just as women do. Studies are now finding that men aged 40 to 55 experience hormonal, physiological, psychological, and chemical changes very similar to what women experience. Both men and women have made fun of women reaching menopause, the time when they no longer menstruate. There are women who live for this occurrence as it means they won't have to go through their monthly period ever again.

I think it's safe to say that no man would be looking forward to manopause. Men tend to think of themselves in terms of the qualities of eternal youth: boundless energy, great looks, and a libido that won't quit. When all three begin to fade, one's self-esteem fades with it. The only way to deal with it is to re-visit the old days: have an affair, get a mistress, divorce so you can re-create your old bachelor pad, get the car that shows everyone how virile you are, marry someone much younger and have a child to show the world you still have it in you — you dog you!

What's different about coming out as gay and being accused of manopause is that you're not leaving your wife for a younger woman or revisiting your youth. You may hook up with someone who is younger than you, you may not. What you are definitely doing will most likely involve sex with one or more men as you acclimate to being an openly gay man and possibly seek a monogamous relationship. Your reasons for doing it are to be who you actually are: a man who is gay, not straight. That's not to say that you won't sow your oats. That's only natural as you now have the freedom to do so and, generally, without any responsibilities (an issue we'll discuss in Chapter 8).

For now, we're still at the point of establishing a strong communication dynamic with family and relatives. In doing that, at some point, both you and your wife will need to work as a team in dealing with children, relatives, and friends. There is nothing that will diminish relations and upset the apple cart faster than conflicting information and reports of what the situation is between you and your wife. And the only way to manage it is both of you agreeing to be consistent in the information provided to others in your communiqués. This holds true no matter with whom you're communicating.

Whatever your agreements concerning communications, everyone you talk to about your coming out and the eventual divorce, will have some emotional reaction and probably an opinion or judgment to go with it. Come up with a game plan between you and your wife so that when you run into whomever in whatever situation, you're prepared. The two of you may have to rehearse what you'll say in order to avoid any social mishaps or conveying conflicting information, especially as concerns your children.

When it comes to your children, depending on how young they are, consistency will save a lot of heartache and misunderstandings. Agree not to let anger, frustration, or even hate for each other get downloaded into your discussions with your children. This is not about getting them to choose sides and ally with either one of you. It's about supporting them through this difficult family period. Stay in tune with what's going on in their world from home life to school, friends, church, and work.

Be careful about putting on a false front. When the truth is finally known, trust could be diminished and resentment could build. You still need to help them face the reality of what's happening to the family and why. And above all, let them know that you are both there for them no matter what happens.

The last area to cover concerning communication involves technology. I'm sure you've read or heard the horror stories about texting, Facebooking, tweeting, chat rooms, etc. Our world has become so interconnected and we have so much ready technology at hand that allows us to capture pictures, take videos, and quickly reach out to one another that digital communication has become a norm — even for people in their eighties and up. Aside from the obvious upside, there is a downside to our use of technology to "stay in touch."

Researchers are discovering that our empathy quotient is diminishing. What that means is that our ability to empathize with another is disappearing. Through constant use of technology, we are shortchanging true communication. What's missing are the visual cues, tone, and inflection that provide clues to the emotional state and sub-text of the person(s) with whom we're communicating.

Texting is a huge culprit as not only has it replaced direct connection with another person, we're abbreviating our language and expression, cutting out what is considered superfluous. Basically, we're resorting to shorthand. Meanwhile, the person on the receiving end is left with having to interpret the meaning behind the communication they've received not only without visual cues, tone and inflection, but now coded in shorthand.

This lack of empathy is showing up in the level of intense violence we see in movies, the expansion of conflict between individuals and groups. We're finding ourselves less moved by the plights of others, a situation of become deadened to the world around us. In order to feel something, we need heightened scenarios to grab our attention, but not necessarily our hearts. Consequently, when bad things happen to people we know, researchers are discovering that we remain unfazed, emotionally distant.

Researchers are finding that a reliance on technology to express our thoughts and feelings actually produces a barrier between us and the person/people with whom we're "communicating." Words can only convey so much. The rest is left to our interpretation, perceptions, expectations, projections, biases, needs, etc. Combined with the lack of visual cues, tone and inflection, the outcome is misinterpretation.

What we're also seeing is live conversations that mirror how we express ourselves when texting and e-mailing. Again, verbal shorthand, as well as a shrinking vocabulary. Considering the fact that the English language consists of over 1,025,109 words and that a new word is created every 98 minutes (Global Language Monitor), this seems counterintuitive. There's so much to choose from, yet we rely on such a small percentage of words to articulate what's in our hearts and minds.

Since you're going through such an amazing period in your life, think about how much you want people to understand who you are, what you're feeling, and what you're thinking. Open the door to the "real" you and discover just how enriching your relationships can become.

As you work through the process of coming out, be aware of the levels at which your communications are occurring. What you, your family, and friends are going through is not to be taken lightly. Our emotional beings require care and consideration, not flippancy and unresponsiveness. Make sure you spend plenty of time face to face with those close to you. No matter how uncomfortable circumstances are, stay present, mindful of your feelings and the feelings of those with whom you're talking. Truly, there is no substitute — digital or otherwise — than spending time face to face with each other and speaking from your hearts.

> "Deep listening is miraculous
> for both listener and speaker.
> When someone receives us with open-hearted,
> non-judging, intensely interested listening,
> our spirits expand."
>
> ~ Sue Patton Thoele
> Author, *Heart-Centered Marriage*
> *Fulfilling Our Natural Desire for Sacred Partnership*

# Chapter 3

# The Next Step: Coming Out to Your Immediate Family

> "How I came out to my wife was completely unexpected.
> I had printed my chat notes from a gay chat line
> and accidently left them beside the computer.
> My wife found them when she was house cleaning
> and I literally felt the blood drain out of me
> when she handed them to me
> as soon as I got home that night."
>
> ~ Disclosed by Grady, a member of the
> Married Men's Coming Out Group

Quite unexpectedly — and as quick as Instant Messaging — a new chapter began in Grady's life.

Grady had been married for 20-some years and had two children. He was relatively high up in a national company, so his family lived quite comfortably. He and his wife shared a home computer. Grady surfed the Net every day. He found a gay chat room and began regular correspondence with a number of men, one in particular. He'd not been to a gay bar or club yet as he wasn't ready to make that foray into the gay world. So, at this point, Internet chat was workable for him at this juncture.

How Grady came out to his wife was not exactly how he'd envisioned this part of the process. Once the "secret" was out, though, he called me to arrange an intake interview to join the Married Men's Coming Out Group. When he explained the above scene, we both had a good laugh as this was a sign of our technological times. Outed via chat notes — imagine!

On closer inspection, what we had here was Grady's subconscious at work. He wanted to disclose his secret life to his wife at some point, but had been consciously putting it off. His "accidentally" leaving the printed chat notes by the computer was his unconscious way of getting off the dime. This is not a method I would promote. A more direct approach is what I advocate. Spouses really don't appreciate being surprised with this kind of news in this manner.

Much has been written about coming out. For most men, this is the scariest part of the entire process. It may involve a lot of emotional upheaval: hurt, anger, doubt, blame, regret, confusion, numbness, overwhelm, embarrassment, frustration, disappointment, stubbornness, distrust, hate, and fear. Accusations will be leveled at you. Misinformation will fly through the air. New boundaries will be set, enforced, violated, and broken. Lawyers may get involved. You may lose family and relatives. Yet, the most important goal in this process will always remain the same: honesty and authenticity to self and others, and truly becoming the man you were meant to be.

**Married Men Coming Out Movies**
Love Life
Mulligans
Making Love
Brokeback Mountain
The Lost Language of Cranes

With the above stated, it's no wonder many men choose to stay in the closet and remain married. The heartache, potential loss, and legal ramifications just seem too much.

So, men trying to hide their true sexuality from the world will often go to extraordinary lengths to remain closeted. At any cost to themselves and creating elaborate webs of deceit, they will lie, manipulate, obfuscate, redirect, sneak around, and fake much of their life. They'll work incredibly hard to ensure that their spouses, children, in-laws, friends, and co-workers know nothing about their secret proclivity.

> "Steve T....a Long Island doctor married to his high school sweetheart and the father of three school-age sons... would do almost anything to keep his family together and his suburban lifestyle intact, even after telling his wife that he is gay.
>
> "She is his 'best friend' and the 'perfect co-parent.' He enjoys the social life of a popular suburban couple, adores his in-laws, and wants to live in the same home as his children.

But he also wants to continue a love affair with a man like himself: married, with children, a lawn to mow, and a comfortable life. And until a few weeks ago, Dr. T. said, 'this was working great in terms of getting our needs met and not disrupting our families.'

"Dr. T.'s wife had agreed she could live with his sexual orientation provided he didn't act on it. So he lied and said his homosexual relationship did not include sex. But she wasn't fooled and forced him to move into an in-law apartment in the family home, a way station to a more formal separation.

"This development has left him stunned, one moment sympathetic to his wife's position and the next disbelieving that they can't work it out. 'I love her, but she wants me to be in love with her,' Dr. T. said. 'She wants to be my one and only. Everything we have will be at risk if, God forbid, we divorce.'"

Jane Gross "When the Beard is Too Painful to Remove"<br>
*The New York Times*, August 3, 2006

Many well-known men are part of this group, but have after many years come out, including: Congressman James Kolbe, Sir Elton John, former megachurch pastor Jim Swilley, Representative Steve Gunderson, Senator Mark Hatfield, Assistant Secretary of the Department of Defense Pete Williams, Calvin Klein, Jann Wenner, Malcolm Forbes, Apple CEO Tim Cook, Representative Robert E. Bauman (for a an exhaustive list, go to http://en.wikipedia.org/wiki/List_of_gay,_lesbian_or_bisexual_people).

Despite all the hurdles — both self-imposed and otherwise — and the confusion and desire to maintain the status quo and a sense of equilibrium, married men still come out because the pain of not being themselves is greater than the pain they'll go through by disclosing that they're gay.

> "There came a time when the risk to remain tight in the bud was more painful than the risk it took to blossom."
>
> ~ Anaïs Nin

In spite of the challenges of coming out, like most married men coming out, you will want to control the process of your coming out to whomever, at your speed, and in your timing. You'll need to be smart about this or else things could get out of hand quickly and in a manner that could be equally painful for you, your family, and relatives.

What you want to do is become the CEO of your life. You don't want to end up describing life as Sasha Purse has, "The difference between my life and hell…is it's better to be in hell." Instead, you want to manage your journey to freedom as Michelangelo described, "I heard an angel cry within the stone, so I carved until I set him free."

## *Coming Out to Your Spouse*

> "My wife called me a homosexual the other day.
> I nearly fell out my closet."
>
> www.sickipedia.org/sex-and-shit/gay/my-wife-called-me-a-homosexual-the-other-day-i-518421#ixzz3wOfLJB33

Life should be so funny! But, life isn't a sit-com or a movie, no matter how much we may wish it to be. The fact is…we have to face the facts. So, when the time arrives to come out, your spouse will most likely be the first loved one to whom you'll disclose. This will take a lot of careful thought and planning. The first thing to think about is when and where, then how to tell her.

If you have children, they should be second in line for your disclosure. In most instances, the news is going to be quite upsetting for your wife and having the children present only adds to the discomfort of the moment for everyone. And, your wife deserves to let her emotions have free rein. It's also emotionally hard on children to see their parents so visibly upset. Additionally, a lot could come spewing out of your wife's mouth as she begins the process of handling the news and it would not be appropriate for your children to be present for this.

Only you know your wife and can predict how she might react. Choose a time that has no emotional charge to it like Christmas, her birthday, Valentine's Day, or your anniversary (I've known men to disclose at those times). Secondly, choose a place where no one else will hear you, especially the children. It could get loud with angry words, swearing, and crying. You also want to make sure that no one else who doesn't belong in this exchange will intrude, especially another family member or friend, whether they're close or not. The only time you might include a third party is if you've been seeing a therapist and the therapist agrees to mediate, though I recommend against this option.

Next is to determine how to tell your spouse. Only you know the dynamic of your communications. For the most part, it's a matter of letting her know that you've been dealing with something for some time that she should know about. The news won't be pleasant for her to hear, but she deserves to know what's going on with you.

Let her know how much you've struggled with finally admitting that you're gay, how terrifying it's been to live with this knowledge about yourself (if that's true), and that you in no way meant to hurt her or the children — but, you can't hide your true feelings anymore and that's not fair to her or the kids. You need to let her know how sorry you are and that she and the children mean the world to you (if that's true; some men can't stand their wives and can't wait to get out of their marriages).

Generally, there will be tears, hurt, confusion, shock, and anger from your wife, and she's going to question upon what your marriage has been based:

> "Did you ever love me? Did you know you were gay before we got married? Why did you marry me? How long have you known? What the hell was going on when *we* were having sex? If you're gay, what does that make me? How could you have children knowing you're gay? Don't you have any respect for me and the kids? How are we to tell family, friends, and neighbors? Have you been with lots of men? What's going to happen now? Are you leaving me for a man — I don't know how to compete with that! Does this mean our son will be gay, too? Are you HIV+? Have you talked to a therapist, doctor, priest/minister? Do you know what you're doing is a sin? What am *I* going to do now? I'll do anything, just don't leave me."

As the reality of your disclosure hits home, your wife will question her own sense of identity, integrity, and beliefs. You've had years to come to your decision to be who you are, but your wife is suddenly faced with rediscovering herself in a way she'd not asked for or possibly imagined. She's going to asking herself, "Who am I?"

Your wife's self-esteem, sense of self-worth, and confidence are going to take a major pummeling. Her point of reference has always been in regards to the two of you as a conventionally married, heterosexual couple. That's been shattered, and she is now going to have to re-order her life, possibly as a divorced woman and possibly as a single parent. A lot of personal questions are going to arise for her:

> "How could I have been so blind? What am I going to do with my life? How am I going to survive financially? Will I be able to trust men again? Will another man ever want me at my age? Did I already know about my husband, but ignored it because I was "in love"? Was I desperate? Was I just too stupid? Was I trying to prove something? Do I know what real love is? How will people look at me? Will I be blamed for our marriage breakup? Is my church going to condemn me along with my husband? Where will I stand with my church? Is the faith I have in my religion wrong or misplaced? Am I just as bad and culpable as my gay husband? Am I the reason he turned gay? Do I still love my husband or am I just being dependent and emotionally needy? Can I find true love again? Is my understanding of marriage just a Cinderella fantasy? Can I trust *myself* anymore?"

Your wife is going to feel abandoned and stranded in a world she no longer recognizes because her social, religious, and family equilibrium has been thrown off kilter. So much of her belief system and values around your marriage that she was familiar and comfortable with have evaporated. Again, she is going to wonder who she is and where exactly she fits in society and how that works operationally. Have the rules changed or is it just that the media is having a field day with the issue of married men coming out?

Many wives are going to look at themselves in the mirror and not feel confident that they know who they are anymore, and possibly question their own sexuality in terms of who they are as a sexual being, what they truly want and what works for them, what they're willing to work with and compromise on, and even whether they might be in the closet themselves.

The institution of marriage has been rapidly evolving since the 1960s when established conventional lifestyles and institutions were confronted with the idealism of the counterculture movement. From then until now, for many people, marriage and marriage ideals have been refashioned so much so that the meaning of marriage is no longer as B&W as it used to be. This realization will add another layer of self-doubt for your wife. She may begin to wonder if she'll ever survive this unwelcome change in her life and just what her life is going to look like after the dust has settled.

Needless to say, your wife is going to go through many of the same emotions and processes you've been going through. For anyone questioning their identity and upon what it is based, bewilderment, disorientation, anger, fear, guilt, shame, loss, distrust, uncertainty, emptiness, listlessness, and grief are going to define many of his or her days. Your spouse will be no different.

Your wife could easily and, quite understandably, feel that she's a victim and that you betrayed her. She married you in good faith believing you were who you said you were and that you had the same future mapped out for each other. Now you're "the man behind the curtain," a man who can't be trusted with her life and heart, and in some cases, an imposter, a liar, and a manipulator. That's pretty damning. You'll be repeatedly apologizing — make sure you mean it. It's up to your wife to come to terms with whether she feels she's a victim or not, but you can sure push her in the direction of feeling like a victim if you're not sincere in admitting that you're sorry.

It will take time for your wife to believe you and trust in you again. Be patient and don't attempt to force things to move more quickly to suit your agenda and needs. That will only make this process more challenging and potentially hurtful. Respect and consideration for what your spouse is going through is imperative.

One thing to be very careful about is asking for forgiveness right away.

First of all, forgiveness is a truly individual and contextual thing. It's not automatically achieved just because one says, "I forgive you (or myself)." Forgiveness is something that will most likely be a long time in coming, possibly taking a lifetime or never fully coming about. A lot of emotions are tied up with your coming out to your spouse. They need to be addressed and lived with over time to sound out their full depth and impact. As with so much in life concerning our emotions, there are layers to peel back, understand, and resolve.

To be clear, forgiveness is not conditional, not a matter of bargaining, such as, "I'll do this, if you do that." To do so creates an open-ended situation where full forgiveness is never actually given. The seeking of forgiveness is then replayed and strung out over time, and can continually be used against each other. When asking for forgiveness, simply communicate to your wife that you're sorry to have hurt her and that that was never your intention. Be gentle, understanding, not demanding, and compassionate.

And be aware that forgiveness is not about forgetting. A woman will never forget this happening in her life, just as you won't forget your coming out.

Secondly, society, religions, and various therapies stress forgiveness as key in one's ability to move forward with their lives. That is very true. Just understand that forgiveness isn't a thing to check off on one's "to do" list. It is, instead, an ongoing process. Before you can forgive yourself and your wife forgive you, you will both need to deal with two other concepts: surrender and acceptance.

- Surrender means "to give up, abandon, relinquish, or let go." That's hard to do when you're emotionally invested in your marriage and way of life. We all develop expectations and create frameworks that give meaning and structure to our lives. You and your wife did the same in your marriage. But, once you've disclosed to your spouse that you're gay, that's going to require re-structuring and re-defining what your relationship is, what new dynamic you're going to maneuver within, who both of you are, and how life is going to look during this process and in the future.

The need to let go will then become a significant component in your reality and the more resistant either of you is to that, the more difficult the process will become. That doesn't mean denying your feelings and needs. It does, though, mean facing up to facts, and that's where acceptance comes in.

- Fact: You are gay and you want to shift your life to be structured around that reality. Your wife, whether she likes it or not, is going to have to eventually accept this jarring fact. It's referred to as "accepting what is." Avoiding or denying "what is" will only lead to more hurt, confusion, disappointment, and frustration for both of you.

If children are involved, this could make their lives very unsettling and scary. They won't necessarily know what's going on, but they will react to the emotional environment you and your wife are creating (more on that later in this chapter). Be very conscious of what and how you both are expressing yourselves when around your children. If you think "accepting what is" is challenging for adults, imagine what it's like for children who don't have your years of life experience and frame of reference.

Another fact is that most people would rather things didn't change. It just makes life so much easier. But the fact is that change is a constant. Your having come out doesn't mean you are going to go back into the closet just because your wife doesn't want to accept that you're gay. You are who you are. As painful and upsetting as this is for your spouse, you need to stand firm. You also need to do what you can to support her in understanding the situation, that you are a gay man, that this isn't the end of the world though it may feel like it, and that she will get through this major life shift.

Surrender and acceptance require patience, consideration, and empathy for everyone involved in your coming out process. Your spouse will experience ups and downs, days of ennui and despondency, as well as an embracing sense of release and freedom. Don't be dismissive of any aspect of this emotional process for either of you. Being sensitively and mutually supportive will aid everyone in this turbulent period.

Very importantly, you need to understand that your wife is coming out also. As a first step, she will need to come to terms with her understanding of what homosexuality is, her beliefs about it and what it means to her, as well as deal with societal myths, misrepresentation, and misinformation.

Your wife will then go through her own disclosure process to family, neighbors, friends, co-workers, etc. She'll experience the same fears and anxieties you underwent: the potential for rejection, loss, fear of her, blame, humiliation, cold pity from others, public aversion, excommunication, and even hate.

You cannot and should not be the only support for your wife's process. She will need to talk to others, especially those experiencing the same circumstances. One important resource is the Straight Spouse Network whose missions is: "We serve straight spouses, post disclosure couples, families, and the community by reaching out to increase visibility of straight spouses and accessibility to support; healing and empowering straight spouses to cope constructively; and building bridges between spouses, within families and with the larger community through support, education, and advocacy."

Doing a Google search will provide a listing of additional support resources that includes support groups and workshops, as well as publications and books.

Between just the two of you, your wife will need to feel that she can freely express herself and that she is being heard. On your part, prepare yourself to listen as openly and compassionately as you can. You're going to hear a lot that could be quite uncomfortable and hard to take in.

Having said that, at some point, anger and recrimination toward you will begin (some of the following may appear quite strident and unreasonable, but trust me, they were repeated to me by men in the group):

> "How could you do this to me after all I've done for you and I bore your children? How could you do this to the kids? You're a bastard and a liar. Now I know why you've been acting strangely. You're sick and need help. If you've given me or the kids AIDS, I'll kill you. Where can I get tested for HIV? You better not have had any of your men friends in this house or in our bed. I don't want the kids to know. I don't want the neighbors to know. I want an immediate divorce, and I get the house and custody of the kids. You're a pervert and if you've ever touched our son, I'll kill you. I'm going to take you to the cleaners. I don't want the kids to ever meet any of your disgusting men friends. You must move out immediately as I won't have your perversion in this house. God takes care of people like you. Because of you, I'll never find another man at my age — I'm used goods, all washed up."

You will hear a lot and you need to be willing to admit that you agree with some of her recriminations and accusations. You also need to be able to stand up to those comments that aren't true or completely factual. Don't get caught up with minutia, which will get you off track in dealing with the real issue at hand.

Her pain is going to be palpable. Whatever you do, don't go stoic on her. Let yourself be vulnerable with her. After all, you did marry her and you may have had children with her. Your marriage is based on something and you need to have that come through. This way, she won't feel completely abandoned by you and let feelings of worthlessness overtake her. Her self-esteem is definitely going to take a hit. Even though you're the bearer of upsetting news that's going to upend your family's life, old emotional habits between you will most likely kick in.

You can still support her to a degree, though she may initially want to keep a lot of distance between the two of you. Genuine gentleness, consideration, gratefulness, and compassion will go a long way toward re-establishing communications with her.

Speaking of communication, one thing not to do is unleash your whole history surrounding this subject. The last thing your spouse will probably be able to bear or want to hear is your "story." She'll be awash with her own emotions and empathy for you will probably not be at the top of her list. To quote Richard Nelson Bolles: "I have always argued that change becomes stressful and overwhelming only when you've lost any sense of the constancy of your life. You need firm ground to stand on. From there, you can deal with that change."

Give your spouse plenty of space to grasp the totality of your disclosure — however long that may take. At some point, she may ask for details so that she can begin putting two and two together and can regain some semblance of reality that makes sense to *her*...not you.

> I received a call late one night from Sherman. He was in a panic. He and his wife had gone to dinner and she had started asking deeper questions about their marriage and his decision to come out. During the conversation, she became more and more upset. Finally, in tears, she rushed out of the restaurant. Sherman, quickly paid the bill, but by the time he exited the restaurant, his wife had completely disappeared.
>
> Sherman jumped into his car and began roaming the streets trying to find her. She was nowhere to be found. He was in tears by the time he called me worried sick that something had happened to her. She was very petite and someone could easily take advantage of her. The important piece of information, though, was that she had told Sherman she was going to kill herself.
>
> I knew the part of town they were in and said I'd be right over to help find her. I drove around for about two hours and was unable to find either Sherman or his wife. I returned home and called Sherman. Amazingly, he was home and hysterical, still unable to find his wife, and in despair that she was truly going to kill herself. He blamed himself saying it was all his fault.
>
> I inquired as to what exactly he'd told her over dinner that would distress her so. Out came a story replete with all the drama of a movie-of-the-week. Sherman had felt such a rush of relief when his wife had started asking more involved questions that he mistook her desire to know more as the signal to tell all. And he did — all the fear, heartache, and gay experiences he'd had since before he met her and during the years of their marriage.

Being that they were both in their early twenties and married for about three years, they were emotionally in over their heads.

She had apparently gone into overwhelm with the tsunami of information and his emotional deluge. I asked Sherman if he'd called their friends and all the people she knew. He had. Suddenly, Sherman caught his breath. The front door of their apartment was opening — it was his wife. Without missing a beat, she lit into him and unleashed her own torrent of emotions dating back to before they married. The next time I saw Sherman, he was completely exhausted.

Suffice it to say that unloading on anyone tends to backfire. In this type of situation, it is best to consider the feelings of your spouse and only give enough information that works for her. Let her determine how much she can handle, and when she wants to know more, tread gently.

As with any challenge, time is going to play its part in this process. Have no illusions here: Your wife is going to need plenty of time to deal with this major change in her and the family's world. Be available without enabling her to emotionally blackmail you or to let her slip into a victim mode, which is very possible. Much of the focus of this upset is going to come out as, "It's all about you," an accusation you'll potentially level at each other.

> "The reason you're going to make a great fag
> is that most of you guys are just like dogs anyway....
> You do whatever with whomever pleases you
> and don't seem to care about the consequences."
>
> ~ Author Terry McMillan
> (in an alleged letter to her gay husband)

Fundamentally, this situation is about both of you. Each of you will be in pain and each needs to acknowledge that fact. You may be the cause of the breakup of the marriage and/or family, but everyone's heart is going to be battered, including yours. As hard as it will be to remain compassionate, it must remain a keystone for everyone throughout this process.

Since separation is generally unavoidable, legalities with property and children will come into play. Whatever your actions, as with any separation and/or divorce, do not use your children as pawns by getting them to ally with you or set your wife up as the bad guy — and don't let her set you up as the bad guy either. That's unfair to everyone involved. Though the fabric of your family is unraveling, there is no need to help it disintegrate unnecessarily. Despite the awkwardness and pain involved, let your kids see positive role models in this process as much as possible.

Lawyers usually get involved or, depending on how your relationship is adapting to this change in your marriage, a mediator could be appropriate. Therapy, both individual and couple's, is usually beneficial so that the two of you are not left to figure everything out on your own. The unbiased and neutral perspective and insights of a trained therapist can be exceptionally helpful for both of you.

Consider couple's therapy as early as possible. It's called a "window of opportunity" wherein the feelings you have for each other are allowed expression in a safe environment, which creates greater functioning and compassion toward the situation. The longer you wait to do this, the less inclined either of you may feel toward working with each other.

- In some situations, in which a married man comes out to his wife, both willing to stay together so as not to break up what they have for a home life and lifestyle. Some wives are willing to stay in the marriage even though their husbands may be involved physically and emotionally with a man. One wonders how the wife's emotional and sexual needs are to be met in this arrangement. What happens if she decides to take on a male lover? How are the children going to deal with this additional situation if and when they should find out?

- Some men want it all: wife, kids, family, home…and male lover — they just aren't willing to have one or the other. A lot of this has to do with fear of loss. Many men believe that their comfortable family situation will most certainly never be achieved again with a man. But what if a man comes along and they fall in love? What kind of home life could two men have? Would the male lover be able to give the type of love a wife gives? Additionally, the love and relationship dynamic with the children is something most men never want to lose. Would that be maintained? (Visit the following web site for a list of books pertaining to gay relationships: www.rainbowsauce.com/gaynonfic/gayrelation.html)

- Another fear dynamic is fear of the unknown. We all experience that from time to time, yet some men want certainty for their future. The thought that a man *might* come into their life with whom they *might* have a full and loving relationship is too big a gamble. They'd prefer to stay in their current situation being out to their wife and either practicing abstinence or deception. At any rate, they think they won't lose what they already have.

Many people either involved in the coming out process or observing others in this specific arrangement have the perspective of the man who wants it all is that he's being incredibly selfish and insensitive to his wife and family. To them, the guy is simply immature. And isn't that something that's said about many men is that they never really seem to emotionally grow up?

Selfishness is a word that will definitely be put out on the table. Who's being selfish, though? Generally, the married man coming out will be considered the selfish one, perceived as thinking only about themselves, wanting to be gay no matter who's negatively affected. Yet, from the spouse and family's perspective, they'd want their husband and father to remain in the closet or get "fixed" somehow. So who's being selfish?

This is difficult as each person involved wants to feel safe, secure, comfortable, and untroubled by life's demands, etc. But, for the most part, that isn't real life. Each day brings challenges we must either face or not — and change will definitely be a constant in our lives no matter how hard we work to keep things the same. Married men coming out face pain, frustration, confusion, fear and change, which are going to be a part of their personal equation despite attempts to distance ourselves from them. Whether we deal with them selfishly or not is a matter of degree and opinion.

The only way around being selfish is to put oneself in the shoes of the other person(s) involved to gain an understanding of what they may be going through on all levels. Then, it's making decisions that are inclusive and not just about satisfying one's individual needs and desires. It also means helping others to approach this situation in a similar manner.

It's very important to remember that this entire process isn't just about the married man coming out. Whatever arrangements are made, they take a toll on everyone involved and everyone's feelings must be taken into account. Just as with an addiction, everyone eventually gets dragged into its drama, pain, and process. Therefore, the best course of action is sensitivity toward all the parties involved. But sensitivity won't come into play with some spouses, though. Vengeance is determined to be the appropriate way to handle their husband's coming out announcement.

That's what happened with Kiernan, one of the original members of the married men's coming out group. His wife took all their credit cards and maxed them past their limits to the tune of over a hundred thousand dollars. It took Kiernan years to pay them off and, needless to say, they both kept their hate for each other alive for many, many years. They've now managed to get beyond that and talk to each other as they do have grown children. (How Kiernan and his wife came to an agreement that allowed them to be civil with each other again is covered in Chapter 5.)

Hopefully, as time passes, you will begin opening up to each other again. That isn't always the case, but if you truly love, or at least respect and/or care for each other, then there is a real possibility. Remember, your spouse will very possibly feel violated by your news. She may have feelings of having been used, that the trust she had in you has been destroyed. These will be the dominant feelings, along with her very possible loss of self-esteem. She will be going through her own process of trying to understand what your marriage was, who she is, and what the future holds for her. As much confusion as you're going through, she'll also be experiencing a life rewrite. Give her space and be supportive and considerate of her needs.

> "Straight Americans need... an education of the heart and soul.
> They must understand — to begin with — how it can feel
> to spend years denying your own deepest truths,
> to sit silently through classes, meals,
> and church services while people you love
> toss off remarks that brutalize your soul."
>
> ~ Bruce Bawer, *The Advocate*
> April 28, 1998

There are some situations where the wife already knew her husband was gay when she married him. You're probably wondering, "What was her motive?" There are several.

- One is that marrying a gay man is safe and certain things won't be asked of her. One woman I know married a gay man knowing they'd never have sex. She'd been badly abused, raped, and beaten by her former husband and didn't want a repeat.

- Another motive is that the woman is under the delusion that she can change the man, he just needs the right woman to "make him a man."

- Still others are following the dictates of their religion and truly believe that homosexuality is a choice and, therefore, marrying a gay man will change him and bring him into God's favor.

- Finally, there are those who marry a gay man simply because they do love each other and they'd be happier being together, though not sexually, than being apart. And for some couples, that works marvelously. They respect each other and honor their relationship dynamic.

And then there are those wives who, though sad and pained at their husband's disclosure, are amazingly supportive. The two remain close friends in spite of divorcing and breaking up the family as they know it. That is not the usual scenario, but it does happen. The basis for their relationship, no matter what, is universal love, which carries them forward into a lasting friendship.

One thing to be aware of here is determining upon what the continuing, but changed, relationship dynamic is based: co-dependency, fear, power, finances? A gay, married man and his wife can remain close friends and spend time with each other on a regular basis though the man is involved with another man or men. It's important to recognize if the husband and wife are clinging to each other out of emotional neediness, fear of moving on with their lives, and/or unwilling to move out of their existing emotional patterns. The known is always more comfortable because it's what they know and there's a degree of safety involved.

How will the man be able to move into a full relationship with another man if he's still emotionally, and possibly financially, tied to his wife? This gets tricky. The man may still love his wife, even deeply, caring for her wellbeing and welfare. Is the wife able to stand on her own two feet emotionally and financially? Are the two staying close because of the property they hold together or the children? Are there health issues involved? Or, is it about the fear of letting go and moving on with one's life? All of these must be taken into account so that all parties have the ability to move forward positively and healthily with their lives.

> Gene was in his second marriage when he finally came out as gay. His wife, Sarah, though not thrilled with the news, was very supportive and the two shared with each other a great deal of what was happening for them emotionally. They had their moments of frustration, annoyance and anger, but they chose to work hard to remain friends throughout the process.
>
> Today, almost three decades later, they are still very close seeing each other every weekend and talking several times a week on the phone. Gene's male partner, Evan, has

known Sarah for 20-some years, so the three of them have created their own little family unit, since Gene and Sarah never had children. The three go on outings together, as well as join each other for lunches and dinners on a regular basis.

Sarah has become far more independent and enjoys living by herself. Gene stops by from time to time at the house they still own together to do household chores that Sarah can't do. The two are still married, though Gene is settling into the final long-term relationship of his life with Evan. Evan completely understands Gene's love for his wife and his not wanting to abandon her or the love they still have for each other despite Gene's disclosure of being gay.

The situation with Gene, Sarah and Evan is not the norm, but it does happen and shows what is possible. Many couples will find this a challenge they don't want to take on simply because it means coming face-to-face with many of their own personal issues. What can be most beneficial is going to couple's counseling so that a dispassionate and objective third party can assist the couple in wading through the detritus of their marriage.

One thing to remember throughout this process is the initial love that brought the two together and formed the basis of their relationship. It hasn't been lost, just covered over with life's daily vicissitudes. Additionally, it helps to realize that we all have our blind spots that, if looked at supportively, are a means to identify and resolve our individual issues, freeing us to be more unconditionally loving and engaged in any relationship. It can be a very enlightening and empowering process for both individuals.

An important thing to remember is that it's not about being right and affixing blame to the other person. Relationships are a tango. Both parties choose to partner either supportively or not. Truly, it's unquestionably all about unveiling the real person inside — our truest essence — and learning how to love without conditions, agendas, and egoic needs.

Let's return to your wife and her reaction to the news that you're gay. She may not want your marriage to end no matter what. She'll deny you're gay. She'll tell you that:

- you're going through a phase,

- all men do some exploring at some time and that you'll get over it,

- all she needs to do is be a better wife because the entire situation is really her fault,

- she's willing to let you have male "friends" as long as you stay married to her and don't tell her about them, and

- if the two of you pray hard enough, you'll be saved and all will be well.

This kind of rationalizing and bargaining can easily rope you back into the marriage — especially if, when you came out to your wife, you actually stated that you're "confused" about your sexuality. That's an open invitation for your wife to "prove" that you're not gay and to pull out all the stops to keep you in the marriage.

This is quite unfair to both of you, especially to your wife as she's going to forever keep the HOPE shingle out anxiously waiting for you to come back to her and the family. All this will do is extend the entire process, as well as drag out and even exacerbate the emotional rollercoaster everyone will be on. So, be clear with your disclosure. Don't give your wife false hopes of maintaining your marriage.

Now, there are those spouses for whom this information is so overwhelming that their despondency carries over into powerful thoughts of suicide. If this is your situation, you need to seek immediate therapeutic help or, depending on the situation, call for an ambulance or the police. Do not operate under the delusion that you can handle the situation. Let the professionals take over. (There is more discussion concerning suicide in Chapter 7.)

Assuming your spouse has the "usual" response, new ground rules will need to be established. One of the rules may be that you need to live elsewhere, not in the family home. If you are not living in the family home, then an agreement must be reached in terms of when you can be at the house, when you can see the children, how much time you get to spend with them, and whether you can bring them to your new living space.

If you move to a new space and you're dating or already have a boyfriend, it should be some time before you introduce your current paramour to your kids. They need time to acclimate to your not living in the same house, that you and your wife are no longer together, that their family is no longer nuclear, and that they are seeing you in a new space you now call home.

They also need to get used to the idea that the decision you've made to be true to yourself — that of being an openly gay man — is very possibly a foreign idea to begin with because they've not had much real experience with the subject of homosexuality.

Secondly, what's foreign to them is that you want to make love to another man instead of their mother. Their picture of the family has been wrenched out of focus and they're going to try to put it back in focus in a way they can take in. That will take time. Trying to force them to move at your speed could actually drive them away. You may be experiencing joy and freedom with your new life, but you can't reasonably expect them to share in those feelings.

If you do remain in the family home, how you communicate with your wife and behave in front of the children needs to be discussed, no matter how old the children are. Kids easily pick up on energetic and emotional dynamics between parents. They'll most likely be wondering what's going on. You and your wife need to discuss how you want to handle your changing relationship and be very clear and consistent in your communications with each other and your children. Agree on when you feel would be a good time to let the children know about the situation.

## *Coming Out to Your Children*

A gentleman, Skip, called me for an intake interview. He required absolute confidentiality and secrecy as he was a highly-visible and well-known military doctor.

We met at a coffee shop far from the gay community and his home. In talking with him about his situation, he was stuck between a rock and a hard place. He wanted to be a part of the Men's Group but feared word would get out and the military would find out, thus, his long and distinguished military career would end tarnished, with him being discredited in the eyes of the military and world.

His second problem was that he found the idea of coming out to his wife and children difficult in the extreme, even though his son had come out and both Skip and his wife had become part of PFLAG (Parents, Families and Friends of Lesbians and Gays) in order to support their gay son.

The first issue was easily dealt with by Skip assuming a false name and background for the group. No one needed to know his real name and profession.

The second issue was a problem. What it came down to was that he, as a father figure, couldn't let his gay son down by coming out, too. Obviously, Skip was dealing with a self-image problem in both arenas.

One of the greatest fears a father has when considering coming out is the potential for losing his children, either through custody or the children turn away from him. Loss of his children's love can hurt more than the dissolution of his marriage. Why? The father is the one choosing to end the marriage, rejecting his spouse. If the kids turn away from him, they are rejecting him, not vice versa. When the door is shut on you, it cuts more deeply.

This is why when, where, and how you tell your children you're coming out and breaking up the family is so important. It's a double whammy for the kids. You may possibly lose them, though only for a short period of adjustment. You will most likely be seen as the bad guy and you may experience a sense of revulsion by some or all of your children, no matter their age. Hold your course. If you start falling apart in front of your kids, this will not only add to the discomfort of the moment, but show them that you don't have your act together. But this doesn't mean acting like a Stoic or being emotionally aloof. Your children still need to see that you are a human being with feelings. You'll need to maintain your relationship dynamic or your kids may decide they no longer need to respect you as their parent. Then you'll have a real uphill battle in front of you.

Note: If you're dealing with really young kids, full disclosure may not happen until a later date when you feel they can understand what you'll be telling them.

When to tell your kids is, again, important so that you're not choosing a time that's emotionally charged, such as a birthday, Christmas, or any type of celebration. Choose a place that feels safe and is private (the best place is in your home). Make sure you'll have plenty of time for discussion or simply the venting of emotions. You need to be ready to address their anger and tears or closing down. Don't force any discussion point. Let them control the flow of conversation.

They may also accuse you of all sorts of things — as well as being labeled everything that's the opposite of "hero" and "best Dad in the world" — and you need to be prepared to bring clarity to their understanding of what being gay means, as well as what's going to happen to the family. You will probably not need to go into intimate details concerning things of a sexual nature, but you never know what will be thrown at you by your children. As Art Linkletter used to say, "Kids say the darndest things."

Be sure to impress upon your children that you're still the same father they've always known. Just because you've disclosed that you're gay doesn't mean your love for them has changed. Additionally, give your children the tools they'll need to handle your disclosure and homosexuality with family, friends, school, church, and community. Remember, they're now joining you in the coming out process.

> Andrew, a Catholic, had four daughters, one in high school, two in college, and one graduated and married. When he came out to his wife with all four daughters present, battle lines were instantly drawn and emotions hit the roof.
>
> The eldest daughter was absolutely furious with her father, feeling that he'd betrayed her mother. She wanted him to contact Exodus International immediately and go through reparative therapy, electroshock therapy — whatever. The next two oldest, twins, were confused and unsure how to respond to this news. They chose to sit and watch the scene unfold.
>
> The youngest child was completely supportive of her father and started asking questions, which infuriated the eldest daughter who felt her youngest sister shouldn't be supporting their dad as it meant she was condoning his sinful behavior. The two went at each other full tilt with Andrew trying to intervene.
>
> Andrew's wife, though, was very supportive and willing to have him continue living at home even though he had a young male lover whose apartment he paid for. The eldest daughter blew up at her mother and loudly exclaimed that the entire family was going to hell because of everyone's mass denial.
>
> She announced that her father had put the entire family on the road to everlasting perdition. How could he do this to them? He was literally making their lives a living hell — she was never going to come back to their house again until he'd fully repented and renounced his homosexuality!
>
> Andrew's situation is all too common with family members who weigh in with their opinions and judgments. It can get pretty intense and a lot of accusations, misunderstandings,

and misinformation will fly through the air. Your job will be to dispel all the misinformation both about yourself and the gay community.

> "From a religious point of view,
> if God had thought homosexuality is a sin,
> he would not have created gay people."
>
> ~ Howard Dean
> Chairman Emeritus of the
> Democratic National Committee

There is a lot of misinformation spread by those who fear homosexuality. Unfortunately, the gay community's celebration of the male figure, its focus on easy sex, they're outlandish displays at times, and the specter of HIV/AIDS haven't helped straight people feel more comfortable with gay people. But, the heterosexual community is actually not much different if you think about it. They exhibit all the same foibles, addictions, vices, fears, insecurities, and obsessive/compulsive behaviors as gay people do. The only difference is that many heterosexuals believe gay people are more wrong than straight people, something akin to George Orwell's "Some of us are more equal than others" sentiment.

Another misunderstanding about gay people is that they can be "converted" to being heterosexual. There's a lot of controversy and contradictory data as to whether conversion therapy works or not, whether it's helpful or harmful. Much of the research on this subject has found that the majority of gay people attempting to convert have been unable to do so. Yet, there is a small percentage that are allegedly successful.

Exodus International — though it's been shut down in the US and its claim to cure homosexuality has been discredited by many psychologists — believes that through prayer and adherence to religious tenets that gay men can become "ex-gays." Much of their focus is about instilling the belief that homosexuality is a sin and that if a man remains homosexual, he's doomed to reside in hell for eternity. Their entire program is based on fear and manipulation.

What's most important when considering conversion therapy is to truly understand one's agenda in deciding to convert. Many endeavoring to convert want to be "normal," to have kids, be a part of a larger community where instant acceptance is guaranteed by virtue of appearing heterosexual. Others want to convert because of pressure from their religion and wanting to live by their personal religious beliefs. Others experience pressure from family, their jobs and careers, the groups they belong to, and their fears and ignorance about gay people, gay life, and actually being gay.

Whichever direction a man chooses, there will be challenges and pressures from gays and straights, each wanting you on their "team," each with their own opinions, judgments, and rational as to which side is best, correct, and/or moral. If you — or someone you know — are still confused about your sexual identity, working with a therapist trained in this issue can be very beneficial. Don't attempt to go it alone. You need a sounding board, someone to help you organize your thoughts, keep you grounded and out of fantasyland, and to guide you in working to understand your feelings and upon what they are based.

If conversion therapy is not what you're seeking, then you'll want to do some homework to truly understand the myriad aspects of the gay community. Be ready to abolish myths and correct misunderstandings. Know what the story is with AIDS and assure your family that you are not HIV+ unless that isn't the case. If you are HIV+, then be prepared to deal with your children's fear of you, that they may think you've possibly given them AIDS, and the fact that they'll probably think you'll be dying soon. That will be like throwing gasoline on a fire. If you think things can't get worse, think again. Consider family therapy to address the issue of HIV combined with your coming out as a gay man.

> "Prevention, treatment and care are now saving millions of lives
> not only in the world's richest countries,
> but in some of the world's poorest countries as well.
> And for many, with testing and access to the right treatment,
> the disease that was once a death sentence
> now comes with a good chance at a healthy and productive life.
> And that's an extraordinary achievement."
>
> ~ President Barack Obama
> 2013 Address for World AIDS Day

If you aren't HIV+, then be prepared to assure your family that you won't be getting it, that you'll be careful because you want to be there for them for the rest of their lives. Let them know you'll always be their father no matter what and they can always come to you for anything.

This change that's happening with the family is not about them, it's about you being who you truly are. You'll still be the loving father they've always had and nothing will ever change that. Be aware, though, that they may not want you touching or hugging them for a while. You've thrown their world out of whack and the news that you are gay means you're not the person they thought they knew. They will see you as changed: you look and sound like their dad, but somehow you're not.

For the kids, they'll be thinking in terms of their world as they know it ending. Their lifestyle may change for the worse. They're losing you. The family will be breaking up. They'll probably have to choose between you and mom. They may have to move. They may feel stigmatized by everyone they know, fear that their friends will probably think they're gay. You've lied to them for God knows how long, and that you probably don't really love them. How could you love a *man* — gross! Be ready to address all these concerns of theirs.

> "Be who you are and say what you feel,
> because those who mind don't matter
> and those who matter don't mind."
>
> ~ Dr. Seuss

The location and setting you choose for telling your children is very important. At home is your first choice as it is familiar territory and they can always retreat into their own bedrooms if necessary. Whether your wife is there with you is up to what both of you based on what is in your *children's best interests*. Again, do not use your children as pawns and a means to get back at each other or create allies. For the most part, the issues you have in your marriage are separate from dealing with your children. They don't need to know all the ins and outs of your spousal relationship. One day, you may discuss this with them, but right now, the most important thing is their feelings and supporting them in understanding what is happening.

If you're seeing a therapist and the therapist agrees, you could come out to your children with the therapist present. This is a secondary choice as the therapist will be a complete stranger to your kids and since their trust in you will be strongly tested, having a stranger present will not exactly instill trust. Your kids may clam up during the disclosure process simply because they won't feel comfortable. Their feelings of duress may in fact increase. This would obviously defeat the purpose of the disclosure session. So, discuss this in detail with your therapist to determine what would be the most appropriate and best for the children.

On the other hand, it may not matter that a stranger is present. Your kids might still get involved with the session despite the stranger's presence. This will depend on how that stranger's being there is explained. The kids need to know that this is a therapist who is only there to support them and provide feedback and insight into what is discussed, that no judgments will be made no matter what is said during the session, and that the therapist won't be taking anyone's side. This will go a long way in creating an atmosphere of trust and your kids may feel more inclined to express themselves freely.

One thing you definitely don't want to do is disclose to your kids with your boyfriend present, if you have one. That could easily send the kids over the edge. They may feel that they have no say as to how their reality is structured, that they're being manipulated against their will. It'll be too much for them to take in and you could find yourself dealing with a child or all your kids having an emotional breakdown. That isn't the outcome you're seeking. If you need support during this process, either have your wife present or your therapist. It is also not advisable to have a sympathetic relative or family friend present. This is very intimate family stuff, and consideration and sensitivity need to be employed.

Depending on the age of your children, you may need to have separate talks with them.

- Younger kids are not going to be able to understand some of the concepts you'll be bringing up like homosexuality, liking men instead of mommy, divorce, etc. Explain that there are some things you'll talk with them about when they're a little older.

- As for your older kids, be frank with them and be prepared to handle their more adult emotional responses, as well as tough questions. Whatever you do, don't patronize them or avoid addressing the content of their questions. Though their trust in you will be strained, being honest and authentic with them will work to everyone's benefit. They'll also be more inclined to work with you rather than shut you out and not care about your feelings.

- Just as safety and confidentiality are important to you, the same will be true for your kids. Assure them that they're not going to see you on the news, you're not going to embarrass them in any way, their friends won't know, that only the family knows the situation — and you aim to keep it that way unless as a group you decide to change that policy.

- If you have a boyfriend, let them know that they don't have to meet this person unless they want to and they don't have to like him if they do meet him. Also let them know that they don't have to accept your new lifestyle, so you won't be asking them to march in a Gay Pride parade, go to PFLAG meetings, or join any kind of gay support group unless they want to.

- If you're a person already in the limelight in some manner, then your situation may be even more delicate concerning public exposure. If your family is finding out about your true proclivity via the media and not you, then you'll have just as much explaining to do as any other man. You will need to defend yourself and your actions from the standpoint of having already been convicted by your family as being deceitful and dishonest. You'll also need to fence with the media, which will add a whole new level of pressure and stress to the situation.

It's best to come clean with your family first and step through the subsequent process with them privately. If possible, and depending on your situation, vis-à-vis your position/public persona, come out publicly only after thoroughly discussing the matter with your family. They are going to be put in the spotlight whether they want to be or not — and you instigated this without their consent. They need to be as ready to deal with public scrutiny as much as you. They are going to feel caught between a rock and a hard place and feelings of disappointment, shame, embarrassment, humiliation, guilt, anger, loathing, revenge, and fear will very likely come into play.

If you have young children, your parental instinct will be to protect them. Do the best you can with this. Again: be honest, be loving, be open and available to them. Just understand that you won't be able to shield them from everything as information is going to be coming at them from many angles.

Depending on the intensity of the media's interest in you, you may decide to keep your children at home rather than have them continue attending school, sports practice and games, church, and clubs and community events. Prepare your children for some of the things that will be said to and about them and you by their peers and even adults who don't know any better.

> "Nothing in the world is more dangerous
> than a sincere ignorance
> and conscientious stupidity."
>
> ~ Martin Luther King, Jr.

The last thing you want to launch is a media circus with you and your family center ring. The more you are able to maintain family cohesiveness — despite the news of your coming out and upsetting the family's equilibrium — the more you will as a group be able to weather any media onslaught.

Finally, honesty is the best policy. We've all seen large-scale dishonesty at work with politicians concerning their sex scandals and how absurd the situation can become. Those are not people you need to model because, to put it succinctly, they are not role models.

If you want people to feel you still have some shred of integrity left within you, then be integrous — completely. No playing games, e.g., Bill Clinton's "It depends on what the meaning of the word 'is' is" while testifying before a grand jury concerning his affair with Monica Lewinsky. Or Newt Gingrich who was having an extramarital affair at the same time he was trying to impeach Clinton for being involved with Monica.

> "For seven and a half years
> I've worked alongside President Reagan.
> We've had triumphs. Made some mistakes.
> We've had some sex...uh...setbacks."
>
> ~ Former President George H.W. Bush

At some point and depending on the age of your child or children, you may want to let them know that there are a lot of other gay people in the world, too, that you're not the only one — and they all have stories they can share about being gay. With the advent of the Internet, a great deal of information is available that will help give them a birds-eye view of the gay community. This is something you can do together, especially since some of the material may be inappropriate for them and you will want to be able to monitor what they're viewing.

**Partial List of Well-known Gay Individuals Who Have Come Out**

| | | |
|---|---|---|
| Marc Almond | Stephen Fry | David Paisley |
| John Amaechi | Brittney Griner | Peaches |
| John Barrowman | Neil Patrick Harris | Megan Rapinoe |
| Lance Bass | Sean Hayes | Christopher Rice |
| Matt Bomer | Elton John | Bobbie Rogers |
| Derren Brown | Natasha Kai | Portia de Rossi |

| | | |
|---|---|---|
| Rhona Cameron | Adam Lambert | Michael Sam |
| Jason Collins | k.d. Lang | David Sedaris |
| Steven Davies | Jane Lynch | Darryl Stephen |
| Rupert Everett | Luke Macfarlane | Sheryl Swoopes |
| Boy George | Ricky Martin | Wanda Sykes |
| Anderson Cooper | Ian McKellen George | George Hosato Takei |
| Orlando Cruz | Michael | Rosie O'Donnell |
| Alan Cumming | Matthew Mitcham | Tila Tequila |
| Ellen Degeneres | John Cameron | David Testo |
| The Fab Five | Mitchell | Gareth Thomas |
| Jesse Tyler Ferguson | Martina Navratilova | Esera Tuaolo |
| Jodie Foster | Cynthia Nixon | Darren Young |
| Barney Frank | Graham Norton | |

You may know local people who are publicly out of the closet. Your children will have questions about people they suspect are gay. Be ready to discuss those people with your children and allay any fears they may have concerning them.

If you don't know for sure if someone is gay or not, don't affirm that they are — they may not be out of the closet yet or may not be gay in the first place. To put it simply, you could be sued for stating someone is gay when they aren't or they're still trying to hide their true identity. Don't add a class action suit to what's already on your plate.

Also be prepared to discuss questions and concerns about pedophilia, stalking, outing, and other social issues concerning the LGBT community.

After disclosing to your children, it will be the same situation as occurred with your wife. Your kids will need time to come to terms with this monkey wrench in their lives. Give them space, be available to them, and be willing to be vulnerable. Whatever you do, don't shut down. Answer your children's questions, no matter how intimate they are. They will very likely have some of the same things to say to you as your wife. If they seem to be fishing for answers as to how your wife is with this change, encourage them to talk to her rather than avoid dealing with her directly.

In time, as things settle down, the subject will arise as to who else should know what's going on. The most appropriate people would be relatives including siblings, parents, and extended members of your family.

## Coming Out to Siblings, Parents, and Other Relatives

> "I love my parents. Coming out to them
> was sort of coming out to myself.
> I educated them,
> and I wanted our relationship to keep growing.
> I wanted them to be a part of my life still.
> I wanted to be able to share with them
> what I was going through."
>
> ~ Randy Harrison

At some point, you'll feel the need to let your siblings, parents, and other relatives know that you're gay and what's happening with your family. This is another big hurdle with all the same possibilities as you coming out to your family.

Having your immediate family know you're gay is different than their accepting the fact that you're gay. It will take some time for them to get used to this new factor in their lives. They'll be watching you to see if you've changed in any way or they may hide from you. It will be very important to them to feel that you are still the person they've known you to be and that they can trust who you are.

Be consistently available and communicative, especially about what's going on in their world. Let them know you're still interested in them and what's happening with their lives. And be aware that moods will swing back and forth so that on some days, life will appear copacetic and other times completely unhinged — as though life weren't that way before you made your disclosure.

For many men, coming out to their parents is even more frightening than coming out to their immediate family. There's a deep-seated fear of being rejected by our parents, whether they are the people who brought us into the world, or the adopters who specifically chose us from amongst other children. Our parents are the original people to love and nurture us on a level that no one else can. To have them reject us is like being sentenced to hell for eternity. Therefore, disclosing to them is fraught with fear.

> A friend of mine, Ryan, discovered he was gay in his late teens, but chose to hide from that part of himself and has now been married twice. I've known him since 17 and I also knew his family.

> Ryan's father knew I was gay and would do anything to support me, including beating up anyone who attacked me for being gay. But his own son being gay — no way. That he could not support.
>
> Ryan came to visit me in 1991. We'd not seen or heard from each other for nine years so had a lot of catching up to do. He told me that even though he was currently married, he was just about ready to come out. But one thing he would not be doing is telling his father.
>
> I told Ryan I had a feeling that as soon as his father passed away, he would come out as a gay man. What would be great is if he could have that special conversation with his dad before he passed. Well, the day came when his father was dying and Ryan did have that conversation. It was as though a great weight lifted off his shoulders as Ryan's dad told him he loved him and that he was proud that Ryan was his son.

Not all stories end this touchingly.

> Roger thought he knew how his parents would react when he came out to them: his dad would reject him and his mom would fully embrace him. What a surprise for him when just the opposite occurred. His dad embraced him, but mom couldn't accept him for who he is. Her rejection was devastating to him and he ended up on antidepressants for over a year until he finally came to the conclusion that he could never prove himself worthy enough in her eyes and that it was her problem, not his.

This type of story happens all too often. Whether a man has a close relationship with his parents or not, the impact of disclosing to them is still a major undertaking and is deeply felt. Many issues need to be taken into account: the quality of the relationship you have with both parents, their feelings about homosexuality, their religious/spiritual beliefs, their health, and their age.

Everything I've covered concerning coming out to your immediate family comes into play with your parents. The one added component is confidentiality. Agreements must be made as to whom they can tell or not tell concerning your extended family — and those agreements must be maintained. If there is one thing that will get a family off track concerning the topic of coming out, it's all the background talk that can occur and families are great at gossiping amongst themselves. Again, you want to control this process as much as possible. That's why you need to attain agreements from not just your parents but your siblings and other relatives.

Many times, before parents are told, siblings are told first, which gives you a chance to figure out how your parents will deal with this news judging by the feedback you get from your siblings concerning your parents. Be as neutral as possible as each sibling will have their own idea of what your parents can handle and why. If you don't have siblings, then you'll just have to go with your own instincts and trust that your timing and approach are right.

As for your siblings' reactions, it can cover the spectrum.

> In 1983, my sister, Aileen, came to New York to visit for a week and take a break from taking care of our dying father back in Colorado. One night, my sister, my partner, Roger, and I went to a Broadway show and then Aileen and I went to Joe Allen's as she might see some stars and return home with some great stories.
>
> Joe Allen's was packed to the gills with theater people and patrons. I managed to wrangle a small round table in the midst of the crowd. As soon as we sat down, Aileen barked out, "Are you gay?" I responded cautiously with yes and why was she asking. She immediately burst into tears and began yelling at me. She demanded to know if I was ill. I asked what she meant and she responded that she read things. Highly irked with her, I replied that I was HIV negative and "What's wrong with you?" Aileen just kept on crying and accusing me of all sorts of things and bringing up old family baggage.
>
> This exchange went on for a while. The room was so crowded that people were pushed up against us and it was a little difficult holding a reasonable conversation. Aileen kept up with her crying and angry outburst to the point that the people standing around us took notice and began interrupting. I explained that we were having a private conversation, please stay out of it. My sister didn't let up

with her irrational attack and I, getting fed up, eventually asked the strangers surrounding us if they'd like to jump in and comment.

We eventually went back to my apartment and Aileen cried until around 3 am. She stated that I was not to tell our dying father that I'm gay as that would kill him (groan). In my extreme annoyance with her, I blurted out that he was dying anyway, why would it matter? That went over real well. Before I got a chance to fly back to Colorado, though, our father passed on.

I came out when I was about age 17, but not to my family. I figured they knew anyway considering I had been in theater most of my life being heavily involved in music since age five, was a well-known dancer in New York, had at one time been involved with a priest from our parish, and had only introduced them to and talked about one particular man in my life, Roger, for the past five years. It just goes to show you that you should never second guess a sibling's knowledge of you or underestimate their response when the subject is broached either by you or, as in my case, my sister.

Everything covered in this section applies to your siblings. You'll discover who is supportive and who isn't, who's trustworthy and won't disclose this information to anyone else and who will, who wants to polarize around this issue and who wants to stay open and flexible. To repeat: Attain agreements from everyone involved so that you don't suddenly find yourself on a runaway train. You'll need to repeatedly remind family members of their agreements with you as they may forget.

You'll also want to discuss just what confidentiality means because a banner item such as coming out is hard to keep to oneself. Family members will feel that it's okay to tell so-and-so because they're an old friend or relative or just like family. Wrong! People inadvertently finding out about your sexuality could cause irreparable damage to relationships, affiliations, jobs, and careers. It's best to come out when you're ready to the people you trust the most and then expand who you come out to as appropriate for you. You don't need to become an item for the tabloids.

There is the possibility that some of your family members are going to reject you and homosexuality. For whatever reason, your disclosure just won't compute in their world and the only way they can deal with it is to shut "it" and you out. Being adults, they'll have had many more years to let attitudes become deeply ingrained than your children, so that being reasonable just isn't going to happen.

You may never talk to or see some of these people again and they won't let you around their own children. This can be heartbreaking, but you need to realize that the problem doesn't lie with you, it lies with them: they haven't the capacity to meet you halfway concerning this subject. Whether it's religious fundamentalism, fear, or ignorance doesn't matter. When the door is closed on you, it hurts deeply. If you're prepared ahead of time for this potential, you'll get through it much more easily.

> "You could move."
>
> ~ Abigail Van Buren, "Dear Abby,"
> in response to a reader who complained
> that a gay couple was moving in across the street
> and wanted to know what he could do
> to improve the quality of the neighborhood.

Finally, some family members will deny that you are gay no matter what you tell them. "It's just a phase" or "You're just exploring" or "You're going through a mid-life crisis — you'll come to your senses, return to your family, and everything will be back to normal." Sigh....

Understand that emotions are not based on reason or logic. When things happen, people are either reactive or responsive. To be reactive means that no reasoning has occurred, just an immediate knee-jerk action taken that could be for the better or worse. To be responsive means that one thinks before taking action so that the action taken is more appropriate to the situation. Family will most likely be in reactive mode when you disclose. You then need to be in responsive mode to help them come to a more reasonable and calm place. If not, then all hell can break loose and the upset feelings will be exacerbated. You'll get dragged into that hellish vortex.

## *The Emotional Effects of Coming Out for You*

When all is said and done, the process of coming out to your immediate family and relatives can be very distressing, so much so that you may experience overwhelm. Work with a therapist or psychiatrist as you may also find yourself deeply depressed and even entertaining thoughts of suicide. I don't like the idea of being medicated, but sometimes there is no other solution than to take antidepressants — temporarily, and definitely under a doctor's care.

One thing to be aware of is that you may possibly go through a period of grieving. What you're grieving for is the loss of what you've known for however many years and a certain level of safety and comfort you had created. Your life is changing and a lot can be left behind as you move into new territory, both figuratively and literally. You may experience loneliness and even abandonment even though you're the one initiating the change in the family.

A note on grief: It's something that affects people from all walks of life. In her book *On Death and Dying*, Elizabeth Kubler-Ross puts forth five distinct stages of dying: denial and isolation, anger, bargaining, depression, and acceptance. This process is prompted by traumatic events, the passing of a loved one or a pet, and losses of all kinds. Her five stages have been around for years.

Other research has determined that people, though they do experience grief and loss, are far more resilient than described in Kubler-Ross's work. It seems that Kubler-Ross's process was developed from having worked with people who were in the dying process or who had lost someone to death.

In Ruth Davis Konigsberg's book, *The Truth About Grief: The Myth of Its Five Stages*, research included people not dealing with death and dying issues, but other kinds of loss. What she discovered is that most people grieve for about six months, overcome their loss, and then begin moving forward with their lives. Many people go on to thrive, though the sense of loss will remain with them throughout their lives. You might want to read both of these books.

Everyone is unique, so what's important here is to approach your grief in the way that works best for you. There are numerous ways to deal with grief, so do some research and explore what's available. Whatever your choice, be very mindful to not avoid, defer, deny, or suppress your feelings — and don't let anyone try to corral you into doing something that doesn't feel right for you.

The grieving process is an integral aspect of your entire coming out process. Go ahead and feel whatever feelings you're having and don't stuff anything. You stuffed your gayness all this time and that didn't serve you very well, so why would you want to stuff your feelings once again? Truly, this is the time to get real, to be in touch with your core being. Denying, repressing, avoiding, and deflecting will only retard your personal growth and ability to move forward in your life. It's a new day and though you may not be feeling it at the moment, you are a new you, the real you.

If you find you're having trouble dealing with your grieving process, seek professional assistance. There's no need to go it alone. If, after you've worked with either a therapist or psychiatrist you feel you need medical intervention and they feel likewise, then please avail yourself of this possibility.

Should you decide to go this route, be sure you're working with a reputable psychiatrist and that you are closely monitored. I would suggest you not get a prescription from your family doctor as they are not as well versed with psychological issues as a psychiatrist. For a list of the most commonly prescribed antidepressants, visit: www.webmd.com/depression/symptoms-depressed-anxiety-12/antidepressants.

For those who approach life from a more natural perspective:

- St. John's Wort is widely known as an herbal treatment for major depression, and standardized extracts are available over the counter.

- SAMe (S-adenosyl-L-methionine) is a chemical naturally found in all the cells of your body, and has been found to be as effective as antidepressant medications when used in proper doses.

- Ginkgo biloba improves blood flow through the brain, and has helped many people regain mental acuity and improve mood.

- Caffeine not only wakes you up, it can also improve mood, decrease pain, and bring about weight loss in some patients.

As with anything, read labels and directions and be aware of side effects and allergic reactions, if any. Additionally, work with a licensed practitioner to determine what is best for you.

You may, just as your spouse will, very likely suffer self-esteem issues. Working with a therapist will help you sort through the rollercoaster of emotions you'll experience about yourself. You'll go through periods thinking you made a huge mistake coming out. You'll determine that no man is going to be attracted to you. You'll decide that men aren't capable of loving you the way your wife did. Maybe you'll find the gay community too scary or maybe you'll agree with one member of the Married Men's Coming Out Group who stated, "I hate gay people." Perhaps you'll get stuck in a conundrum between what you were taught by your religion and what you feel inside yourself. Whatever it is, you'll have an emotional reaction that needs addressing. And don't do as you may have done in the past: stuff your feelings and avoid dealing with the issues. You've come this far and you *will* make it through the rest of the process.

You're not alone and there are those who can and will support you. So, support yourself by not reverting back to old behavioral patterns or letting fear dictate your life journey. And, as you go through your process, begin putting together your support team of family members, the ones you can truly trust to have your best interests at heart. They will prove to be a lifeline.

On a final note, having gone through the most difficult disclosures you need to make, there is light at the end of the tunnel.

## Chapter 4

## Coming Out to Others

I was an expert in computer-based training (CBT) and had worked on numerous projects for large North American companies, as well as high-profile military assignments. Before CBT, I'd danced in New York, which included modeling. In keeping with current trends, I got my left ear pierced and a very small silver ball earring became part of my everyday wear.

When my partner, Roger, and I moved to San Diego in 1988, my first assignment was to teach a 2-week class at North Island Naval Base. I arrived at the classrooms to have an initial meeting with the client's head instructor and several other personnel, including the Captain.

The Captain showed up late to the meeting which was already in progress. Everyone stood when the Captain arrived, including me. The Captain approached me to shake hands and began his introduction by saying, "I hear you just moved here yesterday from New York City."

I responded with yes, I had. The Captain immediately remarked, not looking me in the eyes, but staring at my left earlobe and the tiny dot of an earring the entire time, "I hear those faggots out there...."

I, being the person I am, retorted warmly without batting an eye, "If it weren't for those faggots, people of color, and all the other people considered undesirable and different, New York wouldn't be the incredible city it currently is and the world would be very sad and lackluster." You could have heard a pin drop. I immediately turned to the rest of the group and suggested we continue our meeting.

At lunch, the Captain approached me and apologized for his remark about faggots. I accepted his apology.

I also explained that I am gay and discussed the inappropriateness of the remark not just because the Captain was meeting me for the very first time and didn't know me from Adam, but the negative ramifications of labeling and using denigrating language as a generic means of communication continues to promote hate and divisiveness. The Captain and I became good friends outside of my training assignment.

I have always been up front about my sexual orientation. I'm neither overt nor covert — no matter what work scenario or social setting I'm in. I don't broadcast to co-workers, clients and people in general that I'm gay, but if the matter does come up, I never deny it. My left earlobe now sports three pierced earrings and I never think twice about it no matter where I am.

Sometimes, the opportunity to come out is handed to us on a silver platter, such as what happened with me. But most of the time, it's going to be a pre-meditated process that involves not only planning who to tell and how to disclose that you're gay, but agreements about what happens after disclosing that information.

The process of coming out to non-family members is one that will most likely take years. This is a long, drawn out process simply because the need to disclose is not as urgent as with family and has different ramifications. Again, you want to be in control of this process, not someone else, so agreements and boundaries will need to be created and maintained.

## *Coming Out to Friends, Co-workers, and Other Important People*

After you've let the dust settle from coming out to family and relatives, you'll begin feeling the need to be out to the rest of the world. Since you no longer want to lead a double life with family, the same impetus that drives that decision will come into play with the wider world. When it comes to dealing with larger circles of interaction, people's reactions to your coming out generally will not have the love component in the mix. They're not part of your close family. Whether you are actively in their lives or not may not matter all that much. Whether you fit into their world views is another matter altogether.

Before we discuss coming out to people other than family, let's get some clarity around the subject of homosexuality. There are some people in society who believe being gay is a choice. Yes and no. Heterosexual men don't wake up one day and say, "I think I'll switch to being homosexual." If they did, that would be a choice. That isn't the case. Heterosexual men are heterosexual because it's intrinsic to their very being — they can't be other than what they are — heterosexual. The same is true for homosexual men: they can't be other than what they are — homosexual. It's intrinsic to their nature.

Here's where choice does come in: to live and be who you intrinsically are *or are not*. This book is about and for men who previously "chose" to not be who they fundamentally are. Rather, because of socio-cultural conventions and pressures, they chose *to be someone they are not*. We can't choose who we fundamentally are internally, but we can choose *how* we want to live externally. We can choose to deny ourselves, to become turtles hiding in our shells, living a lie or to be who we are and live with honesty and integrity. Ask yourself: Why would any man "choose" to be gay in this society when he could be maligned and treated so horribly?

Socially, gay men are seen as pariahs and many times are going to suffer at the hands of people who feel it's okay to abuse, deny rights, castigate, publicly humiliate, openly hate, ostracize, and irrationally judge. There are some who feel it's their civic and religious obligation to mete out "justice" and become the *bringer of death*. Yes, bringer of death. Remember:

- Matthew Sheppard, aged 21, tortured and murdered in 1998 for being gay

- Kenneth Cummings, Jr., 48, murdered in 2007 for being gay, the murderer claiming to be doing God's work

- Steven Parrish, 18, murdered in 2008 by fellow gang members for "possibly" being gay

- Lawrence King, 15, murdered in front of 24 fellow students in 2008 for being gay

- Moses Cannon, 22, shot to death in 2008 for being gay

- Felix Pearson, 19, Kenneth Monroe, 27, and Darriel Wilson, 20, murdered en mass in 2008 for being gay

And the list goes on...

Knowing how gay men can be treated in society, why would anyone "choose" to be gay, be treated badly, abused, bullied, and possibly get killed for it? Gay men need to be who they truly are. It has nothing to do with socio-cultural conventions. It's about the integrity, honesty, self-respect, congruency, and courage that come with being able to live with your real, natural, and true self. To live according to someone else's dictates is to live your life in fear. To quote the Spanish proverb used in the movie *Strictly Ballroom*, "A life lived in fear is a life half-lived (Vivir con miedo, es como vivir a medias)!"

The other component of choosing to be who you are — a gay man — involves determining what kind of gay man. Just as in the heterosexual world where there are many types and expressions of men, the same holds true in the gay world. What many people see and what is generally reported on by the media are the more overt, external expressions such as drag queens, leather men, fems, men in military and work uniforms, and scantily dressed men in skin tight clothes at gay bars, Pride events, and depicted in the arts. What is not focused on are all the ordinary types of gay men who are doctors, lawyers, bus drivers, fathers, coaches, pastors, and men who you very often wouldn't know are gay unless they've told you.

> Doug joined the Married Men's Coming Out Group in the early 1990s. Meeting him, you'd never guess he was gay: he had a blue collar job, dressed blue collar, talked like most men do, and loved sports. But his sensibilities in the Men's Group were completely that of a gay man, though none of the persona and characteristics of a straight man disappeared. He was completely at home in his being and it just wasn't in him to be any of the homosexual behavioral characteristics we all know about, stereotypical or not.

Gay men come in all shapes and sizes. Their expressions of masculinity, variety of interests that straight men have, behavioral distinctions, male habits, emotional range, and personality types are the same that straight men possess. Take a look at Appendix B for a list of 370 male archetypes available to men. (We cover this in Chapter 9, which discusses coming out in the gay community.) For now, enough said on this subject. Let's continue with coming out to people other than your family members.

Anxiety usually sets in with this next phase for the very same reasons we have previously discussed (Chapter 2): there's plenty of potential for being rejected by and losing people in the process. This phase, though it will cover the same territory, will not have as much stress attached to it, as with family and relatives, simply because the people involved will generally not impact your heart as family will. You have had the experience of stating, "I'm gay" to a number of family members and dealt with the consequences. This is not to say that you won't experience emotional pain, confusion, and fear during this phase of coming out. Rejection is rejection and still hurts.

> Patrick's best friend was the best man at his wedding and also his gym workout partner. Patrick agonized over coming out to his friend. He was afraid their friendship might end and that he'd be subjected to all sorts of hurtful comments and questions.
>
> One day, following a gym workout, Patrick told his friend he needed to talk to him about something really important. They found a quiet place without people present and Patrick explained that he and his wife were getting a divorce. His friend was astonished and asked for further explanation. Patrick gave it to him.
>
> Patrick's friend was dumbfounded. He had never suspected and initially thought Patrick was putting a joke over on him. Patrick explained, as his eyes welled up with tears, that this was no joke. His friend immediately hugged him and then jokingly said, "Don't get any funny ideas that I'm coming on to you."
>
> That broke the ice for Patrick giving him the opportunity to open the flood gates and describe to his friend all that he'd been through for years concerning his sexuality, how for so long he'd wanted to tell his friend, and the pain he'd been in.

Never underestimate the people around you and how they might react to your coming out news. You'll experience quite a spectrum of responses that run the gamut from total surprise, denial, fear, anger, disappointment, damnation, concern, support, and love to something as simple as, "I suspected you were." Not being in other people's heads, you need to be prepared for just about anything. Never second guess the outcome and never think that you'll get the same response from one person to the next.

How and when you choose to come out to anyone is up to you, no one else. There will be some people you'll dread telling and others you'll feel won't care. Telling friends will have different ramifications than telling co-workers, colleagues, and clients. Telling clergy and people from your church will necessitate a different conversation than with people in the business world. Each arena will have its own parameters and requirements. Only you can determine and manage the approach and outcomes.

When coming out to friends and neighbors, be aware that you'll experience a broad range of reactions similar to your family, one of them being fear for their children, even if their kids are grown adults (their children are their children and they'll revert to protective measures). One of the most damaging pieces of dis- and misinformation circulating in society and actively publicized by some very anti-gay people is that gay men are pedophiles. Granted, there is a very, very, VERY small segment of society that includes pedophiles on both sides of the aisle — straight and gay. They are not the norm, though when a story breaks in the media about an incident, it receives national attention on a level equal to an assassination attempt on the President. The truth is that the vast majority of gay and straight men have absolutely no sexual interest in children — period.

If a friend or neighbor expresses their concern over this, assure them you have absolutely no designs on their children, that your interest is in finding a like-minded adult you can relate to, talk to, share life with, etc. You may also need to assure a woman that you're not after her husband. And, here comes that male conceit thing: you may possibly need to assure your male friends and neighbors that you're not interested in sleeping with them. It's amazing how many men think that just because they are male you're going to be attracted to them and want to jump their bones — even if they look like Quasimodo!

As a side note, here are a few other false accusations about homosexuals being spread by people of deeply religious convictions:

- Hitler was gay, the Nazi Party was entirely controlled by militaristic homosexuals, and gays were especially selected for the SS because of their innate brutality.

- Homosexuality is a predatory addiction striving to take the weak and unsuspecting down with it.

- Homosexuals have no idea of how to act in the best interests of their country, their intention is to serve none but themselves.

- The goal of the gay movement is to defeat the marriage-based society and replace it with a culture of sexual promiscuity.

- Gays and lesbians live vastly shorter lives than heterosexuals.

- Homosexuality has a disproportionate incidence of pedophilia.
- Gay people are responsible for a "radical leftist crusade."
- Homosexuality carries enormous physical and mental health risks.
- Gay marriage entices children to experiment with homosexuality.
- Gay activists use same-sex marriage to indoctrinate children in schools to reject their parents' values and to harass, sue, and punish people who disagree.
- Practicing gays should be executed.
- Bible-believing Christians will quickly find themselves unwelcome in Rep. Barney Frank's new pansexual, cross-dressing military.
- Homosexuality leads to a loss of stability in communities, with a rise in crime, sexually transmitted diseases and other social pathologies, and a shortage of employable, stable people.
- The biggest hypocrite in the world is the person who believes in the death penalty for murderers but not for homosexuals.
- Most men who engage in same-sex child molestation identify themselves as homosexual or bisexual.
- One of the primary goals of the homosexual rights movement is to abolish all age of consent laws and to eventually recognize pedophiles as the "prophets" of a new sexual order.
- If gays have children, what will happen when they are too busy having their sex parties?
- Allowing gay people to serve openly in the military would lead to an increase in gay-on-straight sexual assaults.

You get the point. In the debate over homosexuality, intense emotionality — fear and hostility — comes into play and people will then say anything to gain allies, prove themselves right — WIN. Essentially, it's just a way to make themselves feel comfortable socially and religiously, a.k.a. emotionally. It's the very basic "fight or flight" scenario. Sadly, they pick and choose and truncate their religious tenets to assuage that fear. To put it simply, emotions are not based in logic and when humans fear something, then anything is possible no matter how far-fetched and unreasonable.

One of the most famous *Twilight Zone* episodes is titled "The Monsters are Due on Maple Street." In the closing narration to the show, Rod Serling states: "The tools of conquest do not necessarily come with bombs and explosions and fallout. There are weapons that are merely thoughts, attitudes, and prejudices — to be found only in the minds of men. For the record, prejudices can kill and suspicion can destroy, and a thoughtless, frightened search for a scapegoat has a fallout all its own — for the children, and the children yet unborn. And the pity of it is that these things cannot be confined to the Twilight Zone."

Back to our discussion concerning coming out to friends, co-workers, and other important people.

There is one possibility that could arise when disclosing to your friends (a male or female friend or neighbor): they will suddenly decide to come out to you, the first person they'd be disclosing to. What do you do then? First, you tell them about this book — really. Then encourage them to talk and you just listen. Your role is not to be the sage dispensing wisdom, but to just listen. Like you, they'll probably have a lot to get off their chests and they need someone to truly hear and see them at this juncture in their lives. This is very important for their self-esteem and emerging identity shift.

At some point, you'll feel there's space to share some of your story. This will let the other person know they're not alone, that they have something in common with another human being concerning this subject. Depending on the situation and how you're feeling during all of this, let the other person know whether you can be a support for them or not. You may decide that with all you're going through, you can't take on someone else's upset. Then again, this may be just the thing you need to pull you out of a potentially myopic/obsessive focus on your own situation (being of service to others, when appropriate, can be very rewarding and fulfilling for all parties involved). You determine what will work best for you while taking into consideration what's going on with the other person.

In the process of coming out to friends and neighbors, stress how important it is for you to not have them blabbing this news to everyone they know, including, if necessary, their spouses. If you've already made an agreement with your family and kids concerning whom they can tell, then you may want to discuss your friends and neighbors telling their own children. Go over what exactly they'd tell their kids so that dis- and misinformation isn't being spread. Let them know you'd prefer their kids didn't talk about your coming out to anyone else, especially their peers.

There may come a time when you might even consider getting a number of these people together to discuss the issue as a group. This is highly unlikely, but it is a possibility. Of course, it depends on a number of factors, most importantly, how much you trust these people and how close you are to all of them. If you do take up this option, you may want to have your therapist present, if you're seeing one. People will have questions and perspectives, some fair and some not, that a therapist will be able to appropriately facilitate.

Many men coming out are going to feel quite paranoid for some time. They'll be wondering if the word is getting out about them, what people are thinking, what's going on behind their back, suspicious of what people are saying and doing, and second guessing people's motives. In your case, (1) you've managed the process as best you can, (2) you can't control people, and (3) relax, continue to just be yourself, be consistent in your communications, and let it go. The last item, let it go, can be a really difficult one to master.

You need to realize that you can only do so much; the rest will take care of itself. You know people are going to be talking about you behind your back — you can't stop that. People are going to develop opinions, perceptions, and perspectives about you and your situation — you can't stop that. People are going to maintain their agreements with you and possibly violate those agreements — you can't stop that. All you can do, which will bring your stress quotient down, is meet challenges the best you can when and if they arise and stop imagining all sorts of nasty things are going on around you.

You will not help yourself by remaining paranoid. It will be difficult for you to be present with family, relatives, and others because your mind will be too busy trying to figure out perceived sub-text and hidden motives. What a waste of time and energy! Your story is evolving in this process and you need to be present to it.

Be aware that you may experience some annoyance after a while because you're going to get tired of coming out to people, tired of telling your story, and even get bored with your story. You may feel like you just want to get on the 6 o'clock news and make a general "coming out" announcement, tell your story, and be done with it. Probably not going to happen.

You will, though, begin to edit your story, cut out some of the drama, and learn to disclose to people in a simplified, matter-of-fact manner. The charge you once felt concerning the subject will diminish as you begin to focus on other things important to you besides "coming out."

One thing I'm consistently telling people is: "It's all a process." All of life is a process, a process of becoming. What that "becoming" is will be a mystery to most of us. All we can do is stay present and aware so that we can truly flow with it. Hints and clues will make themselves known to us, but if we're busy being focused elsewhere, we'll miss them. That only makes life more challenging. So, the idea here is to not put energy into things that only hold us back, but instead remain neutral, open, and expectant. Then watch, observe, and go with the flow.

Now, let's discuss coming out to co-workers. If ever there were a rumor mill, it's within the workplace. This can be one of the more difficult places to disclose that you're gay. Be very judicious with whom you tell, and you MUST get their agreement that they won't tell another soul. You may tell some co-workers and never tell others. It's up to you. What you feel is the most prudent course of action.

You must only disclose to those whom you absolutely trust, and even then, reconsider. To put it mildly, your job and career may be on the line. Someone I know got fired by their very high-profile boss for being gay. My friend sued and the parties settled out of court. Imagine, in this day and age, being fired for your sexual identity. It happens. Be careful.

**Note:** The Supreme Court's recent ruling regarding same-sex marriage — *Obergefell v. Hodges*, June 26, 2015 — has apparently opened a Pandora's Box of upset and resistance. States are now considering how they are to address equal rights for the LGBT community, as well as the rights of all other citizens. In some states, gays can still be fired simply because of their sexual orientation. Stay on top of developments because you never know what kind of illogical reaction you'll receive when you disclose that you're gay. With all the craziness surrounding this issue, it's no wonder a man chooses to hide his true self as society can quickly turn on a dime making him the odd man out.

Conversely, your need to be who you are is going to create pressure within you. Part of you isn't going to care who knows and the other part of you is going to care very much. Part of you will want to no longer live a lie or compartmentalize your life anymore — part of you is going to want to continue to run and hide. It's quite a juggling act and you must decide how complicated it's going to be.

Everything we've covered so far in Chapter 2 and this chapter applies to coming out to co-workers. They're not just your co-workers, they're human beings with all the traits and foibles of human beings. Be sensitive, compassionate, circumspect, consistent, and available. Be careful about being emotional in front of co-workers. People have different ideas of what that means. Some will see it as being touchingly endearing. Others may see it as weakness. Still others will decide you're being manipulative. And some will decide you're gay. Oh, wait…that last one's true.

Outside of family and work, the only people left to tell besides the general public are people you consider important in your life, e.g., your minister/priest/rabbi, someone in public office, a mentor you look up to, a well-liked teacher, an old family friend, etc. Disclosing to any of these people is the same as anyone else, except for the level of respect you have for that person. If you're choosing to disclose to a minister, priest or rabbi, you're probably already aware of what their religion has to say about homosexuality.

You may not come away from your disclosure with the outcome you're seeking — acceptance — in which case you may decide to join another congregation that is more open to and supportive of gay people. Some of these congregations are MCC, the Metropolitan Community Church. Unity, the Unitarian Universalist Church, ECKANKAR, and the Church of Religious Science. There are a number of others to consider, so if you feel you need to move on, do some research amongst friends and on the Internet.

Choosing to switch churches is yet another layer of change that could occur in your life besides just coming out. I'm sure it's not something you want to add to your burden, but the facts of life are pretty clear: many religions have sects that have a strong stance *against* homosexuality. Since your coming out is about total acceptance of your being homosexual, then you'll find yourself at a stalemate, as well as at a crossroads. These sects are not going to budge as their belief rests on the Bible, Torah, Koran, or whatever spiritual doctrine they follow.

Just as you had to do a lot of introspection before finally coming out, you'll need to do the same concerning your belief in and support of your chosen church. Spend time looking at your personal relationship with God and make up your own mind as to what you feel is right. If you choose to switch to another church, just be aware that you may lose friends and end relationships from your prior church that are meaningful to you. What you'd be moving toward, though, are people who have a different understanding of God, love, inclusiveness, and compassion. You'll make new friendships that will work more appropriately with your new life.

**Gay Slogans**

Civil Rights are Family Values
Family is a Family Value
Love is a Family Value
Hate is Not a Family Value
Fix Marriage Not Gays
Protect Marriage, Let's Expand It

God is an Equal Opportunity Lover
God Loves Me Just as I Am
Gay Rights ARE Civil Rights
Homophobia is a Social Disease
Homophobia – Now That's a Choice
Institutionalize Homosexuals – Support Gay Marriage
Please STOP Trying to Recruit Me to Heterosexuality
What Part of Love Don't You Understand?
We the People – that means all of us

In the process of coming out to friends, co-workers and other important people, you will experience some pain as not everyone will agree with your decision to come out as a gay man and they will shut the door on you. Honor that pain and realize that new people will come into your life who will be wholly accepting of who you are. And your true friends are those who take you in lock, stock, and barrel. Those who don't are operating from a very narrow perspective and understanding. So be it. Your life will go on and can be incredibly fulfilling and rich and joyful and full of love. Just be who you are.

## *Being "Outed" by Your Spouse*

If there is one thing that can drive you nuts and also produce great anger in you, it's being outed by your spouse without your consent. The reasons for her doing this include: vengeance, she needed someone to talk to and that person blabbed, it was a slip up and she didn't mean to, she was in a moment of weakness, you aren't being there for her during her time of duress, her life has been significantly affected by your coming out and she has her own story to tell, she was only trying to help you in your process.

If this happens, it's time for a come-to-Jesus meetin'. It is not alright for her to do this under any circumstance. If she's doing this for vengeance, you can actually sue her depending on a state's gay rights laws or even as a matter of slander. If she's done this because she thinks she's helping you in your process, you need to explain to her that this is your process, not hers.

How and when you come out to people must be on your timetable, not anyone else's. Whatever your reasoning is for coming out to anyone, that's your business. If she's "helping" you come out, there may be a hidden agenda at work that she's not even aware of and she's acting on unconscious needs. This is where couple's therapy can be most useful. If you're not signed up for some sessions, then now would be the perfect time.

As for the other reasons she might have, none of them are acceptable and she needs to understand that in no uncertain terms will you put up with it. Her reasoning that you're not being there for her during her time of duress is a weak attempt to get attention and is manipulative. There may be some truth to her accusation, but take care that you're not falling into a trap. Ask her specifically what she needs and then discuss what the *two of you* can do about it. You might even suggest she begin individual therapy.

If you don't do this together, then you may end up doing things you don't want to just to appease her. Meanwhile, she'll be working you over and you'll be getting in deeper and deeper. This could end up in an inappropriate blow up and it may cause problems when it comes to dealing with legal issues. Clear boundaries must be agreed and adhered to in terms of your changed relationship dynamic.

**Note:** It is generally assumed that women are manipulative and men are straightforward. What a myth! Men can be incredibly manipulative, it's just called "being strategic" in their world and usually applied to business. Men are manipulative in relationships, too. Emotions are emotions and we all have needs we want met. Somehow we work it until we get it, or at least try.

For example: you're married and now you've decided to be who you truly are — a gay man. Okay, how have you dealt with this over the years you've been married? By being honest in your relationship? By being forthcoming with what you're feeling and thinking? By hiding things? By managing information? By sneaking around? By being deceptive? By lying?

All of the above are tricks of the trade for those who manipulate. So — not only are you coming out, you're getting real.

Just as you need and want to be treated with respect, compassion and sensitivity, your spouse needs the same in return. What she is going through is incredibly difficult, heartbreaking, a self-esteem and self-worth killer, and not something she asked for. Be there for each other as much as is appropriate. It's a two-way street that if supported, your relationship will develop into something more amicable. Though neither of you may believe it, your marriage can turn into a lasting friendship. You both have to work at it, though, and it will have its ups and downs. Keep mutual respect and the goal of friendship uppermost in your minds and you'll most likely achieve it.

But what about arguments and fights? No getting around it, they're going to happen. There are a couple of things you should agree to in order to get out of the easy habit of arguing.

One: Decide that once you've discussed the past, it's the past. No need to keep re-hashing it as it will only exacerbate old hurts and slights and keep you from moving forward.

Two: If you look at your relationship, there are all sorts of things to blame each other for, most of them minor. And, yes, you're the one upsetting the equanimity of the family by coming out. That's understood. Don't fall into the trap of labeling someone the "bad guy" as once a person is chosen (usually you), then you'll be trying to find ways to make the other person the bad guy in some way so you can be "right." That's really childish. Stop the blame game and stick to the primary issues so you can move forward.

Three: Do not use your children as pawns. They don't deserve such abuse. You are their parents and you still need to come out as positive role models in this process.

Four: Do not make unilateral decisions. Work together to arrive at agreements involving the children, house, pets, friends, belongings, and financial matters.

Five: Consider couple's counseling and individual counseling, which can be of immense benefit to you both and even your children if they are involved in the counseling sessions. This is another way to discuss issues without a lot of emotional drama brought into play. The therapist can keep you focused and on track.

If you're not fighting, what about love making? You must be careful with this one. The one thing you don't want to do is give false hope that you'll drop this gay thing and come back to the marriage. You may still love your wife and there may come a time when you decide to have sex again. With all that you both are going through, having some intimacy and nurturing can be helpful. But you both need to be clear as to what you're doing. Is this a one-time deal? Is it for old time's sake? Do you want this to be a regular thing or an available option? Are you still having sex with men or one man at the same time as with your wife? Is this just for sexual release or emotional support? Is this satisfying a need for both of you or just one of you? Is this something either of you really wants to do or are one of you just being accommodating? Is there a sub-agenda because one of you wants something?

There are a lot of questions that need to be sincerely answered when it comes to reviving sexual relations otherwise a lot of upset and hurt can be derived due to misunderstandings.

Coming out will not be easy for you and won't be easy for the rest of your family. Aside from therapy, suggest that your wife get on the Internet and check out sites geared toward women whose husbands are coming out. Through them, your wife will gain a lot of insight, find commonality with others in the same situation, and discover resources that can help her. There are blogs and chat rooms, and she may find a support group in your area to join.

Your wife may have some trepidation at first, but the first step is always the scariest. Once that first step is taken, she's on her way toward getting the support she needs in this process. In a way, she's also coming out by connecting with others to whom she can say, "My husband is gay." She'll go through the same process as you in determining with whom she wants to share this news with and when. And then the day will arrive, believe it or not, when you both decide it's time to be out to the entire world.

## *Going Public*

Going public with our sexual identity is something we shouldn't have to do, but our times are such that people still get tied up in knots about the subject. We've all seen what happens when people in the public eye get "caught": entertainer George Michaels, Sen. Larry Craig, Rev. Ted Haggard, Gov. James McGreevey, former Rep. Mark Foley — and more. All the more reason to manage your coming out process so that those who fear or are offended by homosexuality can't start calling the shots for you.

As was stated earlier in this chapter, coming out can take years. For some married men coming out, they want the world to know right away, no more hiding. They're ready to go to Pride Parades, visit the bars, be seen in gay neighborhoods, be seen with gay people, go to gay events, fill their house with gay objects, and even put a gay flag out in front of their house — whatever. They don't care who knows.

Others bide their time, which may be your case. You may want to take it all in at a slower pace, not immediately have a boyfriend, start to get to know some gay people, rent gay-themed movies, read gay-themed books, etc. There's no rush, as you're in a fact-finding mode and want to see how things resonate with you.

One thing you'll discover is that being out in public is not really anything big. Of course, there are some neighborhoods where you might want for safety's sake to be a little more circumspect just. But, for the most part, the world has too much going on to really focus on you and your being out. Having made the decision to be out all the time, you'll experience a level of freedom you've not felt before and then eventually, you won't think twice about who you are to the world, you'll just be yourself all the time.

Finding support will help you in going public. Is there an LGBT community center you can visit? They'll have all sorts of activities to check out, as well as support groups that might be of interest to you. LGBT centers are very important cornerstones in a gay community. The range of services they offer, the issues they confront, and the support they provide are a sure refuge and safe haven from the rest of the world and a home where you can truly be yourself. They are tremendous repositories of information for all things LGBT. Google LGBT (you'll find millions of listings) and you'll find centers and additional links connecting you around the country and world.

The Internet has a gold mine of resources to explore. What about joining a gym that caters to mostly gay people? How about Match.com, Grindr, M4M, and other such services? As you meet gay people and develop friendships, you'll have the chance to expand what you know about the gay community and all things gay. It's a world unto itself and you'll determine what works for you and what doesn't.

> "To know what you prefer,
> instead of humbly saying 'Amen'
> to what the world tells you
> you ought to prefer,
> is to keep your soul alive."
>
> ~ Robert Louis Stevenson

Meanwhile, as you're busy exploring and getting comfortable with being out, there are ongoing issues that need to be addressed with your family that deserve your utmost attention, the subject of the next chapter.

## Chapter 5

# Issues within the Family

JT is originally from Brazil, Portuguese his first language. He wanted to live in America, met a young woman from San Diego, they married, and now had a young daughter.

When JT met me for his intake interview, he disclosed that he was gay, had a guy he was sort of dating, he didn't have a job, his wife worked, and that things were rough at home. He adored his young daughter and was afraid of losing her completely in a custody battle because he had only been in this country for a couple of years and his English suffered. He was currently enrolled in an ESL course striving to improve in that area.

JT joined the Married Men's Coming Out Group. Over time, he disclosed to the group just how bad things were on the home front. He took his shirt off one night to show us the bruises on his body. He explained that they were caused by his wife hitting him with whatever she could. He had been brought up that you never hit a woman, so he never tried to stop her, just avoid her blows.

Additionally, it turned out that her entire family was threatening him with physical harm and death, going so far as to brandish a gun at him, if he didn't stay in the marriage. His wife's father and brothers, who were with the Police Department and who were much larger than JT, had on several occasions surrounded him and done a number on him: swinging bats and 2 x 4's, yelling threats at him, and smashing his car headlights. His wife's threats extended to not just physical abuse, but complete custody of their child and JT never seeing his daughter again.

JT was at a loss as to what to do and quite frightened. He was suffering from depression and was considering escaping back to his own country unbeknownst to his wife and her family. He had even thought about kidnapping his daughter, but knew his wife's family would track him down and kill him. With her family being part of the SDPD, he knew that the cards were stacked in his wife's favor and he didn't stand a chance. He was going to lose, no matter what.

The irony of this story is that with his wife's physical abuse and her family member's threatening JT as they were, they were giving him even more reason to *not* stay in the marriage. Who'd want to be involved with a family like that? Can you imagine years from now still being a part of that family, their hanging over you like the Sword of Damocles?

Out of the 70-some men who had been members of the Married Men's Coming Out Group, JT's was the only one whose story involved violence and dire threats. He had called the police on more than one occasion and had even spent the night in jail when the police believed his wife's story and not his. He was having a very difficult time getting people to believe that he was the victim of spousal abuse. The fact that he had trouble expressing himself in English wasn't helpful. He didn't dare claim that he was being threatened with physical harm by members of the SDPD as that would cause her family to retaliate on a level he had yet to see. For JT, there was no hope. He stopped coming to the Men's Group and then disappeared. I have no idea where he is, how his life has fared, or if he is even alive.

JT's story illustrates one end of the spectrum — one not very positive. For the most part, the journey for married men coming out is somewhere in the middle and includes the stress that separation and divorce issues encompass that anyone would experience, straight or gay.

## *The Specter of Separation and Divorce*

No one wants to go through a divorce. It's messy, emotional, disruptive, confusing, generally costly, potentially polarizing, always divisive, and requires a great deal of stamina. But separation and divorce are usually the end product of a married man coming out. In the coming out process, there's the actual disclosure phase and then the phase dealing with the nuts and bolts of breaking up the marriage and family. Property has to be dealt with, perhaps business dealings, custody discussed and agreed to, schedules rearranged, visiting rights established, alimony, perhaps the wife going back to work, re-formulating parental authority dynamics, dividing belongings, deciding whether to allow the children around the boyfriends of either parent, how vacations with the children are going to work, who gets the children during holidays, and even dealing with future wedding and commitment ceremony issues. It's a lot to deal with. Some of the issues will occur later down the line, while others will require immediate attention and decisions made.

**Note of caution:** It is very important to not make financial decisions without the aid of a lawyer and possibly an accountant. Some married men coming out feel so guilty for the pain they are causing their family that they end up providing far more than what is practical or appropriate to their spouses and families in alimony and support. This can cause all sorts of extended headaches, as well as exacerbate frustrations and escalate resentment and anger. Children can get caught in the crossfire and relationships become strained and even terminated — all because of money issues that weren't handled in a reasonable manner. So, if you need to, hire a lawyer who will help you stay on track, see things from a sensible perspective, and keep your emotions on an even keel.

Eventually, most men coming out will want to establish a new lifestyle that entails having their own space, which means moving from the family home. They want to be able to have whomever they choose in their space without judgment and without impinging on their wife and children in any way.

Before a move is made, though, the first thing that needs to happen is a discussion with your wife letting her know you plan on moving out. Your wife may have already precipitated this by demanding you remove yourself from the premises or you may be initiating the discussion. However the talk happens, it again requires sensitivity and caring from both parties. This initial talk may cover a lot of issues surrounding your moving out and an impending divorce. You'll want to do some thinking about this, as well as research so that you know your rights and the legal ramifications in your state. Be ready to provide information and answers, but don't even consider using what you know as a weapon. Remember, turnabout is fair play. We've all read about rancorous divorces. There's no need to go in that direction, but if you do, be ready for your wife and her lawyer to play dirty, too. Instead, consider working toward an equitable parting that leaves both of you feeling your needs have been met as much as possible.

With your first talk, you don't have to resolve everything. Some of the topics you'll cover require a lot of thought and further discussion as they are complicated and no easy answers will be readily available. Values and beliefs are going to come into play that may be in conflict with the other person's values and beliefs. Be patient and open in this process, and listen. And give yourselves time so that no one feels that they're being rushed, manipulated, or coerced.

Something to be aware of is the different permutations of what constitutes a family. For some married couples where the husband is gay, the love and connection between the two is strong enough that they choose to stay married and live together in the same home. This is termed a "mixed-orientation marriage." Another type is very similar, but both spouses are seeing others. Both parties have agreed to monogamous relationships outside the marriage. This is known as a "closed-loop relationship." Finally, an "open relationship" allows each spouse to date whomever, but stay in the marriage.

At some point, the time will come when one or both of you feel it's time to tell the children about the impending divorce — if it's come to that — and you moving out of the house. The same consideration applies with the kids as when you came out to them. Depending on their age and understanding, they may already have an idea that this is happening. Don't underestimate them and don't assume anything with them. Ask questions and be ready to answer theirs. Both parents need to be prepared to handle the next phase, which involves a shift in parent/child dynamics.

## *Parent/Child Dynamics*

Kids are generally pretty smart and can be pretty wily about the parent/child dynamic. You are probably already practiced in dealing with them on this level, so we're not going to spend any time on that. Instead, what we'll focus on will be your role as a parent with divorce on the horizon.

Parents play several roles with children: enforcer, caretaker, instigator, creator, nurturer, sage, playmate, judge, fixer, the "no" person, the "yes" person, good guy, bad guy, etc. These roles are divided up between the wife and husband, sometimes evenly, sometimes not. Both parents move back and forth as an authority figure. When in the process of a divorce and when you've moved out, which parent has what authority will become an issue. One parent wants one thing, and the other parent wants something else. One wants to be permissive in some areas, while the other wants to be permissive in other areas. Both do not necessarily coincide with each other. Communication is the only way around this. At heart in all of this is what's in the best interests of the children. Your beliefs and values will, again, come into play, yet it is still what's best for the children that must be kept in mind. This will take discussion — not arguing, not entrenching, not polarization, but discussion. Communication is the key.

Most people think they know how to communicate, yet developing solid and useful communication skills is not something many of us take the time to work at. There are a ton of programs, books, videos, CDs, and DVDs on the market featuring gifted trainers and coaches focused on communication. Check them out and see if any appeal to you. Of course, any of these will require work and persistence. A lot of us just wish we could take a pill and voila, instant master communicator. Ain't gonna happen.

There is one rule of thumb, though, that you can easily employ that will help tremendously: learn to listen, listen to learn. If you're dominating a conversation, then it's all about you even though you think you're having a two-way conversation. You're not really listening to or engaging with the other person because you're so busy talking.

Listening is an art and requires two things from you: (1) be silent, and (2) stay present. By staying present, you'll actually hear what the other person is talking about, you'll hear sub-text and nuances, and you'll truly be able to engage with the other person. You'll be able to comment appropriately and ask questions germane to their topic. Now you're really connecting with someone — and that's the purpose of conversation in the first place and the cornerstone of all our relationships. A web site you can visit that will provide you with a lot of information about communication is: www.coachingintelligenceinstitute.com.

Another aspect of communication is to understand just where we learned to communicate the way we do. Essentially, our families are the primary means of our communication dynamic with others and even in our own heads. To learn more about communication and relationship dynamics both within the family and on the job (we tend to recreate our familial dynamics at work), the book *Don't Bring It to Work: Breaking the Family Patterns that Limit Success* by Sylvia Lafair, PhD, will take you far in understanding yourself and others.

> *Don't Bring It to Work* explores what happens when patterns originally created to cope with family conflicts are unleashed in the workplace. This groundbreaking book draws on the success of Sylvia Lafair's PatternAware™ program Total Leadership Connections. Throughout the book, she shows how to break the cycle of pattern repetition and offers the tools that can turn unhealthy

family baggage into creative energy that will foster better workplace associations and career success.

Lafair identifies the thirteen most common patterns that correspond to characters familiar to anyone who has ever worked in an office: Super Achiever, Rebel, Persecutor, Victim, Rescuer, Clown, Martyr, Splitter, Procrastinator, Drama Queen or King, Pleaser, Denier, and Avoider. To help overcome destructive behavior problems, she maps out the three main steps for becoming aware of patterns and finding the way OUT:

- Observe your behavior to discern underlying patterns

- Understand and probe deeper to discover the origins of these patterns

- Transform your behavior by taking action to change

The book includes a wealth of real-life anecdotes and practical, workbook-style exercises that clearly show how anyone can get beyond old, outmoded attempts at conflict resolution and empower themselves to make profound differences both at work and in their personal lives.

Inside jacket flap of<br>Don't Bring It to Work

Okay, back to being a parent and the shift in dynamic that occurs with divorce.

The temptation to maneuver either parent into a good guy/bad guy position will be easy. The outcome of this is putting your children in the middle of a tug of war. Is that what's in the best interests of the children? Hardly. What could prove useful here if the two of you are really having a tough time coming to amicable agreements is to work with a family mediator — and I don't mean another family member, good friend of the family, etc. You want to work with someone who doesn't know either of you so that they're neutral in the mediation process. As you work with the mediator, you'll begin to apply the tools you learn to all of your discussions with family members, both immediate and extended.

Your children will very possibly attempt to play the good guy/bad guy game also. Both parents need to stay in communication with each other so as to avoid getting sucked into this situation. That may not be to your liking — staying in contact with each other — as you are getting a divorce and you both need space in this process. But, it's all about the kids. You don't necessarily need to be warm and fuzzy with each other, but you also don't need to be perfunctory in your communication either. Discuss what's going on with the kids, their schedule needs, their activities, their state of mind, how they're doing with the news of the divorce and changing family situation, etc. You're still their parents, you love them, and they deserve your energy, time, input, and love.

Meanwhile, you and your spouse need to agree as to who has the last word concerning decisions involving the kids. Usually, this falls to the parent the kids are living with, but that's really all up for discussion depending on what the topic is, it's level of importance, and its impact on the family. You may need to remind the kids that both parents have authority over them, not just the parent with whom the kids are living.

## *Child Custody*

For various reasons, there is usually one parent children gravitate toward more so than the other and with whom they want to stay. And it isn't so simply broken out as the females with the females and the males with the males. If you have more than one child, sometimes the children are split concerning which parent with whom they want to live. Other children refuse to be separated from each other and can't decide between the parents. Then there are those who don't want to be with either parent. It can get complicated. Sometimes, it just comes down to the parents emphatically stating that the kids are staying with so-and-so — that's it, no discussion.

Sometimes, the easiest solution is for the children to stay with the mother, particularly if she stayed at home taking care of the house, the kids, and their schedules. Many men aren't used to juggling all these things and will go into overwhelm if they suddenly have to take care of everything. Others will thrive on the challenge. Some women will have to seek employment so day care centers or babysitters/housekeepers who cook will become a significant cost if younger children are involved. Then there are the usual costs involving children, e.g., clothes, school supplies, dental and medical, extracurricular activities, toys, allowances, outings and trips, etc. You'll need to determine how costs will be split fairly.

It's going to be a day-by-day proposition as you all adjust to the new living arrangements. And just when you think you've got everything ironed out, something will come up to throw a monkey wrench into the works... such is life. You'll figure ways to resolve any surprises.

One issue that can become thorny is one parent wanting sole custody of the children. This is where lawyers or mediators will make an entrance. You need to know what your rights are and what the custody laws are in your State, so do your homework. Some wives are going to think the worst of your new gay bachelor pad and not want the children exposed to it. They'll want you to only visit the kids at the family home and/or out in public places. They may also insist that the kids never meet your boyfriend(s) as it would be too upsetting for the kids or that their religious beliefs reject this option.

Other wives will have the opposite thinking and suggest that the kids have overnights on weekends, play dates during the week. If they feel you're in a steady enough relationship with a man, they'll allow the kids to meet him and even spend time with both of you on a regular basis.

Now, the same for all of the above holds true if *you* have custody of the kids. Your wife may at some point begin dating. Are you ready for another man to be the object of her affections? What about the kids meeting and spending time with this person? You probably won't know anything about this guy and, being the protective father you are, you'll want some kind of assurance from your wife that he's not a felon with a record, won't abuse your kids in any way, doesn't have addictions of any kind, isn't some kind of con man, and doesn't have some kind of weird philosophy/lifestyle/religious belief/mental aberration/belief system with which he'll try to inculcate the kids. You'll also be concerned that he might upstage you in the Dad Department or undermine your authority with them.

Finally, there are the actual divorce proceedings. If you've done your research and you're working with a lawyer or mediator, you'll work things out. If you have children, remember the effect all of this is having on them and make sure that the decisions you and your wife are making take the kids into consideration. Do not make decisions based solely on your needs or those of your soon to be ex-wife. Yes, you need to take care of yourself first, but not to the detriment of loved ones. You'll find the right balance.

> Roland has three children whom he adores. He was a member of the Married Men's Coming Out Group I was facilitating and regularly talked about his kids, how much they meant to him. He didn't want to do anything that would hurt them, they were his life.

Then he met Edward, falling head-over-heels in love with him — this was the one. Edward lived in San Francisco and was married. He was planning on coming out to his wife and getting a divorce. Roland and Edward began making a lot of trips back and forth between their two cities trying to see each other as often as possible.

Roland started looking for jobs in the Bay Area and he and Edward began looking for a house to buy together.

Then Edward called to let Roland know that his wife was pregnant and that he couldn't possibly leave her at this time. Roland had already landed a high-paying job with the school system. Meanwhile, the men in the group felt that Roland was not thinking clearly, especially concerning moving away from his kids, who were relatively young, in order to be with his lover who now had a baby on the way.

The outcome: Roland moved to San Francisco anyway leaving the kids with his former wife.

Once Roland moved to the Bay Area, I lost track of him and have no idea how things worked out between he and Edward, or with his own kids. One can only hope that Roland stayed in close communication with his children and either made trips down to San Diego to visit as often as possible and/or flew the kids up to the Bay Area to spend time with him.

Which brings up an interesting phenomenon: The call of love is very powerful for most people and hardly anyone would choose to ignore it. Its draw is such that we sometimes lose sight of ourselves, the facts of our situations, and our responsibilities. The hope is that we can juggle it all and win in the end. This is a hard one, especially when you consider that many married men who come out are looking to hook up with someone. They're not sure what a gay relationship looks like and how it would operate, but they know what they're attracted to and love just might enter the picture no matter how old they are.

Lawrence came into the group at age seventy. His wife of 40-some years was dying from emphysema and was in the hospital. He wanted to come out to her, but felt with her being in an end-stage condition that coming out would add mental and emotional stress to an already unpleasant situation for her. After several meetings with the Men's Group, he decided to leave well enough alone.

Meanwhile, he announced that he'd met someone whom he really, really liked. What should he do? His wife, whom he loved, was dying and he wanted to be by her side, but he also wanted to seriously explore this new relationship's potential.

The possibility of experiencing love's rush again can truly knock us off kilter. Love is a wondrous thing and wouldn't we all want to experience it more than once? Yet love can be elusive, at times difficult to discern, and can be false like fool's gold. How we comport ourselves while in its throes is important. Keeping a level head seems counterproductive and oxymoronic, yet try we must. So, if you have children and that special someone appears in your life, do your best to keep an even keel. You may feel like everyone is pulling at you wanting your attention and time and energy, so it's up to you to set appropriate boundaries for all of them — and yourself.

The bottom line in all this is how to balance your needs with the issues surrounding child custody. Make sure you have time just for yourself, no distractions of family, boyfriend(s), work, and the gay community. You need inner sustenance just as much as the next person, so take care of your physical, mental, emotional, and spiritual health. Everyone will benefit.

## *Moving Out of the House*

The day will come when you actually move out of the house into a new space. You'll feel the excitement of a fresh start and at the same time the pangs of leaving the family behind. It's leaving the known for the unknown and swapping a full home for an empty house.

Some men move without their children's help. Others enlist their kids so they know where Dad will be located. It helps to create a lifeline of connection so that Dad isn't just disappearing off the face of the Earth. Discuss the move with your wife and kids so that they remain a part of the picture and give them the option of helping or not. This would also be the time to re-confirm visiting schedules, play dates, school schedules, etc.

The majority of men move somewhere in the same locale as it's familiar, they can remain close to their children and their support group of friends, and they don't have to leave their place of work and find a new job. It's also easier when it comes to meetings with lawyers concerning custody, property, and financial issues. Other men want a completely fresh location from which to start their new lives as gay men. They opt to move to a different city or state. The idea of starting anew where no one knows you is appealing and you can be whomever you want. No one needs to know your background unless you decide to tell them. It's sort of like reinventing yourself.

Sometimes the move to a new city or state is prompted by the fact that there isn't an active gay community close by. Having come out, men want to find fellowship and commonality — and a date. They generally want to get immersed in the gay community, which is part of becoming comfortable in one's new persona as a gay man. Sharing one's life experience is key and allows bonding to occur — a boost to one's self-esteem, sense of belonging, and placement in the world.

Then there are the situations where the wife is the one to move out. She may stay in the same area or move to another city or state. And she may take the children with her. Again, discuss the move with the children. Go over the visitation schedule with them. You might also want to review the schedule for when you'll be calling them, and the various ways they can stay in contact with you, i.e., phone, letter writing, e-mail, text messaging, online hangouts, and Skype. The day the move occurs will be a sad one for everyone. Let your kids know how much you love them, you'll miss them terribly, and that you'll talk with them very soon and often. Physically bond with them — and I don't mean via handshake. All of you need reassurance that you're still connected to each other and a long bear hug can really cement that.

How your kids are feeling on the day of the move may preempt touching goodbyes. Be sensitive to how they're feeling and just let them know they can call you at any time, you're there for them, and you love them. That may be as far as you get as they may have closed down or are put out with you because you've disrupted their lives, broken up the family, etc. Try not to take it personally, just let them be in their feelings. Don't try to fix the situation, just be caring.

Once the move has been made, reconfigure your space so that it becomes yours. You'll definitely want reminders of your kids still there, but a little cleaning house will be helpful. Make it a space that works for you. This is part of your re-identification process. If you need to have a garage sale, do so. If things need to go in storage, make it happen — whatever it takes.

If you're moving into a new space of your own, the same applies. Take the things that matter with you and then begin creating a living space that says, "I've arrived!" You'll quickly begin adjusting and working out a new daily routine. The poignancy of the move will dissipate and you'll find other things upon which to focus. Keep yourself busy so you don't get maudlin. Be sure to honor your feelings and take time to be just with you. In time, your life will fill up with new activities and friends, and you'll have moved into creating a new life as a gay man. Some men will want to jump into the gay community headlong. You may want to dip your toes and take your time. That's okay. There's no rush. Do it at a pace that works for you.

## *Wrangling with Relatives*

Families being what they are, allegiances usually come into play and lines are drawn as to who supports you and who doesn't — whether the relatives are from your side of the family or your wife's. Family members are also generally good at volunteering their unsolicited opinions and proffering their unwanted advice. Obviously, certain members will side against you and think all manner of bad things about you and what you're doing. Others will support you and your cause. Still others won't care.

Having people's support is gratifying and you'll appreciate what they have to offer. With those who are on the opposing team, let them have their say. At some point, though, let them know that you understand and appreciate where they're coming from, but the matter doesn't really involve them — it's between you and your wife. Explain to them that though it isn't a pleasant situation, you've made a decision that allows you to live with yourself in spite of the hurt it's caused everyone involved.

Create boundaries that work for you without just cutting people off. Closing the door on some relatives will cause them to probably do the same to you and their backlash within the family circle could cause additional heartache for everyone. In the process, you'll discover who gets the bigger picture and has compassion and who is just plain dense, obtuse, and/or just mean and vengeful. Whatever the situation, always take the high road and appeal to a person's higher sensibilities. As long as you're not being aloof or superior, this will work to your advantage.

## *Marriage*

Now we come to a really interesting situation: you, your ex-wife, or one of your children decides to get married. Obviously, there's going to be some sort of ceremony. Who to invite? Do you invite mutual friends? How will family members handle the situation? Do you invite your kids and relatives to your commitment/wedding ceremony? Do you invite your ex-wife? Your ex-wife has invited you, can you bring your partner?

If your child is getting married, do they invite both parents? And their parents' boyfriends?

TV movies have covered this situation and it can get complicated... and messy...and open old wounds. At heart, weddings and commitment ceremonies are supposed to be happy occasions celebrating two people's love for each other. It pre-supposes that differences will be set aside so everyone can focus on the happy couple's union. But, people being people, there are those who won't let a sleeping dog lie and they're going to let their feelings be known in some way. Don't let that spoil the occasion for you, especially if it's your own ceremony.

Congratulations! You've met the man of your heart and the two of you have decided to honor your relationship with a wedding ceremony. If you and your ex-wife have remained friends, invite her and her significant other. Invite your children. Depending on their age, you may want to have a conversation with your ex-wife first, assuring her that the ceremony will be just like any heterosexual wedding (if that's the case).

> Dixie and Brenda invited me to their commitment ceremony and I attended it with my boyfriend. When we got there, we didn't know anyone, so we had a chance to meet some new people.
>
> Then the ceremony began and the happy couple made their entrance: wearing very little, their very overweight figures bulging out over their barely containable leather skivvies and between the netting of their black mesh stockings. Nipple rings were evident with chains connecting to not just their two nipples but to each other's. Each wore a top hat and spats over their patent leather shoes. They were radiant in their joy — the attendees were stunned.

So much for the "usual" ceremony. As we all know, the gay community knows how to dress up any event. Just watch a Gay Pride Parade and you'll get quite an eyeful. At times, you'll think you're at Carnival in Rio. When it comes to weddings, they can turn out to be quite theatrical and not exactly come with a G rating. Keep this in mind when planning the guest list.

Concerned parents will want to know that nothing untoward or unseemly will occur at a union so that the children are protected. Some will not want the children at the ceremony because they don't support unions between two men and don't want their kids thinking such unions are acceptable. If that's the case, then it's possible your kids won't be attending. Again, it's a matter for discussion and with the parent with whom the children are living. At some point, the children are going to find that Dad is "married" to another man and that when they're visiting you, that person will be present. Former wives with a religious background disapproving of homosexuality will try to control what their kids are exposed to and what they hear. You may have to live with this until the kids are old enough to make up their own minds as to what they think about homosexuality.

If you've dropped to one knee and proposed to your man (or vice versa), then one thing you'll want to consider is marriage counseling. This may sound antiquated or even silly, but two men getting married have some of the same issues as heterosexual couples and a few more simply because same-sex marriages are still not the norm. The following article provides some reasons why to seek marriage counseling: http://purpleunions.com/blog/2012/11/5-crucial-topics-for-the-same-sex-couple-to-work-out-before-walking-down-the-aisle.html.

Now, you may one day be informed that your ex-wife is re-marrying. Are you ready for that final letting go? Will the "new husband" try to replace you with your kids? Would you want to attend the wedding if an invitation is extended? Can you bring your boyfriend/partner? Are you ready to contend with her family again? Are you up for what people might say to you in the way of disapproving looks, snide digs, left-handed remarks, and re-visiting old issues? Think about what you may be letting yourself in for and whether it's worth the trouble.

If one of your children is getting married, the question at hand is whether you can bring your boyfriend/partner with you. Some mothers won't hear of it as people will talk, she wouldn't want some kind of scene to occur, and/or since she doesn't approve of your lifestyle then she doesn't want it flaunted in front of other people. This could get rough as you may be faced with an ultimatum or the child getting married will be given an ultimatum from one parent. Ultimatums are selfish and the person leveling them has forgotten that the day is not for them. It's for the couple getting married. Ultimatums show a lack of maturity, so it's time to straighten things out and put the focus where it should be — on the child getting married.

But, what if the ultimatum is coming from your child? What if they don't want you there? Or if you do come, you can't bring your boyfriend/partner. That's very painful because they're rejecting you and also saying that they're embarrassed to have you with them in public. It could also be that they don't approve of your lifestyle. It's time for a heart-to-heart between you and your child.

If you do go to the wedding of either your ex-wife or one of your children and your boyfriend/partner accompanies you, agree on how you'll introduce him, as well as how you'll refer to each other in front of people. What you don't want to do is fumble in front of people, otherwise, they may think you're embarrassed to be who you are. You want to stand strong and confident, especially if you're giving your daughter away. And if people disapprove, that's their problem, not yours.

You are who you are and just because you're gay, very little changes about your fundamental character. Some people, though, think being gay changes everything. It's up to you to show them differently. All that they know about you is still in place, they just need to set their "gay" filter aside and see you for the person you truly are. In order to do that, as I've mentioned, you'll need to do some introspective work to make sure you're congruent with your identity.

## Chapter 6

# Identity: The Path of Self-Acceptance

Kiernan, whom I mentioned in a previous chapter, came to the Married Men's Coming Out Group one of the angriest men I've ever met. His biting tongue was like a rasp and could easily flail the skin off you. Where did all this anger come from?

The dissolution of Kiernan's marriage was rancorous with his wife maxing out their credit cards and putting him in debt for years. Kind words were never used when her name was mentioned.

What added to Kiernan's bad mood was the fact that he'd worked for the Department of Defense for many years in a high-level, stressful position that necessitated his fighting like a pit bull on many an occasion with other departments, higher ups, and mind-numbing government bureaucracy.

Kiernan had been an alcoholic when he was much younger, but he'd been a member of AA for over two decades. His communication style was curt, directorial, non-nonsense, and entirely lacking in compassionate overtones. In short, he came across as a mean and angry man, and crossing him was not something you wanted to try.

Kiernan and I had a number of talks and I found out that he was interested in being of service to people in need, that underneath the gruff exterior was a man wanting to transform himself. We talked about his helping people with AIDS. He was compassionate. It was just that in public settings, his fear got in the way and he reverted to what he knew, which would accomplish one thing for him: survival. What he wasn't getting was that this "style" was also off putting to the people around him. He got the job done, but connection with the people around him was only at one level.

Then Kiernan discovered the spiritual following of the Self-Realization Fellowship (SRF) and he began reading their works. He also began classes under the tutelage of a yogi. And the crusty exterior used to provide protection from the world began sloughing off. Kiernan changed rather quickly. By then, he had left the Men's Group, but the men stayed in touch with each other and they got to see his transformation. It was remarkable.

While Kiernan is still a master of zingers, he has done in his life what people term "a one-eighty." I would venture to say that he has gone farther than anyone else in the group to not just come out as a gay man and be identified as such, but he has stretched beyond the confines of that label to find an even greater version of himself. In 2009, he completed a life-long dream of touring Asia, visiting many holy sites, especially the home of Paramahansa Yogananda, the founder of SRF, in India.

I attended Kiernan's 25-year-pin ceremony in AA, a wonderful milestone for him. I was so proud of him. But what has been even more remarkable is that Kiernan chose to face himself on all levels and realize how he'd become his own ball and chain. His all-encompassing spiritual work was just the balm and key he needed to find a more authentic version of himself and undo the fetters of his self-imprisonment. He no longer needed to be a combatant in the world, but a participant. All part of his journey to soaring like an eagle.

If ever there were an area that needs some work, it's one's identity. We all think we're clued in to who we are and what we're about, yet there are parts of ourselves that remain obscure or hidden — places we don't want to look into because they're too painful or scary to contemplate. And that's how we trick ourselves into avoiding our issues, whether they're emotional, psychological, mental, or spiritual. We build up in our minds that whatever that issue is it's so damaging, hurtful, frightening, or massive that we'd crumble.

In spite of what we choose to hide from about ourselves, we still need to be able to move from day to day dealing with myriad challenges of all kinds. Many of us relegate "issues" to a back burner saying that we'll get to dealing with it sometime in the future, which usually means not at all unless something forces us to face ourselves. Coming out as a gay man is just one such "push" that can initiate our getting in touch with ourselves on a deeper level and achieve freedom.

A simple definition of freedom is: to not be shackled by anything that keeps us from being our true selves. The metaphor that comes to mind is either being trapped on the ground or being able to soar like an eagle. Fundamentally, the choice is ours. It may seem that life, family, events, physical challenges, etc., are telling us differently. It is a matter of choice when it comes to deciding how we perceive anything and what we want to do about it.

Kiernan turns the adage "you can't teach old dogs new tricks" inside out. He was already in his mid-50's when he joined the Men's Group. He not only came *out*, he came *into* himself — quite a feat. But if there is one thing Kiernan doesn't do is back down from a challenge. Thank God for one of his character traits: the temerity and tenacity of a pit bull!

Kiernan isn't the norm. Though each man in the Men's Group worked on himself, much of what they were focused on dealt with divorce, children, and becoming part of the gay community. I was always hearing about the dating scene, gay events, and the accouterments of the gay lifestyle. Few dove into the roots of their character and life issues. They mostly just wanted to be able to say, "I'm gay," and then work out the rudiments of gay life. What they were looking for was to find some sense of normalcy in a community and lifestyle many people consider abnormal. (On a side note, the Gay Men's and Lesbian Community Center in San Diego used to be located on Normal Street and that's where the Men's Group met. Such irony!)

## *Oh, to be "Normal"*

"Man's main task in life
is to give birth to himself,
to become what he potentially is.
The most important product of his effort
is his own personality."

~ Erich Fromm

Okay, what is "normal"? In this book, there's no such thing simply because every individual on this planet is just that: individual. The universe in our minds is separate and distinct from everyone else. Therefore, to strive to be normal is a dead end. What we call "normal" is the attempt to fit within the socio-cultural conventions and patterns that allow us to feel a part of something larger than ourselves wherein we are allowed to "be ourselves" to a degree and find a level of acceptance with which we're willing to live. For most people, that's fine and they aren't really interested in rocking the boat. But when you're a married man coming out, you have no choice but to rock the boat.

And, what's normal in one universe is not necessarily normal in another. Many heterosexuals have a problem with the manner in which gays and lesbians comport and sport themselves. I've always found it interesting that the consistent manner gays and lesbians adopt to express themselves out in public is the same way heterosexual people behave, but this is mostly found in clubs and certain settings, like Las Vegas where you get to pay to see people flaunt themselves. There, it's called show business or work — and it's considered legit.

What's the difference? Generally, the difference has to do with whether you are expressing yourself or watching others do it. Amazing how many people are willing to live vicariously. That way, they can be safe from the judgments of other people. Watch the parade going by and get your kicks, but look and act normal. Is that living authentically?

Life's many distractions make it very difficult to live authentically. We are constantly being pulled this way and that way by glitter and flash. It's constant, pervasive, and can be all consuming. We've become such an ADD (Attention Deficit Disorder) culture that we don't even see what we've become. We're in it to our eyeballs and think we're getting the most out of life. We're just like everyone else — normal. It's ironic that many of us think we're doing just the opposite, being an individual, being different, not normal. We're our own person. Really?

This is where the idea of life as illusion comes into play. We're so involved in our lives thinking we're going in such and such direction and being such and such person. On one hand, we're striving for independence, to be individuated, yet striving to fit in at the same time. What a confusing rat race.

If we're not striving to be normal, then, what are we striving for? To be ourselves, uniquely identified in a world of wannabes and homogeneity. But, where to start? Self-reflection.

## *Self-Reflection = Clarification = Identity*

Self-reflection sounds gentle enough and non-threatening, yet it can feel like being thrown off a cliff into a black abyss when in the depths of it. Despite that analogy, self-reflection yields some of the most enlightening and uplifting passages to clarity.

> One day, I got a call from Nate. I had to hold the phone away from my ear as he was yelling. He wasn't angry, just couldn't stop yelling at the top of his lungs.
>
> He started telling me he wanted to join the Men's Group because he was gay and I redirected the conversation by asking him why he was yelling. He told me an amazing story.
>
> Nate had been a drug user, methamphetamines. One day, he drove out to the desert with two of his "friends." All of them were high. Nate had a stash of drugs in the trunk of his car and let the other two know about it. Out in the middle of nowhere, he pulled the car over so one of the guys could relieve himself. All three got out of the car. Nate's two friends immediately jumped him, beat him to a pulp, and drove off back to San Diego leaving Nate to die in the hot desert sun.
>
> Nate was found a couple of days later by some hikers and rushed to the hospital. There was brain damage: Nate would no longer be able to speak at normal volume, only yelling; his cognitive abilities were reduced to that of a person born with a mental disability; and he would be confined to a wheel chair having lost major motility in his legs.
>
> This episode had apparently happened several years prior to Nate calling me and he was now used to getting around on his own in his wheel chair and, instead of yelling when wanting to express himself, he used a machine on which he could type what he wanted to say and then have it immediately print out.
>
> Nate and I had the chance to talk privately on several occasions. Although he was attending the Men's Group, he felt that he achieved more by just spending time thinking about his life. What he had determined is that he, like so many other people, had taken life for granted

and drugs allowed him to avoid turning his life into that of being a clone of everyone else. He wanted to be free of society's cloying sameness and just experience life as a stream of consciousness.

His assessment was that he substituted one drug for another: societal similitude and comfortableness for escapism. He now realized that drugs have the effect of affecting and even damaging one's brain so that you're disconnected from yourself. He'd done to himself, in an irreparable manner, what he thought society does to people over the long run through what essentially amounts to hypnosis — disconnecting one from self. Now he was paying the price, but felt that if he was learning who he was through his challenges and then the process of self-reflection, then it was all worth it in the long run.

The journey of life is all about identity: Who are you and what is your purpose? Hopefully, what you learn along the way to answering these questions is clarification. What you gain in the process of self-reflection is self-acceptance, self-love, and learning to love others unconditionally. Sounds simple and in our more shining moments, we experience all three with ease. Most of the time, though, we're caught in the throes of dealing with life's challenges both large and small, ordinary and extraordinary. They constantly distract us, pulling us off our center and out of balance, driving us to make decisions and take actions we wouldn't ordinarily make in our "right" minds. That's the process and it is one long, extended lesson designed to test, strengthen, temper, and expand us. Depending on your perspective, it's a most wonderful process.

One way of beginning the process of discovering who you are is to create what I call an Identity List. Disarmingly simple in appearance, it has reduced men to tears. In its simplest form, it's a list of 25, one-word descriptors about you. They are all positive and describe you. An example list would include descriptors such as: compassionate, loyal, giving, affable, genuine, funny, supportive, inquisitive, persistent, patient, organized, tolerant, pacific, reliable, flexible, practical, loving, accommodating, nurturing, thoughtful, creative, silly, spiritual, honest, and ethical. Notice that there are no negatives and no descriptors based on work or roles, e.g., I'm a father, coach, singer, couch potato, golfer, millionaire, etc.

To get you started, on the next page is a list of descriptors. Choose the ones you feel apply to you. Select as many as you like and then pare the list down to just the top 25.

| | | | |
|---|---|---|---|
| ○ Patient | ○ Hardworking | ○ Methodical | ○ Clean |
| ○ Inclusive | ○ Enthusiastic | ○ Adaptable | ○ Level-headed |
| ○ Fun-loving | ○ Knowledgeable | ○ Caring | ○ Adventurous |
| ○ Engaging | ○ Honest | ○ Enterprising | ○ Funny |
| ○ Upbeat | ○ Precise | ○ Faithful | ○ Diligent |
| ○ Assertive | ○ Persistent | ○ Forward-looking | ○ Gentle |
| ○ Giving | ○ Curious | ○ Reliable | ○ Individualistic |
| ○ Perceptive | ○ Multifaceted | ○ Compassionate | ○ Quick-witted |
| ○ Strong | ○ Growing | ○ Imaginative | ○ Robust |
| ○ Helpful | ○ Passionate | ○ Gregarious | ○ Self-directed |
| ○ Sincere | ○ Considerate | ○ Stimulating | ○ Nurturing |
| ○ Playful | ○ Discrete | ○ Loving | ○ Resilient |
| ○ Appreciative | ○ Intellectual | ○ Athletic | ○ Professional |
| ○ Lenient | ○ Tireless | ○ Intuitive | ○ Studious |
| ○ Constructive | ○ Valiant | ○ Fair | ○ Complimenting |
| ○ Friendly | ○ Industrious | ○ Forgiving | ○ Graceful |
| ○ Experienced | ○ Thoughtful | ○ Motivating | ○ Discerning |
| ○ Dedicated | ○ Silly | ○ Versatile | ○ Loyal |
| ○ Open-minded | ○ Content | ○ Organized | ○ Distinctive |
| ○ Ethical | ○ Practical | ○ Lighthearted | ○ Trusting |
| ○ Intelligent | ○ Supportive | ○ Musical | ○ Forthright |
| ○ Tenacious | ○ Responsible | ○ Optimistic | ○ Incisive |
| ○ Skillful | ○ Cultured | ○ Insightful | ○ Stable |
| ○ Encouraging | ○ Spiritual | ○ Cheerful | ○ Tolerant |
| ○ Generous | ○ Formidable | ○ Pacific | ○ Determined |
| ○ Dynamic | ○ Sophisticated | ○ Unbiased | ○ Contemplative |
| ○ Stylish | ○ Conscientious | ○ Progressive | ○ Kindhearted |
| ○ Flexible | ○ Polite | ○ Resourceful | ○ Sensitive |
| ○ Empathetic | ○ Artistic | ○ Thorough | ○ Easygoing |
| ○ Accommodating | ○ Sharing | ○ Energetic | ○ Inspiring |
| ○ Confident | ○ Affable | ○ Creative | ○ Receptive |
| ○ Objective | ○ Persuasive | ○ Sensible | ○ Philosophical |

Looks easy, yet it's deceptively difficult. Why? Because few people sit down and take the time to look carefully inside themselves and positively describe who they are. They feel silly, guilty, egotistical, uncomfortable, weird, embarrassed, bored, scared, numb, angry, sad, disconnected, worthless, ashamed, hurt, blank — it's all unfamiliar territory for most men. What is does, though, is give you a chance to consider how you think of yourself, not how other people see you. It's a self-evaluation, as well as a tool for insight into you. You may surprise yourself. For most men, it takes them quite some time to put the list together. They're used to describing the world around them in certain terms and describing themselves within a narrow band of focus.

The next step, and this is where the tears come in, is to write a short sentence for each word using that word. For example: the first word in my example list is "compassionate." A sentence illustrating the word as it applies to me would be: "I am very compassionate about people who are struggling because of a lack of education." Each sentence needs to be different from any other sentence. The second word in my list is "loyal." You wouldn't write: "I am very loyal about people who are struggling because of a lack of education." Doesn't quite make sense and it's rather like cheating. Take the time to write 25 discrete sentences that, when you're done, describe you and your life.

Part of the difficulty in writing these sentences is that we can end up describing ourselves according to what our significant other, family, friends, community, church, work, and society wants or dictates. The result is that we're now describing them, not ourselves. As a reminder, the purpose of this exercise is to really delve deep into discovering who you truly are, who you feel yourself to be deep in your heart. It has absolutely nothing to do with the rest of the world.

Many men, when doing step two, start thinking about their lives and begin experiencing regret and shame for things they've done and not done. Pain begins building and their feelings start welling up. That's a good sign — it means they're not as disconnected from themselves (their hearts) as they may have thought. For you, stay with your emotions, feel them, acknowledge that they are integral to your being, don't judge yourself in the process, and know you're growing because of it.

What needs to happen next is for you to really anchor to the list you've created. Print the list and sentences and post them somewhere where you'll see them every day as a reminder of who you are. Print just the 25, one-word descriptors, put a copy in your wallet, and read it whenever you're feeling down in the dumps. We tend to forget just how expansive we actual are, relying on just a few descriptors with which to get by on a daily basis. If you're doing that, you're doing yourself a disfavor, both to you *and the world around you*. It's like choosing to be one-dimensional when you're actually 3-dimensional; like choosing to consistently use only 5,000 words when there are over a million available in the English language.

If creating the Identity List just isn't going to be something you'll do, then here's another exercise: look at yourself, up close, in a mirror. What do you see? How do you feel looking straight into your eyes? Now, say out loud, "I love myself." Say it over and over until you truly believe it. Once again, you may feel a number of unsupportive feelings in this process. Just go with them and still do the exercise. Once you're at the point of believing yourself, then begin describing your attributes, e.g., "I am a good and loving father to my children." "I help people as often as I can as a way of giving back." "I share what I have so that I can connect more deeply with people." Try doing this exercise every day for a month and see how you and your life change. It could be subtle, it could be grand.

## *Nurturing #1*

It all comes down to recognizing and acknowledging #1: you. Life pulls at us constantly to feed it our energy, time, and focus. We get so caught up with life that we forget about ourselves except to deal with the mundane aspects of life, such as eating, getting to work on time, making phone calls we've got to make, paying bills, taking care of chores, etc. Our lives have become so complicated and full of distractions that we've got ourselves off track, oftentimes lost and confused wondering where our lives are going and if life has any meaning anymore.

> Brandon came into the Men's Group and was an immediate star: handsome, gregarious, vivacious, and funny. He spoke his mind with ease and had no trouble engaging the men about his life and trying to figure it out now that he was coming out. He held a great job and everything about him seemed charmed.
>
> A year went by and Brandon got himself a boyfriend, a nice-looking guy whom everyone liked. I didn't see Brandon for a while once he left the Men's Group, only occasionally running into him at Gay Pride or in the gay part of town.
>
> Years went by and I moved from San Diego to Santa Fe, NM. Kiernan, whom I wrote about earlier, and I stayed in touch. He often ran into men from the group and kept me updated as to what was going on in their lives. His news about Brandon was heartbreaking. Brandon's boyfriend turned out to be a drug user and dealer and he got Brandon hooked. Kiernan had run into Brandon at Stepping Stone of San Diego, a drug and alcohol treatment and recovery center serving the LGBT community, and didn't even

recognize Brandon, he had changed that dramatically. Kiernan described him as looking like he'd been lost in the desert for years, suffering all its deprivations.

Brandon's daughter was relocating in another state and he wanted to move so he could be nearby. But, he had lost his great-paying job and his finances were non-existent. He was truly down and out and obviously depressed. The handsome, gregarious, and vivacious Brandon we'd known would most likely be gone forever, sucked dry by drugs.

Brandon's story illustrates what happens when we're pulled off track so far that we're completely disconnected from our true self. We stop nurturing ourselves and come up with any number of rationalizations to reinforce why we're not taking care of #1. Even if it depletes us in mind, body, and spirit.

To nurture oneself is key to staying emotionally and mentally healthy and happy. Let's get clear as to what I mean by nurture: *to raise or promote the development of; to educate; to bring up or train; to cherish, to hold and treat as dear.* So, this is not just about going to a day spa and being pampered, though that can be a part of it. To nurture yourself is an ongoing process of checking into what your needs are, understanding what those needs are based upon, and then taking appropriate actions to support your development, education, training, and cherishing yourself. That includes: doing things in moderation; taking time to just be with yourself; putting aside the distractions of life for quiet time with yourself. It also means making sure that what you're putting into your body — physically, emotionally, mentally, and spiritually — keeps you in optimum condition and consistently uplifts you. By surrounding yourself with people who are positive and life-affirming, you can let go of those things that hold you back from being a greater version of you.

Nurturing also includes getting back to the basics of what really makes you happy deep in your heart, going after what you're truly passionate about, and discovering and supporting what you really like about yourself. Be prepared to make some changes in your life as you really center on these things. You may find that you need to let go of some people in your life, just as Brandon needed to when he discovered his boyfriend was a drug user and dealer. Think how different life would be for Brandon if he'd "just [said] no," (thank you Nancy Reagan). Some people made fun of the former first lady for the simplicity of her approach to dealing with drugs. But when it comes down to it, just by saying the little word "NO," we've decided in a split second to change the course of our lives. If that were only Brandon's story....

Letting go could also include changes to where and how you live, changing jobs and careers, losing/putting on weight, trying new things, changing your haircut, changing your style of clothes — all sorts of things that are focused on you cluing in to what really makes you tick, what feeds your soul. Then you support what feeds your soul by surrounding yourself with friends and an environment to augment that. Now you're beginning to lead an authentic life, first by being honest with yourself and then taking action. That honesty will then work into all your relationships and people will pick up on it. You are now becoming a force for good in your own world and in the world at large.

You are no longer directed by old patterns, no longer needy, no longer finding yourself in co-dependent scenarios with other people. You are now what in the 1980s was called "Master of the Universe." The difference in what I mean and what it meant back then is that you are your own master and have no need to be someone else's master. It's not about power over others, but the power to be yourself. No one calls the shots concerning your life but you.

## *Highs and Lows*

One area I've not really touched on, but that definitely is a part of nurturing yourself, involves substance abuse and addictions in general. This isn't a new subject for humanity. We've dealt with addictions for a long, long time — a struggle that has claimed an untold number of lives, destroyed marriages and families, tanked careers, and irreparably hurt the people near and dear to us. Addictions suck the life out of us, yet we still get hooked by them.

As an FYI, one aspect of the LGBT community that is quite prevalent is the abundant use of drugs and alcohol. In 2012, the Center for American Progress released a new issue brief stating that "...an estimated 20 to 30 percent of gay and transgender people abuse substances, compared to about 9 percent of the general population." Why?

There are a number of reasons. First, the most obvious is that the LGBT community has been suppressed, attacked, and vilified by society for countless years. The stress of having to hide one's true self combined with the fear of religious, societal, community, family, and work reprisal has caused members of the LGBT community to compartmentalize themselves strictly for protection and survival in such a hostile environment.

Second, American society has made alcohol an exemplary accessory of life to the point that it's advertised everywhere and seemingly integral to the success of any type of gathering.

Third, recreational drugs—used for escapism, relaxation, enhancement, and thrills — are an ever sought-after commodity. Life is rough, we want relief. Now that the state of Colorado has legalized marijuana with other states soon to follow, it's open season on the idea of integrating recreational drugs into everyday life without the threat of arrest.

All three reasons create a lethal cocktail of dissociation. Once again, disconnection from our true selves. And the rationalizations to keep up with the "socializing" component of daily living are such that we're made to feel like we're a boorish oddball and party-pooper if we don't participate and partake.

The purpose of my bringing up this subject is not to dissuade you from enjoying yourself, but to make you aware of the fact that drugs and alcohol are present at the majority of LGBT activities. It's your decision as to how you want to deal with this aspect of our community, first for yourself and then as concerns other people, e.g., a person you're interested in dating, someone you've decided to be in a relationship with, or a group you want to join.

There are a ton of addictions and, thankfully, there are support groups and therapists that can support us in untangling ourselves from the tenacious clutches of addictions. The following link provides initial insight into various 12-step programs that pattern themselves after Alcoholics Anonymous (AA). http://en.wikipedia.org/wiki/List_of_twelve-step_groups.

If you're struggling with an addiction or think you have a problem with something, seek help. Take stock of your life, your habits, the friends you're keeping, and any behaviors that are holding you back from truly being yourself. It's not an easy or comfortable thing to do, but it could be a life-saving step in the right direction.

*"The first step to recovery is admitting you have a problem."*

You are changing roles in your life. You thought you needed to be one thing, e.g., a husband, father, leader, breadwinner, handyman, etc. You will still be some of those things, but now you've added another dimension, that of being a man who loves other men. It's not a huge distinction, unless you make it so, but it will call for some changes on your part. You are becoming a more multi-dimensional person and not suppressing an integral aspect of yourself. What kind of gay man you become will be based on what kind of man you already are. Now you're going to just expand on that and see what new dimensions you discover about yourself.

# Chapter 7

# Loss

Jessy had grown up and lived in several foster homes before being adopted at age four. One of his foster siblings, Sasha, who was a year ahead of him in school, was his absolute favorite sister. She was a model of vivacity and effervescence that he wished he had. Everyone loved her. Even though there weren't legally brother and sister, they considered themselves to be just that.

Jessy came out to Sasha when he was in college. She seemed okay with this news. They had both been in theater most of their lives and were used to all sorts of characters. Years later, though, Jessy's being gay became an issue when Sasha had become a born again Christian. When they had a chance to spend some time together in 2005, Sasha was obviously struggling with her Christian beliefs about homosexuality and her love for Jessy. She wanted more than anything for Jessy to be saved and repent his sinful way of life.

Today, they no longer talk as Sasha, who belongs to an evangelical church group where she met her current husband, doesn't answer the phone messages he leaves her or Facebook postings on her wall. Even when her own mother died, Jessy received no acknowledgement of the condolences he sent Sasha. Jessy is resigned to the fact that he'll probably never hear from or see his favorite "sister" again, which, when he thinks of her, brings a pang of sadness and heaviness to his heart.

One of the most devastating aspects of the entire coming out process is the potential for loss. It can occur in several ways, but the two most prevalent are when someone chooses to shut you out of their life and when, against your will, someone is taken away from you such as what can happen in child custody cases. The potential is very real and this is very often the primary reason why a gay man would choose to stay in his marriage.

In earlier chapters, we've discussed what you can do to maintain lines of communication and approaches to dealing with loved ones to avoid losing anyone. You will definitely need to put a lot of attention and energy into these factors depending on the level of your relationship with each person. For many men, staying at least friends with their wives is extremely important to them. They may have developed a close and supportive dynamic with their wives in spite of their true sexual identity. Losing that unconditional support would create a large void in their lives and trying to replace it when stepping into the unknown of a new lifestyle and community is daunting and very risky. They may never find that level of relationship again.

With children, having a child's love is something very special. When they came into the world, they were totally dependent on you for all their needs — and they loved you without question. As they've grown, your dynamic has adapted itself to fit their age and shifting needs with middle school and high school being the most difficult to traverse. But the core of your love has always remained in place. Your children reaching young adulthood and beyond will necessitate yet another shift in your dynamic. Some men are already in that stage and others whose children are still young have yet to reach it. Whatever your situation, remember what your relationship is built upon and use that as the fulcrum to weather the ups and downs.

When you come out to your children, put yourself in their shoes to appreciate their upset, frustration, anger, fear, and hurt. Your announcement and the impending breakup of the family could traumatize them, so working with a family therapist is a credible option. Do what you have to, without allowing yourself to be manipulated, to ensure that you and your children remain close.

> Sam has only one child, a boy. When he came out to his wife, she was rather understanding, and the two of them managed to remain amicable throughout the divorce.
>
> She met another man and the two decided to marry. The two planned on moving to Portland and she wanted her son to live with her. As upsetting as this was for Sam, he felt that his son being with his mother was more important. Sam and his ex-wife came to an agreement concerning

visiting rights and how often his son could come to San Diego to stay with his dad. Both parents wanted to make sure their son felt loved and that neither parent would be out of his life.

Sam made numerous trips to Portland over the years and his son had regularly scheduled visits to San Diego.

Eventually, Sam's former wife moved back to San Diego. She has since passed away. Sam's son, possibly feeling shame about his father's long-term gay relationship, chose to not communicate with Sam for some time and their relationship was strained for several years. They are just now beginning to communicate once again.

It's nice to know that Sam's story is a norm we see in any kind of family make up, whether straight or gay. With all the men who came through the Men's Group, none of them had a relationship with their children go astray, except for one person. His daughter was deeply disappointed in her dad and they fought bitterly about his coming out as a gay man. She eventually reached a point where she felt they could no longer know each other and she shut him out of her life for good. For the most part, the other members had their falling outs, but they made it through them as they all wanted to remain in each other's lives.

As I said, the norm is to not lose children in this process, but there are exceptions. Some family members and relatives may decide no other option is reasonable for them except to say "good-bye" for good. Most of the time, this has to do with their religious belief concerning homosexuality.

Vince, who was not a member of the Married Men's Coming Out Group, is 57 years old, a minister, married with two adopted girls, and gay. He has never had sex with his wife — she has no idea he's actually gay. They've been married since the mid-1970s. His family has absolutely no idea what the real story is with him. As a minister, his belief is that the Bible is wrong concerning homosexuality, but he would never espouse this belief to his congregation.

Since high school, Vince has had sexual relations with many men. When living in Boston and newly married, he would prowl certain areas of the city and find pickups. He has never spent the entire night with a man.

His two adopted daughters are now in their mid-twenties. One is a grad student at Berkeley and the other just graduated from ministerial college. The minister-to-be's stance on homosexuality follows religious dictates and she is quite adamant about it being a sin against God. Knowing this, Vince plans to never come out to his family as he believes he'll lose all of them. He continues hoping, though, to have a full-fledged relationship with a man at some point in his life.

You can see the convoluted thinking men can go through as they try to come to terms with being homosexual. The potential for loss is huge and something to contemplate in order to determine a path to take. Vince has chosen his path, but notice his disconnection from the facts in hoping to have a relationship with a man at some point in his life. How could that possibly happen? Is he just going to divorce his wife and maintain his secret? Where's the respect due his wife and children?

Hope always springs eternal for finding love, and many people — men, women, straight, gay, all ages — hope to find that special someone who fulfills their heart's needs. It does happen. The reality, though, is that most people won't find that fairy-tale version of a lover, but they will find someone who gives their heart a run for its money. They'll experience their journey together for as long as it lasts. Mazel tov, salud, glückwünsche, felicidades, gratis — congratulations!

Another reason for someone making you persona non grata could have something to do with their having been sexually violated when they were young and you are a symbolic reminder of that trauma — it's too painful or frightening to know you because of what you represent. There are some people for whom being in close proximity to a homosexual scares them for no other reason than it's too different from their sense of reality for them to handle. They have no idea why you scare them, you just do. Then there are those for whom you being homosexual cuts too close to home. They're in the closet about their own feelings, so it's best not to be around you so as to avoid spilling the beans or falling into the "guilt by association" trap. You might recognize all of these as being the underpinnings of homophobia — no matter how irrational and unreasonable as they appear.

Wesley had made plans with his partner in 1986 to visit Santa Fe to determine if they wanted to move there. They'd done a lot of research on many aspects of the city and felt it was definitely worth checking out.

Wesley had relatives living in Albuquerque. His aunt was one of his favorites. She was from Buenos Aires, Argentina. He loved her exotic looks, her playfulness, and her creativity. They used to play duets on the piano, her long, red fingernails clicking on the keys. They'd laugh and laugh.

Wesley's uncle had been the captain of a battleship in WWII, though he never acted like a military man. He, too, was fun-loving and really enjoyed playing host to company.

Not having seen either for many years, Wesley called Albuquerque to see if they'd like to have two visitors for a couple of days. They were delighted. Wesley said he'd call again to confirm the dates when they'd be in town.

The next time Wesley called, the delightful response he'd received from his aunt and uncle had definitely chilled. His uncle told him that he and his wife thought Wesley was a terrific person, but it just wouldn't do to have him stay at their house with his "friend." Sorry.

Deducing what had happened, Wesley called his family in Colorado. What he found out was that his mother had told his aunt and uncle about his being gay. Turned out that his aunt was a born again Christian and having such sin in her house would have been unthinkable. Having the two men stay in their home might have been misinterpreted as sanctioning their sin.

Wesley never spoke to or saw them again.

Loss occurs both ways. Wesley's relatives initiated closing the door, but then he finished the job by deciding he didn't need people like that in his life. His aunt and uncle had supported his dance career and were proud of his accomplishments. Yet, when the idea of having two homosexuals in their home presented itself, the kid gloves came off and their real feelings were made known. This often happens where people are okay with your being gay — at a distance — but not okay when it's up close and personal. In Wesley's case, both parties experienced loss.

So, be aware that if people choose to not have you in their lives anymore, they are experiencing a certain amount of hurt also. If it's a family member or relative, the pain will be that much more amplified. The person shutting you out may feel you've betrayed them, let them down, turned against the family, manipulated and lied to them, abandoned them, purposely sabotaged your relationship with them, destroyed the family. Worse, they may think you are doing this to get even with them or someone else — there are many reasons. Whatever the reason and however unreasonable it may appear to you, strive to be compassionate — and be patient. Who knows, some day you may re-establish your relationship. If the damaged relationship is with your children, give it time, keep the lines of communication open by being available to them, and be consistent with your message of love and support for them.

Sometimes, re-establishing old and dear friendships combined with the disclosure of being gay doesn't end with the outcome we hope it will.

> Ben is very connected to friends and colleagues through Facebook, LinkedIn, Classmates, and several other social and business networks. Every once in a while, an old friend from high school or college will come to mind and he'll search the Internet for him or her. One old friend from college, Isaac, popped into his head one day. The two had been very close, though Isaac was straight.
>
> Doing his usual in-depth search, Ben found Isaac working as a writer for a company in upstate New York. He was still very involved in community theater as a director and playwright. Ben found his e-mail address and wrote him a warm e-mail that wasn't too long and overwhelming, informing Isaac of what he'd been doing for the past 30 years.
>
> The response he received back was a shock. The tone of Isaac's very short e-mail was cold and distant. Isaac, who had been married since 1980, wasn't interested in re-visiting their friendship, had been married to the same woman all these years, and was very content with his life.
>
> Ben was taken aback and hurt. What had happened in all the intervening years? Ben thought about a particular incident in college where he, Isaac, and Isaac's girlfriend were all lying on Isaac's bed. Isaac and his girlfriend were snuggling and Ben was positioned about two feet away. Isaac stretched out his arm toward Ben, placing his hand close to Ben. Ben was unsure what was happening or

what to do, though what he wanted was to take Isaac's hand in his own.

Then, about five years later, Ben had been visiting several theater friends on Long Island and Isaac surprised Ben by suddenly showing up. The two had hugged each other with great joy and enthusiasm. Later that night, Isaac had driven Ben to the train station. Both expressed their love for each other as friends and the evening had ended with the two hugging each other tightly. That was the last time Ben had seen Isaac.

Ben thought deeply about Isaac's e-mail response and wondered what the sub-text was. He had never "come on" to Isaac, never intimated that he wanted to explore anything deeper with him other than just being close friends. What was going on?

Sadly, when reaching out to reconnect with people from our past, the feelings and situations that had once been were no longer active. So much happens in a person's life and when we've not been in touch for many years, the disconnection can be final. For Ben, he was left wondering if the reason Isaac had mentioned that he'd been married to the same woman for 30-some years was that Isaac was actually in the closet. It could be that Ben's contacting Isaac was opening that closet door, something Isaac wanted to keep closed and locked for good.

Men who are either in the closet or afraid of their close feelings for another man — even though the relationship isn't intimate — are afraid that old feelings will surface and have to be addressed. This could turn their lives upside down. If you're telling them that you're gay, they may also be in fear that you are contacting them after all these years because you want to get involved with them.

Most straight men don't have "gaydar," yet when they experience a close friendship with another man, they may wonder "Is he gay?" They may even entertain thoughts of what it would be like to have sex with their friend. Those thoughts never really disappear. So, your contacting them again immediately re-activates those thoughts — and feelings — whether grounded in fact or not. Caution, trepidation, and outright fear can be the response.

Now if you're choosing to reconnect with old male friends whom you've known as straight, be aware that they may have harbored thoughts of your being gay, but they never questioned you about it. Your coming out to them will confirm what they suspected — and they may fear that you're coming after them to take care of old business. Often, this is too much for most heterosexual men to handle. They'll walk on eggshells around you or even give you the cold shoulder. Sometimes, though, just the opposite happens.

> Jim and Neil met when they were 17 years old, still in high school. For the next four years, they became deeply involved with each other, though Jim became very involved with a young woman, Felicia. Neil moved to New York City when he as 21 and Jim married Felicia. They divorced six years later. Jim went on to marry a second time while Neil had two long-term relationships with men.
>
> Though miles separated Jim and Neil, both fully explored separate lives and life experiences, the two stayed in touch over the years and remained intimate whenever they got together, an infrequent occurrence. There was even a period of over seven years when they weren't in touch.
>
> Forty-one years later, Jim flew to where Neil was living as he needed a long weekend away from work. It was then that the two realized they were truly and deeply in love with each other, always had been, and that it was time they became life-partners. Neil packed his household into a truck and moved to join Jim in LA. They've been together ever since. At the time of their epiphany of love, Jim was 58 and Neil was 57. It's never too late!

Another Hallmark Movie of the Week! Wonderfully, this story is 100 percent true. It does happen and as the old adage goes, "There's nothing new under the sun." The problem with this story is that it appeals to the unrealistic romantic in us. We all want that true love to come into our lives. Some of us spend a lot of time trying to find it and end up disappointed. But then, there are the old flames, heartthrobs, or even distant crushes we reconnect with who surprise us and are ready to jump into bed with us — and maybe even a relationship. This is the point where I say, "Tread carefully."

What is so very important to understand at this stage of your life is that the person you were years before is not the person you are today — and the same can be said of the other individual. Old passions can blind us to reality and the next thing we know, we're in a messy peccadillo. Additionally, your heart needs to be nurtured with care, not put through a meat grinder. But, then again, you could finally be moving into the real thing with a man. Whatever you do, try to go in with your eyes as wide open as possible. Otherwise, you're just setting yourself up for more heartache and potential loss.

## *Secondary Types of Loss*

Secondary to the types of loss we've covered so far is the fear of losing one's lifestyle, home, job, career, money, inheritance, and position in life. Depending on your situation, any of these may produce intense anxiety or may not be a concern for you. How you choose to deal with it is what it's all about — and men will jump through all sorts of hoops to safeguard relationships and avoid losing anyone or anything.

In the six years I facilitated the Men's Group, I heard all manner of stories of how men went to extremes to avoid losing anything that was of great importance to them. They'd do whatever it took, including hide information, manipulate information, manipulate people and situations, fabricate stories, and outright lie — and they lived this way for much of their lives. What they created was an incredible web of deception that even Hercule Poirot would find hard to untangle.

What this did to them emotionally was create cognitive dissonance: trying to simultaneously support two contradictory facts or ideas causing a person to experience anxiety, guilt, shame, anger, embarrassment, stress, and other negative emotional states. In order to survive the dissonance and reduce the tension they were experiencing, rationalization was employed to ameliorate their uncomfortable feelings. Most were able to somehow make it all work until the day came when their emotional pain was too great to continue living with it and they took the step to come out. In one case, the person didn't survive.

> Chaz was one of the original members of the Men's Group. A nice looking Brit, he was a Tony Award-winning lighting designer for theater and opera productions. He'd also received the British Olivier Award and 25 other major awards and nominations, including the New York Drama Desk Award and the Los Angeles Drama Critics Award.

Chaz struggled with his identity even though he'd accomplished so much in his life and was constantly in demand around the world. He knew he was gay, had come out to his wife and son, worked in a world known for its preponderance of gay people — yet struggled with the idea that being gay was okay. He just wasn't feeling a level of acceptance from people he knew, which really amounted to his own self-acceptance.

Always on the lookout for a partner with whom to spend the rest of his life with, Chaz did what he could to make himself more attractive, including wearing a toupee. He visited the gay bars, got involved with on-line dating services, and dressed casually. No luck. For him, it seemed that if he had a lifetime partner he could accept himself through the other person's acceptance of him.

In January of 2007, Chaz took his life. He was only 54 years old. In talking with Chaz months before he committed suicide, he was despondent because he wanted a male lover, but couldn't fully even accept himself as a gay man. The dichotomy he had experienced finally overtook him.

Chaz's cognitive dissonance was something he couldn't resolve and it eventually overwhelmed him. Other men dealt with their dissonance in different ways such as abusing alcohol and drugs, refusing to get involved with the gay community in any way, going back to their marriage, and over indulging in sex. Any of these meant a different kind of loss: loss of self. We've all had our moments of this, when we lose sight of who we are. Brandon, whom I mentioned in Chapter 5, did just exactly that by going down the tubes via drug use. Other men rationalized away their dissonance with a cavalier attitude: it's just gay culture so it's okay, I only do this once in a while, it's not hurting anyone, I can easily manage this, it's only for a short period, etc.

The web of deceit we choose to live eventually catches up with us and we experience a whole new level of pain, which can send us into a tailspin that causes us to hit rock bottom. Through rationalization and deception with ourselves and others, what we are essentially doing is hypnotizing ourselves to the point that we actually are creating a form of psychosis. Psychosis literally means an abnormal condition of the mind, and is a generic psychiatric term for a mental state often described as involving a "loss of contact with reality."

So there's another form of loss a person can experience on their way to becoming and actually living as a gay man: the fear of losing contact with reality. This isn't high on most people's list of things to fear. Let's face it, psychosis doesn't rate very high on the list of mental disorders. Going off the deep end, yes, but not developing a psychosis — that's nothing a drink or snort or role in the hay can't alleviate. The problem with losing contact with reality is that we usually have no idea we're caught in that state. This is where being in a support group, such as the Married Men's Coming Out Group, can be helpful.

The men in the group were always catching each other on their rationalizations and skewed beliefs regarding almost everything. If they felt someone was losing touch with reality, they called them on it, questioning just what was really going on. Thus, the self-hypnosis people tended toward was avoided for the most part. There were some, though, who valiantly struggled to remain in their hypnotized state as long as they could.

> A young man, Yale, was a professional who had recently come out to his wife. They'd been married just a couple of years.
>
> In the Men's Group, he tended to laugh when questioned about something that hit too close to home emotionally or factually. He'd laugh as a way to side-step dealing with the issue and then would never answer the question except in an offhand and flippant manner. It was like pulling teeth with him to have him get real and face himself.
>
> Yale's belief was that looking at the truth was going to be too painful and that the others in the group would judge him. Thus, his rationalizations tended to be steer him and the group toward something lighter. Making jokes was his way of deflecting the focus from him and his issues.
>
> Yale mentally knew that the men wouldn't judge him, one of the group's cardinal facilitation rules. But the fear of losing the respect of the group was enough for him to act in a manner that ended up not supporting him. In spite of his attempts, he lost the respect of the group anyway because he wasn't being real with them.
>
> It took many months of working with Yale in the Men's Group for him to finally break through his self-hypnosis.

Yale was completely unaware of his behavioral pattern and gave us that deer-in-headlights look when we pointed it out to him. He was so hypnotized that he was living one life while thinking he was living another. Humans do that. It's no wonder we sometimes sit and wonder what life is about when we start to get a clue that the life we're living is an illusion. Or, to put it another way, that we are living our psychoses.

The point of mentioning all of this is that one of the things a man coming out fears is losing those aspects of himself that he holds dear. The concern is that somehow he'll lose sight of who he is, that he won't know himself anymore, he'll be wandering the world like an amnesiac caught in the Twilight Zone. Coming out necessitates changes in just about every aspect of your life. You can't avoid it. Instead of offering resistance, the best thing to do is to go with the flow and see where it takes you. You'll suffer far less stress and who knows what you'll discover about yourself and the world around you. All it takes is a second to make a decision and then take your first step.

How many of us felt the pangs that change brought when we graduated from high school and moved on to college, perhaps one not in our hometown? Did the same pangs arrive several years later upon graduation from college? How about when you moved from your parents' home or to a new city? We all experience uncertainty when dealing with the unknown and the same occurs when leaving the well-worn clothing of the heterosexual lifestyle for the God-knows-what lifestyle of a gay man. And what do you do when you remove the veils of illusion and you decide to leave your psychosis behind? Essentially, you may have to re-invent yourself to a degree. That takes introspection (Chapter 1). Remember, learning is a lifelong process.

Let's look at one other emotion experienced by Yale: shame. Though he was in a group for married men coming out, his underlying shame about being gay caused him to avoid addressing his very real issues.

Shame is rampant in the gay community. Society has done a great job of instilling it in us and they're still at it through making fun of us to bullying, shunning, ostracizing and even murdering us to show the world who's the boss, who's right, and who has power. Shaming is even used in the gay community against its own members. We've been taught well. Yet, ironically, we celebrate our gayness through Gay Pride parades and festivals as a way to show the world that though they try to put us down, try to "change" us, and even try to eradicate us that we've the strength and wisdom to recognize our innate power, our beauty, our depth, and our divinity.

But shame is one of the emotions that digs deeply into our psyche. It's incredibly difficult to resolve it within ourselves. It does a damn good job of demolishing our sense of self-esteem and self-worth, our sense of belonging and acceptance. At its core, shame is about fear and feelings of inferiority. In Yale's mind, being honest in the men's group was to be avoided because he felt the men would judge him. He didn't want to be perceived as inferior, didn't want the humiliation that would come with their judgment.

Once Yale opened up to the group, he became more thoughtful in how he expressed his feelings. He was no longer avoidant or gave flippant answers. He truly realized that the men's group was there to support him. The only thing Yale lost in the process was the illusion that there was something wrong with him.

What you may lose in terms of old patterns is really about growth. As you review your life patterns, determine if any are in any way holding you back from what you want in life. If they are, it's time to shed them. Then, search within yourself before you decide to immediately replace them with a new pattern. In whatever way you decide to work with your patterns, you're going to learn through the process what works best for you and develop a more discriminating eye as to what is healthiest for you. Just be honest in your appraisal in what to let go of and what to take on — and why you are choosing either.

The other losses mentioned earlier besides loss of family members and relatives can be divided into two types: (1) friends, colleagues, and clients, and (2) home, job, career, lifestyle, money, inheritance, and position in life. Let's look at the first group.

## *Coming Out to Friends, Colleagues, and Clients*

This secondary group has different reasons for whether you would come out to them or not. You'll need to handle each on a case-by-case basis in context to the specific person; what group they are a part of, e.g., friendship group, work group, etc.; and/or level of importance to your job, career, and group/community standing.

> One guy in the Men's Group decided to broadcast to his entire work group that he's gay. The fallout was similar to having dropped an atom bomb. Some people didn't know what to say or do, so just stood there feeling incredibly

embarrassed and uncomfortable. Others freaked out, starting crying, swearing, blew up and verbally attacked him, and some stormed out of the room. Others were confused and wanted to know more. Some were compassionate.

His supervisors on up to the president of the company called him into a special meeting to discuss his company-wide "announcement." He didn't leave the meeting feeling warm and fuzzy. Instead, he was written up and put on a kind of probation for an indefinite period: he was not to discuss his being gay with co-workers, he was not to bring gay issues or paraphernalia into the workplace, and he could not bring a "friend" to any company events. They didn't specifically have a problem with his being gay, just that he was publicly "out" about it. What was being enforced was something akin to the military's directive "Don't ask, don't tell."

The above incident occurred back in the 1990s. In today's world, the above would be cause for lawsuits. Though this story is dated, it's still a good example of an ill-considered disclosure.

Think carefully about who you're going to tell and how you're going to do it. Making a public announcement certainly has dramatic flair to it, but it doesn't take into account how people may take the information you're delivering. Sensitivity is required here just as much as when you came out to your family. Granted, you may reach a point where you just don't care who knows and you're getting antsy about getting on with your life, but it's still a matter of delicacy.

You don't have to plan this like a royal wedding, and likewise, you could do better than handling it as though storming the Bastille. Be sure of whom you can trust to remain confidential about your disclosure — you know how well the rumor mill works and you want to manage the situation as best as possible. If rumors get started, then all sorts of misinformation can spread and you'll have to add damage control to your task list.

Additionally, think about the kinds of reactions you could get, anything from love to hate and in between. That's one reason why telling a group could be difficult to handle. One-on-one works best so that you can focus all your conversation on just that one person and their feelings. This will also give them a chance to not have to worry about someone else being present. What you want to avoid in this process is editing on either your part or the part of the person you're telling. Both of you must feel free to express yourselves without fear of someone else not agreeing with you or the other person, judging you or the other person, the person you're telling feeling as though they need to suppress/edit themselves to save face, and/or be cautious around the other person. Doing it simply is the best approach.

Disclosing to friends, co-workers, and clients involves an initial small circuit of people — which is attached to a larger arena called: the community in which you live. Once you begin the process of letting people know about your circumstances, then word is going to begin spreading. Make sure you're ready for this as you never know who you're going to run into who may broach the subject. You won't be able to control your coming out process entirely, but you can manage it effectively if you take the time to really think about what you're doing, how you're going to do it, and whom you're going tell.

Sometimes, you'll have the emotional impulse to just blurt out the truth of yourself. It's an in-the-moment thing and understandable. Before you do, take a deep breath and count to 10. Make absolutely sure you want to disclose this information at this time to this particular person. There may be ramifications you're unaware of that may make life difficult for you — as if you didn't have enough challenges already.

Again, in disclosing to people, there is the potential for losing individuals or even an entire group. One man, Roland, whom I mentioned in Chapter 4, was asked to leave his church and people he'd known for years entirely. He switched to the Metropolitan Community Church (MCC), joined their choir, and felt much more at home to express his sense of God in an inclusive community setting. So, some of the changes you may have to make will not only involve letting some people and/or groups go, you may find yourself finding new locales in which to be yourself, which could include a new place to work, a new church, a new community service group, a new social group, etc.

You may run into a situation which you've probably already experienced in your life and that's when you lose someone over a period of time. In this case, for some people, your being gay is going to be the 800-pound gorilla in the room all the time. They'll feel they can't relate to you anymore simply because of this one facet of your personality. When in conversation with you or working with you, they'll feel they can't be themselves because they "know" this piece of information about you. Your being gay is going to be in their face acting as a barrier they just can't get past or around or through. Don't take it personally — it's their issue, not yours.

# Married Men Coming Out

The following true story was told to me by my close friend, Martin Rutte. This happened a number of years ago between his mother and his aunt.

> After my father, Harry, passed away, my mother, Lily, took in boarders to both help with the rent and to keep her company. Henry was one of the boarders. He lived in a single room upstairs, she downstairs, and he worked as a short order cook in the restaurant at the end of the block. He looked after my aging mother by getting her any groceries she needed, playing cards with her, and providing her with a sense of safety with his presence in the house. He didn't smoke, which was very important to her — no chance for a fire should he smoke in bed — and he always paid his rent on time. Henry's only friends were the people in the restaurant and one older woman. He was quiet, well-behaved, and he provided companionship for my mother and she for him.
>
> One day, my Aunt Sally came to visit my mother. Henry happened to be out. As Sally walked by Henry's room, she looked in the open door and spied a row of teddy bears on his bed. She immediately knew what this meant. She came barreling down the stairs, dismay on her face and alarm in her voice. My mother, thinking something was terribly wrong, rushed to her.
>
> "Lily!" my aunt cried out.
>
> "What, Sally, what?" replied my mother.
>
> "Henry's gay," said Sally.
>
> "What does that mean?" my mother asked. She really didn't know the word. This was the 1970s in the working-class section of a mid-sized Canadian city.
>
> Aunt Sally then used the Yiddish word "faygelleh" to explain it to her. My mother paused, thought about it for a moment, and then shrugged nonchalantly as she said, "Gay, shmay, he pays the rent!"

It does say something about how shallow some people can be: They only see you, accept you, and let you into their world if you fit within the limited confines of their little box of perception. It's all about comfort levels. You need to decide whether they are the kind of person you want in your life. They may be nice people, but the gorilla is always going to be present. If you want to take on helping them get around the gorilla, that's your choice. Just be aware of the possibility of how that relationship could become co-dependent. You need to be you and not spending time and energy on people who need to be indulged just so *they* feel comfortable.

The point is that you may lose this person in slow motion. People have already come and gone in your life: you've lost track of each other, you've lost interest in the relationship as you don't really have anything in common anymore, the originating purpose and dynamic for the relationship has changed, etc. The relationship will dissolve in slow motion.

## *Losing Home, Job, Career, Lifestyle, Money, Inheritance, and Position in Life*

The second set of secondary losses one can experience — home, job, career, lifestyle, money, inheritance, and position in life — can be just as devastating as losing a family member for some people. Moving out of the family house will be upsetting as you're changing what's familiar for the unfamiliar and unknown. You have no idea what's going to happen to you now. You will most likely be living by yourself. You'll be left to your own devices and decisions that only affect you living in that new space, no one else. You'll adapt and eventually figure out a system of living in your new quarters that works for you.

Losing job and career can also be quite upsetting. Just because you came out doesn't mean that your entire life needs to be turned inside out and upside down. But, if you think about it, if you do lose your job for being gay, which is now against the law, you can sue the company if you want and have the wherewithal to do that. Or, you can look at this as an opportunity to find a place to work that is more in alignment with who you are, your talents, and what you have to offer. Do you really want to stay with a company that fundamentally is opposed to who you are? What kind of daily tension would you be working under and how would that affect your relationship dynamics with co-workers? How would that affect your ability to do top-level work and be creative? Would the unspoken pressure to conform eventually wear you down to the point you sink into depression?

As the saying goes, when one door closes, another opens. That's opportunity knocking and it's really about how you think of yourself and whether your career supports who you are. Are you doing work that truly feeds your soul? Do you have a heart connection with the company's mission and vision? Do you feel your primary talents are being utilized in a way that's fulfilling and expansive? Do you feel fully appreciated for what you bring to the table? If the answer to any of these is "no," then losing your career may be just what you need to move in the direction that ties in more with who you are and your purpose in life.

It's all about meaning in life. No longer is it about living to satisfy socio-cultural conventions as determined by other people and their agendas, values, beliefs, and fears. It's your life journey and it has to have meaning for you. That necessitates letting go of what is considered "important" by others and concentrate your efforts on what gives meaning and depth to your life. You can stop living just to be secure and comfortable, which lets your life energy get sucked out of you. The purpose of life is to live, not find a rut to fit into. You'll never find out just how far you can stretch, what you're really made of, and how extraordinary you are if you settle for being comfortable.

Another potential loss involves money. This can happen because of losing your job, changing careers, and even losing an inheritance. Financial loss is high up on the Richter scale of life stressors and none of us enjoy going through that. It may happen and it may not. You may need to work with a lawyer, your bank, and a tax expert to ensure you stay on top of your finances. That also goes for your partner in the event something should happen to you.

> Nolan opted to stay married to his wife. He felt a deep loyalty and responsibility to her for having come out. They had two grown children with their own families with whom Nolan spent as much time as possible. Nolan also had a male lover, Philip. The two lived for many years in San Diego in a home they both owned. Philip was considered part of Nolan's family and attended many family events, which were held around the country. Everyone was fond of Philip.
>
> While out of the country, Nolan had a heart attack and died. Philip was back here in the States when he got word. He informed Nolan's family members of Nolan's passing and they all worked together to return Nolan home and make arrangements for his funeral.
>
> The next thing Philip knew, he was being forced out of the home he and Nolan owned and had lived in for so

long. The family felt Philip had no rights as Nolan's gay lover to any of his property or inheritance even though it had been bequeathed him in Nolan's will. Philip ended up out on his ear and without any of the mementos of his life with Nolan to take with him.

When it comes to money and property, never underestimate how people are going to react to attaining it or losing it. Nolan and Philip had no idea Nolan's family would respond as they did. Philip was incredulous — not to mention deeply hurt — and took Nolan's family to court, but lost as the courts at that time did not recognize gay relationships on an equal basis as they do the marriage between a man and a woman.

Since the advent of the US Supreme Court's ruling legalizing same-sex marriages, various groups and states have contested the ruling. They've also challenged the Equality Act of 2015 concerning gay rights. The battle for equality has yet to be settled, so it's important to stay on top of what's occurring with state and federal laws as you consider marriage and all that it entails. For more information, check out Lambda's state map that provides updates on the Equality Act as it pertains to workplace and public accommodations: www.lambdalegal.org/in-your-state. If you are in a committed relationship with another man, see a lawyer and understand your state's laws concerning gay rights.

People get really funny around money and property and possessions. Some men who come out are threatened with losing their parents' inheritance unless they stay in the marriage. Sometimes, wills are re-written so as to arrange inheritance for one's grandchildren, thereby bypassing the gay parent. It's a form of threat and manipulation to ensure one's comfort level in their own head, keep their pride intact, uphold social standing, and maintain control of their world and other people.

What a person who does this is failing to see is that a family dynamic with one gay parent who wants out but is being coerced into staying in the marriage is headed for unhappiness and conflict — for everyone. No one is going to win just for the sake of appearances and ego and trying to control reality. It's going to be another 600-pound gorilla in the room all the time. Yet, people still do this. If this is your situation, then you need a lawyer and some major heart-to-heart time with your parents and siblings.

The last area to mention is the loss of social position. We've seen what happens to people in public office or with high visibility who are caught in compromising situations. They can definitely experience loss of status and social position. Eventually, they and society get over it and go on with their lives. Sometimes it takes re-inventing themselves. Some make public apologies trying to save face and go on with their careers. Others stay in the game and keep at it knowing that they'll get through it and life will continue.

The thing about social position is that it's only good for as long as a fickle public is interested. We live in such a fast-paced world full of so many distractions that we've become a rather ADD culture. We quickly tire of what's considered noteworthy and are always looking for the next attraction or bit of stimulation. Events are quickly forgotten and the initial excitement around the event develops a patina of disinterest.

If you are in a situation where you'll lose social standing, please do not choose to hide or lie about who you are. People will actually hold you in higher standing for being truthful, though they may still shut the door on you. That's their prerogative and you just need to be aware of that. In the years to come, some people may still treat you as a topic of disdain, but there may be one person who will say, "At least he was truthful with us."

## *Loss through the Suicide of a Loved One*

There is one last possibility of loss to discuss: what happens if by your coming out, a loved one commits suicide? It's a terrible thought to consider, but it has happened. Due to the level of stress, overwhelm and change being thrust on a family, one member may reach a point where ending their life is the only option they see available. The upset and potential trauma loved ones can experience by your coming out needs to be carefully monitored. That's why keeping the lines of communication open and active is so very important.

We have no idea what's really going on in someone's head as life serves up its fare. We may think we're being straightforward in communicating something and the person(s) hearing us actually perceives something else. Encourage everyone in your family to talk to you and with each other. If anyone begins to withdraw, work with them to get them to express what they're feeling. Don't leave them to try and figure things out on their own.

At heart, most people don't like change, especially if it's forced on them. They want things to remain the way they are, everyone living the role they're supposed to, life is predictable within the parameters that work for them — at least it's what they know. Change could mean they may have to leave their home, experience the potential loss of the lifestyle they're accustomed to, social embarrassment, and possibly losing you. Desperation can set in and then the mind will begin to hallucinate all sorts of unrealities, which means the number of options to consider will begin shrinking. It's a debilitating downward spiral.

Again, sessions with a therapist can be most helpful in avoiding misunderstandings, misconceptions, and sinking into deep depression. Thankfully, suicide is rare in the scenario of a father/husband coming out, but family members can become disappointed, discouraged, and quite depressed in the process of dealing with your coming out and the changes it brings. That goes for you, too. Do you have someone you trust you can talk to? Better yet, work with a therapist. Friends are good to have, but they are most likely lacking a therapist's training.

My friend, Steven Griffith of High Performance Coaching (Chapter 6), has two other axioms he uses in his work: "We transform our relationships one conversation at a time," and "We are meaning making machines."

"We transform our relationships one conversation at a time," is obvious. We have the chance whenever in conversation with anyone to elucidate, expand, inform, re-direct, connect, uplift, and change. As you go through the coming out process with family and any others involved, realize that how you express yourself and what you communicate is vitally important. Have real conversations, not just chit chats that do nothing to truly bond you with the other person. What will be derived is a deeper connection because you'll have created more meaning in your life.

This is where the "We are meaning making machines" comes into play. We want meaning in our life, so we constantly seek it by giving meaning to the world around us. The more you choose to connect with the people with whom you're in conversation, the greater meaning you'll have in life in general. And your life will be transformed for the better.

## Chapter 8

# Relationships

Terrence joined the Men's Group having already come out to his wife and kids. He was having his ups and downs with the process and felt that being a part of the Men's Group would be a great help to him in trying to figure things out.

One night, Terrence explained that he'd run into a man, Owen. Terrance had had quite a crush on Owen many years ago. It turns out Owen was also gay and had come out. It turned out that he had had feelings for Terrence back in the day, too.

Terrence wanted to know what to do. Was he kidding himself and just trying to recapture an old dream? Was he hallucinating that there was something real, or was there actually something between them that he should pursue? His heart was overwrought by this quandary.

After much discussion with the group, he decided to go on a date with Owen. At the next Men's Group meeting, he reported that they were in love and it was for real.

They've now been together for almost two decades and have since moved to Florida, opening a Bed & Breakfast.

Ah, fairy tales. The good news is that this story is true, though not the usual story one hears concerning the dating scene, gay bars, on-line chat rooms, parties, the brunch scene, and Internet dating services. Most of the men who came through the group had got involved with all of the above at one time or another. There were plenty of stories about conquests, first loves, dashed hopes, and getting bored or disenchanted with the whole damn relationship thing. Yet, each was seeking to quench an inner need. For most, it was more than just getting out there and getting laid. It was about finding love, companionship, safety, security, and solidity as a gay man in the gay community. They wanted to settle down to a lives very similar to the ones they had just left with their wives and kids.

There are a plenty of gay men who are against the idea of "settling down just like heteros." They feel it's a cop out for the gay community to pattern themselves after straight people, what with winning the right to marry and having children. And considering how poorly the rest of the population has treated homosexuals historically, why would we want to be like them? What's the point of being gay and unique if we're going to appear straight?

What's the point of being a human in a relationship — no matter what the gender combination is?

Human beings want companionship, understanding, acceptance, and love. They want to have a special someone with whom they can share the joys and beauty of life. They want the comfort of coming home to someone who's there just for them, someone who is supportive of who they are as a person, someone they can have all the little commonalities that bring them together beyond any other relationship, and it's the two of them facing life together as a team. It creates the safety, security, and solidity in one's life that makes it all bearable. Life is rough and sometimes harsh. How nice to come home to that one individual who is there for you and you can be there for them.

For a long time, the gay community was not known for these sentiments. It was all about partying and sexuality and lots of hot bods. But that's been calming down to a degree as everyone, both gay and straight, becomes more accustomed to having a gay presence in the greater culture. Since 1969's riot at the Stonewall Inn (now designated a National Historic Landmark) in Greenwich Village, which brought national attention to the gay community, gay people have had a double coming out: in their personal lives and very publicly as a group and community. It's been a blossoming process of coming into one's own and getting comfortable in it.

Over forty years have passed since Stonewall. Incredible things have happened for gay people that are positive and negative, ugly and beautiful, deadly and uplifting, incidental and far-reaching. It seems that we're now at that stage where we're getting over the initial rush of it all and settling back into our lives. It's not about being "normal." What we're discovering is that there is a middle ground in life between being fa-a-a-bulous and conventional.

We covered cognitive dissonance (Chapter 7): trying to simultaneously support two contradictory facts or ideas causing a person to experience anxiety, guilt, shame, anger, embarrassment, stress, and other negative emotional states. One of the outgrowths of this occurrence is that we begin to compartmentalize our lives: in some circumstances we're gay and in other circumstances we're straight. Doing this will eventually cause you to feel like you're leading a double life — and you will be. You've essentially become a split personality behaving as one of two different people depending on the situation you're in. The question is: What kind of relationship are you having with yourself and with the world around you?

> Warren was a former president of a national association, a practicing life coach, and brokered the sale of antique African artifacts and art. He'd been married for years and had two college-aged daughters. Via the Internet, he found and began chatting with a middle-aged man, Ken, who also turned out to be married. They arranged to meet in person and began an affair that lasted several years.
>
> Warren managed during that time to live two separate lives. He continued his life with his wife and daughters, including occasionally having sex with his wife, and in his public life, he was perceived as a married man.
>
> Meanwhile, he was meeting Ken, who was also married, as often as possible in motels and hotels, doing things about town together, meeting for lunches and dinners, and taking trips out of town together. Eventually, he invited Ken into his home, dinners with his family, and even began working him into all aspects of his business and professional life.
>
> The relationship broke off after several years when it was clear that neither was going to get a divorce and that Warren was deeply committed to leading two lives, never intending to leave his wife and daughters. He also believed that his professional standing would suffer immensely if he were to come out. Better to stay in the closet and quietly have someone on the side to satisfy his needs.
>
> Warren got involved with another young man who was married, again, working that young man into his business. That affair lasted about a year before ending in disappointment, both professionally and emotionally. To

this day, Warren remains married, his wife and daughters clueless as to the double life he leads.

Ken, on the other hand, separated from his wife after dating another man for a few years and was living a "gay" lifestyle. In 2010 he reconnected with a man he had known since age 17, and they are now in a committed, long-term relationship.

The pain that eventually develops in relationships such as this one involves both parties losing out. The married man who is having relations with men on the side is essentially unavailable to anyone, including himself. Yes, there's the excitement of engaging with a new lover who turns you on and being involved clandestinely, but it eventually begins wearing you down. The "game" becomes too complicated and you will begin feeling more and more that you want to live openly and honestly.

Most of us aren't cut out to live the life of a secret agent. We will reach a breaking point and either come out or end the relationship. If we don't come out, what usually happens is that we find someone new to distract us. We end up moving from relationship to relationship — simply running away from ourselves, playing at relationships, avoiding our issues, and never giving ourselves the chance to know something greater and more authentic. We become exactly what many women complain about concerning men: emotionally unavailable.

Tons of material exists concerning how to have a fulfilling and enduring relationship where you're understood and accepted for being who you are and vice versa. It wasn't until the 1960s that anyone began openly questioning what kind of internal relationship we have with ourselves. Since then, the self-help market has exploded with myriad methodologies for discovering and developing a relationship with self. The effect has been wonderful as men and women have made the effort to find out what their needs are, upon what those needs are based, and developing a centeredness and balance through their process of self-discovery.

After talking with a friend who told him he needed to get a life, Jeremy finally came out at age 38. He'd been married for 12 years and realized that he truly wasn't happy, though he loved his wife.

Early in Jeremy's marriage, he and his wife attended marriage counseling. The counselor advised they divorce as he was sure Jeremy was gay. After that, Jeremy's wife refused to attend more counseling as she denied that Jeremy was gay. But, after seven years of marriage, Jeremy's wife had an affair. Jeremy was devastated, but hung onto the marriage for another five years. The trust they'd had in their marriage was severely damaged, never returning to what it had been.

Then, while they were still married, Jeremy's wife met her husband-to-be at work and the sparks flew for them. Meanwhile, Jeremy was finally coming to understand that he truly wasn't happy or fulfilled, that he wanted to be with a man, so he asked his wife for a divorce.

The two went through the usual emotional roller coaster. At first, she was bitter, going through numerous issues since Jeremy's announcement that he's gay. The two continued living together for three months until she couldn't take it any longer. Jeremy moved into the gay section of town. Once again, they sought out therapy and though Jeremy's wife resisted attending, she finally admitted that going to therapy meant they really would be getting a divorce. A year later, she'd married her co-worker from work.

Jeremy went through a lot of changes, some of them difficult. He realized that he wasn't fulfilled at his place of work and moved to a new company where he's blossomed. He is now a supervisor with a staff to manage. His family supported him beautifully through the entire process of his coming out.

Like many people, Jeremy found dating difficult and somewhat daunting. He discovered that the pool of potential husbands was limited in the gay world. It took him 10 years to find a man with whom he would want to grow old. He and Martin, the man who has his heart, were married in 2008.

Two decades later, Jeremy's former wife is still married to the same man. She and Jeremy have remained friends through all his boyfriends and her second marriage. Jeremy feels he is much freer in his life, enjoying it so much more fully.

Amazingly, with all that's available on the market, men are still choosing to compartmentalize their lives and avoid being a whole person at all times. True, fear drives many to lead a double life, but at some point, the pain of discontinuity is going to become great enough that something needs to give. The healthiest choice is to come out: acknowledge that you're gay, come to terms with that fact, and then begin the process of integrating that facet of yourself into the rest of your life — despite the challenges that may come your way.

For some men, that's asking too much. Instead, they choose to self-medicate themselves with drugs, alcohol, pharmaceuticals, sexually acting out, becoming a party boy, becoming a recluse and/or leading two separate lives, which can become very problematical. All of those are either debilitating or destructive methods for avoiding being who you truly are. The pain it causes those you're involved with is also something to take into account.

## *Relationships: Do You Wanna Dance Under the Moonlight?*

Relationships consist of peaks and valleys: boring stretches of highway, exhilarating twists and turns, cliffs of doom, serene pastoral glades, patches of confusing fog, crags of indecision, rivers of upset, canyons of feelings, and sometimes a terrifying black abyss. Sometimes, I wonder if that's why we get into relationships — there's plenty of drama to be had.

Being a married man who has intimate involvements with men lets you experience much of the above. At heart, though, what we're looking for is that incredible feeling we get when that special someone touches us, suddenly shows up at our door, says our name, wants to be with us all the time, and perhaps tells us, "I love you." It makes our world once again a place of harmony, bliss, goodness, joy, and beauty — we're engaged with life and thriving. Why, then, are relationships so difficult to traverse?

> Reid and Doug came to the Men's Group already a couple. Reid had two children, Doug had none. Reid was laid back and willing to just go with the flow. Doug was neurotic and full of angst, and just couldn't seem to let things be...he worried constantly.
>
> Both were concerned as to whether their relationship would last. They'd both been through difficulties in

previous relationships and wanted this relationship to work. The problem was that they couldn't seem to meet each other's needs. One wanted one thing, the other wanted something else. Each had different expectations of the other and different ideas as to what constitutes a relationship.

Eventually, they arrived at the decision to separate, as they couldn't see eye to eye. Neither would be happy in the long run. They separated and Reid moved to Florida.

Opposites attract, as the saying goes — but only if the needs of each are being met, otherwise, there will be friction. It's interesting the demands we put on each other when in a relationship. We want to support the other person by giving to them in ways that work for them and "expect" the same in return — even though we may say it doesn't matter or don't voice this thought or think about it. It does matter.

We want to know that the other person is there for us, that they want to engage in and with our world and be an integral part of it because it has meaning for us. We want to feel that the initial happiness we felt when first becoming involved with each other will deepen into a lasting, touching, and special relationship of significance not experienced with anyone else. It means that we matter in someone else's eyes and heart. It does wonders for our self-esteem and sense of self-worth.

Yet, struggle we do. In every relationship, whether platonic or romantic, there are three things humans want: to be understood, accepted, and loved. If you were to ask anyone which of the three is the most important, they'd probably answer "loved." In reality, to be understood is the most important. We can be loved and accepted by just about anyone, including our pets. But to be understood and accepted unconditionally is what supplies the lubricant that makes the inner composition of the relationship work effectively.

My boyfriend, DD, and I went to the opening night of Gay Pride in San Diego. It was a chance for everyone to dress up in costume or drag as the kick off to this 3-day event. We decided to go in fun drag.

DD was dressed ala Norma Desmond from "Sunset Boulevard" and included a white turban from Lana Turner in "Imitation of Life." I wore a wild and long blond fall ala Charo, a cowboy hat, a shirt and vest, striped pants, gray snakeskin cowboy boots, and makeup that included 2-inch long eyelashes. We obviously weren't what would be considered serious drag.

While we were watching the entertainment, someone came up behind me and tapped me on the shoulder. I turned around to find a short and very drunk lesbian holding a beer. She told me that I was the most beautiful woman she'd ever seen and wanted a date with me, that she was in love with me.

I tried to explain that I was a guy in drag. The woman refused to believe it. I took off my hat and lifted up my wig for her to see. She began crying uncontrollably as her bubble of beauty had been burst. Two male friends of hers came up and walked off with her explaining to DD and me that she'd had too much to drink. DD and I laughed, wondering what other weird proposals we might get that night.

DD looked at me and told me I was the ugliest drag persona he'd ever seen and the woman *had* to be drunk out of her mind to fall in love with me. Gee, thanks!

The woman was in "love" with me and "accepted" me for whom I appeared to be, but would she "understand" me? Obviously, the relationship would never have worked.

And that's what we do in romantic relationships. We get these ideas of who the other person is — and who we are to them — and expect that we'll somehow meet in some incredible and passionate vortex of emotion we call love and all will be right with the world. Unfortunately, what we forget is that we bring along baggage: all the issues we either forgot about, avoided, suppressed, or are completely unaware of that we've accrued along life's journey. So, what we're offering the other person is a mixed bag: we're this wonderful person you're getting involved with and, oh, by the way, there's this other stuff, but "pay no attention to that man behind the curtain."

Put all that together and we're supposed to somehow *u-n-d-e-r-s-t-a-n-d* the other person and vice versa. And that's where things start getting confusing, we begin to get frustrated, and the relationship begins to slowly disintegrate — unless we take the time and make the effort to not just understand the other person, but understand ourselves in the process.

So, what are the basics of a relationship that will help us "understand" each other's needs. They include: trust, honesty, consideration, patience, compassion, integrity, respect, sincerity, gratitude, communication, compromise, cooperation, love, space, recognition of our dreams, acknowledgment of our foibles, emotional growth, energy, time, and choosing to be present as much of the time as possible. There is a line from the movie *The Joy Luck Club* where one of the mothers tells her upset daughter, "I see you — I *see* you." What an acknowledgement. "I see you" says it all, that I truly *understand* you for the person you are. With that comes the acceptance and love we seek.

How, then, does that work with the baggage we bring with us? First and foremost, even though you recognize the feelings you have for this special someone, is to really get in touch with your feelings and know what they are based upon:

> Why are you "in love" with this person? What do you want from them? What do they represent for you? What role are you playing? What do you think they're going to satisfy for you? Where did you get your ideas of what comprises a love relationship? Are you doing this for yourself or some subterranean agenda of which you're unaware? Are you trying to prove something? Are you trying to avoid something? Are you running to in order to get away from? Are you on some type of schedule that needs to be met, as though you have a biological clock ticking? Is it because all your friends are in relationships and you're not? It's the thing to do? Are you being pressured by anyone like family or friends? Are you giving in to the other person because it's what they want, but not necessarily what you want? Are you trying to live some old fantasy you've had since childhood? Are you feeling desperate, lonely, disenfranchised, depressed, unwanted, in emotional pain, bored, or frightened? Are you doing this for the fun of it, but you have no intention of creating something lasting? Does this person make your heart do flip-flops? Is this person actually destined to be just a notch on your belt? Or is it simply that you're in love with love?

There are a lot of reasons for why we choose to get involved with someone on such an intimate level. And this is where understanding yourself comes into play and is so vitally important. You've no doubt heard about people going from relationship to relationship. Why? Because they don't know themselves, which essentially comes down to just "playing" at having a relationship.

The baggage you're bringing with you is actually providing an obstacle to greater happiness on your part, and conversely, the happiness of the other person with whom you're involved. In reality, you're not truly available. How could you be when all this "stuff" is in your way to being completely present with the other person? Combine that with keeping your true sexuality from your wife and kids, relatives, friends, co-workers and clients by hiding information, manipulating information, manipulating people and outright lying and you've not exactly got a winning combination going for you. Is having a relationship worth it or even doable? Yes!

The number one reason for having a relationship is to learn about yourself. It's a chance to get in touch with who you are and evolve through your interaction with the other person. Why? Because they're going to push a lot of your buttons forcing you to come to terms with all sorts of issues. Boy, what fun! Okay, so that's not exactly a great reason for going into a relationship, but that's one of the positive things that could happen if you think about it. You, and they, will get a chance to grow, mature, evolve as a person. The outcome is that you'll both hopefully come to *understand* each other, the #1 need human beings have.

The second reason for getting into a relationship is that you'll create connection. None of us, for the most part, wants to go through life all alone. We like to include people with whom we have things in common and make us feel like we're wanted and appreciated. We want to make sure we're part of something larger than ourselves and that our experience of life is in accordance with other people — that we're not some kind of nut case. Connection also helps us get out of our own head as we're forced to relate to other people and all their baggage. That connection also gives us a chance to compare our sense of reality with other people's, as well as share in life's myriad mundane activities. All of this leads to something called "heart."

> Rand came to the group very excited by what we were doing, feeling he could add immeasurably to our discussions. He often questioned what men expressed, gave his opinions, and let everyone know how knowledgeable he was. He gave the feeling that he could facilitate the group himself. This proved to be a turnoff for group members.
>
> Although Rand was dealing with being a married man coming out and was already involved with a man, left the

group after a few meetings. His feeling was that the other men didn't appreciate him or understand him.

What he was missing is that the men did understand him: he had a need to be superior to everyone else and used his knowledge not as a means to create connection, but to set himself apart from and above others.

"The longest journey a man must take is the eighteen inches from his head to his heart." Rand never got this concept. His reality was all about being intellectual. And for some people, their relationships with other men are going to dynamically work well if both men are operating on the same wave length. Sometimes opposites will work well this way — as long as each person's needs are being met and they both feel they're understood.

Most of us though, prefer to be with someone where the heart connection is in strong evidence. We want to "feel" the love between us and then experience expressions of it on a consistent basis. That's one thing women complain about concerning men: once the courtship is over, men go back to being sophomoric, which means focusing on manly things, acting immaturely, doing the man thing, and letting the more expressive — read: female — capacity fall by the wayside. Men tend to reside in their heads, and women in their hearts.

Current thinking is that men are hardwired this way and there's plenty of evidence with childhood scientific studies to support that. Yet, there is also the matter of training and how one is brought up (nurturance). Essentially, we can all learn to be more heart centered if we understand that we'll not be made fun of, belittled, demoted, shamed, emasculated, and outcast — that we're still a man.

Both genders give males a hard time about this. A man who is considered "soft" is referred to as girl, girlie-man, femme, pansy, lisper, limp wrist, swisher, fag, faggot, whoopsy, homo, bung holer, fudge packer, screamer, flamer, friend of Dorothy, family, Judy, sister, queen, queer, diva, and nancy boy — and the guys suffering being called these names are often not even homosexual. It's a way of disparaging a man, which makes the other person(s) feel superior.

That's how immature people can get, when their own self-esteem is so low that they need to put other people down via name calling in order to feel better about themselves. "Sticks and stones may break my bones, but names will never hurt me" — a little rhyme many of us learned in childhood. One can strive for this, but the truth is that we all get hurt to some degree by name calling. That's why we're enjoined to develop thick skins, which is only good to a point, otherwise, we become hardhearted and shut people out.

Creating heart connections with people and that special someone is what gives life greater depth and meaning. Without heart connections, life would be more like Dickens' *Bleak House* or Dorothy Gale's black and white Kansas life, Andrew Wyeth's painting "Christina's World," or the movie *Pleasantville*. When you choose to open your heart to another, you discover new horizons within yourself and life takes on new meanings. "You can't stop loving or wanting to love because when it's right, it's the best thing in the world. When you're in a relationship and it's good, even if nothing else in your life is right, you feel like your whole world is complete." (Keith Sweat)

The second component for a healthy relationship is not expecting or wanting anything from the other person, just their acceptance of our love for them. They don't need to analyze what we feel for them, just feel it. And the same from us to them. One of the mistakes we tend to make is to put conditions on our love, e.g., if you do this for me, I'll do that for you; you need to do this in order for me to feel loved; don't do that or I'll withhold my love, etc.

## *Chariots of Fire*

All relationships are challenging in some way, to some degree. Depending on why you're getting involved with this special person and what baggage you both bring to the merry-go-round, you're in for an interesting ride on your chariot of fire. You may find yourself trippin' the light fantastic or just trippin'. Again, the purpose of it all — from the highest perspective — is to learn about yourself and what it means to truly love unconditionally. Some of the situations you can get in could be real eye openers.

> Alex is very bright, intellectual, and energetic. He is highly engaged in his line of work and loves the challenge of understanding where people are coming from in a rather Hollywood Tonight fashion.
>
> Alex called up one evening explaining that he'd met a guy who was really, really interesting and wanted some feedback. The two had been dating for a month and he

was concerned that his gut reaction was to *not* continue being involved with this person, but he couldn't get to the kernel of what was bothering him.

In his usual fashion, he was able to describe the man in great detail from habits to behaviors, physicality, clothes, and intellect. Knowing Alex's background, it was easy to determine what the crux of the matter was: Alex had managed to find a male version of his ex-wife, a person for whom he had an intense dislike.

Whoa — what a surprise he got! For all his smarts, he'd fallen back on old patterns to find a new person just like his ex-wife. The reason he did so was that he was unconsciously going with what was familiar to him emotionally. He was truly surprised to realize that he was operating via his habitual comfort zone in seeking a relationship with a man rather than breaking new ground as an emotional being. And he's not the only one who has made this choice. Notice that I didn't say "mistake." The reason being that everything we get involved with is a chance to learn something else about ourselves. Alex, prompted by his gut feeling to call me, learned what he was actually doing. He now had the chance to make a different choice. He took the time to step back to gain a greater perspective on what he was doing. From that new vantage point, he was able to find someone more in alignment with who he currently is rather than a prior version of himself.

Knowing ourselves, our habits, and patterns is important so that we're not just cycling through the same old relationship issues, only with someone new. One could say by doing that, we're portraying a version of insanity because our expectation is that we'll use the same old pattern and somehow get different results. Just because the person you're with is the same gender doesn't mean you've bypassed your old relationship issues. Human beings are human beings are human beings. Somehow and at some point, you'll need to come face to face with who you are, how you operate, and the core of your issues. It's not as bad as you might surmise. It will have some discomfort, but you can do it. A lot of very scared men have made it through the process of self-discovery and found it wasn't as bad as they imagined it could be. Imagination is a wonderful gift, but it can also get in your way if allowed to run rampant and combined with your fears.

Before we continue with dating and the dating game, the issue of when to start dating needs some discussion.

For many of the men who came through the Married Men's Coming Out Group, their need to break away from their heterosexual lifestyle was so pressing that they began getting involved with men even before coming out to their wives and children. There are many ways of doing that: the Internet, chat rooms, porno sites, Instant Messaging, texting, apps for men seeking men, Craigslist, MeetUp, phone calls, Skyping, trips to places known as gay pick up areas, gay neighborhoods and stores, sex toys outlets, gay areas of parks and beaches to parties and clubs. A number of men found someone they wanted to see more than just casually and so began the game of hiding their affair.

For some men, they wanted it all. They came out to their wife and kids, wanted to not lose their wife's love, told their wife about their gay lover, and wanted their male lover integrated into their life as well.

> Leon was a very considerate man, soft spoken, always wanting to make sure other people's needs were being met. He had two daughters who were on opposite sides of the aisle concerning his being homosexual. Leon's wife was very supportive and felt he didn't need to move out of the house even though their relationship was now not going to involve intimacy.
>
> Leon met a young man about 18 years younger than himself. He was head over heels in love with him and it seemed the young man felt the same way about Leon. Leon lived in a house he owned on Coronado Island and also rented an apartment in town for his lover.
>
> Leon was very pleased with this arrangement. He and his lover spent a lot of time together and Leon's wife accommodated this. Leon's one daughter who didn't approve of his being gay, wanted him to stop being gay and just be at home with the family. But, Leon was steadfast with having it all.
>
> Months later, it all fell apart. Not only did Leon's lover decide to call it quits because Leon wouldn't move in with him full time, Leon's wife gave him an ultimatum of either moving out and being gay full time or give it up and stay with the family.
>
> Leon became so stressed that he became deeply depressed and his health began to deteriorate rapidly into a

condition that couldn't be reversed. He passed away two years later.

Leon seemed to have missed the signals he was being sent by his lover and his wife. Initially, they went along with his arrangement as it didn't upset the apple cart too much. But needs were not being met, people were feeling abandoned, not respected, and their feelings were not being considered. What was missing was clear communication. Was Leon being immature for wanting it all? Some people will feel that he was and others will think it was his right.

There's a spiritual saying that encapsulates this type of situation: "Our freedom ends where another's begins." Sure, do what you want in life, but don't infringe on another's freedom just so you can have yours. We must each take responsibility for our thoughts, words, and actions while at the same time owning up to our own needs and supporting ourselves appropriately. That can be a bit of a high wire act, but once we become practiced at it, it becomes second nature to find an easy balance.

Here's another relationship situation some men find useful and a perfect setup while still married is dating another married man.

> A man wrote advice columnist Ann Landers about his situation. He was married, had children, and was intimately involved with another married man. The two families often entertained each other in their homes including holidays. The husbands got together as often as they could with neither wife suspecting their relationship. Both men were committed to their families and were not in love with each other, but their frequent encounters fulfilled their sexual need to be with a man. Was what the two men were doing wrong?
>
> Ms. Landers replied that she saw nothing wrong with their trysts as long as no one was getting hurt in the process. Was he sure their wives were clueless and what would happen if they were to find out? What effect would it have on their wives and children? Were both men prepared for this possibility?

Aye, there's the rub: What if someone finds out? Obviously, people are going to be hurt that you've been clandestinely having an affair — with a MAN — behind everyone's back. We've covered a great deal of what could happen when discovered. What it comes down to is self-respect and respect for those whom you love. What would you feel like if the tables were turned? Unfortunately, the emotional tug and sexual desire of being involved with another man is such that some men often make the decision to still get involved in spite of what the consequences could be. It takes real maturity to moderate one's emotional needs and sexual drive. For many men, though, that's just not going to happen because of the powerful urge to express themselves sexually and emotionally with a man.

What is also unfortunate is the fact that there are still many men who feel that they're Masters of the Universe and can do whatever they please. Because they're male, they're not accountable to their families — the king of the castle answers to no one. That kind of brutish belief seems to be gaining ground. Just take a look at the misogynist and homophobic lyrics and behavior of so many rap videos to which young people are inured. The lifestyle, behaviors, and attitudes are what they emulate. It's all bigger than life and it's got clear rewards attached to it: wealth, sex, visibility, and fame. How does one complete with that?

In the Men's Group, member's beliefs, values, and attitudes were always scrutinized and challenged if they didn't ring true. Only one person got away with remaining convinced that two-timing his wife and still having sex with her was okay because he was a guy. He wasn't in the group for very long as he felt that the men were trying to persuade him to be completely gay and that's not why he joined. He wanted it all and just wanted to feel good about it. Well, if he wasn't feeling good about his actions and attitude, perhaps he was trying to tell himself something, but his lack of maturity got in the way of personal growth.

There's not a lot that can be done with this kind of entrenched attitude. A person like that wants what they want when they want it. They're very clear about it and don't much care who might suffer for it. As selfish as that seems, men still behave in such a manner. The antidote is to appeal to their hearts and take into account how the people they say they love will feel if and when they find out the true situation. Plus, how would they feel if the situation were reversed and they were being treated this way?

This leads to another interesting issue about how one is treated in a man-on-man relationship. It's a phenomenon that's received a lot of attention in the last twenty years, something called being on the "down low" or DL. Simply put, it's a heterosexual man — single, dating, engaged, or married — having sex with men on the side, but he doesn't consider himself to be gay.

We've all heard stories about fraternities and men's locker rooms and the sexual hijinks that can occur in both. There are plenty of men who can attest to having experienced hazing rituals, hand jobs, blow jobs, circle jerks, and even anal intercourse with other heterosexual men. Some of us are just stuck with fantasies. Sigh....

This "not identifying as gay" thing has caused a lot of confusion on both sides of the aisle. It's also caused some heartache for those who are involved with a man who is only in it for the sex, not a relationship, and they're certainly not going to engage their heart. What, then, is the story?

Jane Ward, author of *Not Gay: Sex Between Straight White Men*, states in her book description "By understanding their same-sex sexual practice as meaningless, accidental or even necessary, straight white men can perform homosexual contact in heterosexual ways. These sex acts are not slippages into a queer way of being or expressions of a desired but unarticulated gay identity. Instead...they reveal the fluidity and complexity that characterizes all human sexual desire."

Essentially, the book points out that sexual fluidity is a part of each of us, but because of social, cultural, religious and political strictures, men are not given the ability to openly express their fluidity. The stigma of "homosexuality" still carries heavy censuring. Coupled with society's need to categorize people into male/female and hetero/homosexual, much of male sexuality remains covert and/or relegated to the fallback adage that "boys will be boys."

What this means for a gay man who falls in love with a man on the DL is disappointment and despondency. Basically, it's becoming involved with a man who is emotionally unavailable. If this is your situation, you could wait it out hoping that your man on the DL will wake up one day and want to spend the rest of his life with you. Most likely, it ain't going to happen. In the overwhelming majority of cases, men on the DL truly identify as straight and will continue to either look for a relationship with a woman or maintain the marriage they're already in — and they will continue to seek out men with whom to have sex.

If you're looking to be in a loving relationship with a man building a life together, then a man on the DL isn't the man for you. Being aware that there are men out there who are comfortable with being on the DL is important, just as it's important to know of the other types of men you'll come across on your journey. You'll find the one who's right for you.

One interesting facet of this phenomenon was reported in the September 29, 2015 issue of LGBTQNATION:

"A sexologist in Winter Park, FL says he could 'literally work 24 hours a day, seven days a week' because of all the people cheating on their significant others thanks to websites like Craigslist and Ashley Madison.

"'The volume is that great,' Michael Rothenberg, sexologist and owner of onlinesexualaddiction.com, tells the *Orlando Sentinel*.'

"Rothenberg says many of the patients he works with are closeted married men who use the Internet to find other guys to have sex with."

The need for sexual release, gratification, fulfillment, experimentation, and/or thrill is an immense driver in most men. They'll do whatever it takes to get "it" and the ways to arrange a connection with another man are countless — even if it means possibly getting caught and outed in a very public way, such as what happened with the Ashley Madison site when it got hacked.

If you choose to use the Internet as a means to connect with someone, just be aware that the person(s) you're connecting with may not be entirely truthful as to who they are and what their agenda is. There is a relatively new Internet phenomenon called "catfishing." This entails trolling the Net via Facebook and dating sites for hookups — from getting laid to seeking marriage — masquerading as someone else. The reasons for doing this are myriad and the rouses can be quite elaborate appearing to be absolutely for real.

The outcomes are often disastrous and can produce tremendous anger and heartache. So, approach dating with caution. If your gut is telling you to avoid something or someone, then it's best to follow your instincts.

For most men coming out, it seems they want and need to get into a relationship as soon as possible. They want the full effect of what it's like to be with a man emotionally, mentally, physically, and spiritually as soon as possible — they've waited years and can't wait any longer. The Men's Group was good at helping someone in this mental state understand that there was a lot at stake. It would benefit the person if they took some time to be just with themselves: integrate the significant changes occurring in their life from dissolving their marriage, reviewing the life and lifestyle they're leaving, creating a shift in their relationship with their wife and children, coming out to people, discovering new things about themselves as they also experience change, and contemplating what they feel they're moving toward.

On the other hand, there are some men who aren't willing to rush into anything. For them, it's a matter of going through the process of coming out in a step-by-step method that allows them the time and space to contemplate their every move. They want to make sure that every action taken is one that will ensure few mistakes are made and that choices are made with the best of intentions. They want a high degree of communication and thoughtful consideration brought into play to avoid upsets with their wife and children, friends, co-workers, clients, and that eventual date with a man.

Finally, and rarely, there are a few men who are willing to wait until their divorces are final and they've moved out of the house before they even entertain the idea of seeing another man. For them, very definitive lines are drawn as to what they do and when they do it. The idea of overlapping activities just doesn't work for them and can sometimes be overwhelming mentally and emotionally. So, the best approach is to evince a line-item process — a check list, if you will — wherein each step is a process unto itself and one doesn't move to the next item until the prior item is completed.

This well-ordered approach doesn't work for most men, but for those it does, it provides a level of ethicalness for them. They don't want to be considered cheating on their wives and families, which to them is a moral issue. Basically, it comes down to other people's needs being met before self, but keeping one's goal in clear sight: coming out and leading life as a gay man.

For all the various approaches, one thing is for sure: at some point, you're going to meet a man and go on a date. After having been out of the dating scene — much less the gay dating scene — this could be a real roller coaster ride.

## *Dating Roulette*

The ever-practical Mae West sums up dating nicely: "Don't cry for a man who's left you, the next one may fall for your smile." And, "Save a boyfriend for a rainy day — and another, in case it doesn't rain." Sigh....

Dating, no matter what gender combination you're going after, is heaven and hell all wrapped up in one provocative package. You want to date, but it scares the heck out of you. You want a man, but will a man want you? You're ready, but is the world ready for you?

The dating scene in the gay world is fraught with misconceptions and myths. People are people and they're going to be looking for certain things. Yes, there is a prominent section of the gay community that's focused primarily on looks and style: buffed, tan, handsome, boyish, playful, sexy, making good money, and stylishly together. That group — the "A list" — is often described as rather one-dimensional and shallow. The rest of the gay community is up for grabs and includes all types, sizes, backgrounds, and needs.

When a new crop of married men joined the Men's Group, I'd plan a Friday or Saturday night out doing a tour of the different types of gay bars. Some of the men were terrified of going, but with their comrades accompanying them, they managed to buck up.

The first bar we'd hit was rather benign: scantily clad and incredibly buffed go-go boys were dancing to thumping music on bar tops and platforms, their family jewels well publicized. The men in the group were falling all over themselves in lust and "appreciation." One young group member was running around exclaiming, "I'm in love, I'm in love." Basically, it was a bunch of kids let loose in a candy shop.

From there, we'd proceed to different types of bars, each one progressively more intense in its focus, the next to last bar rather scary in what it provided patrons. By then, the group would be exhausted from an overload of stimulation and we'd make one last visit to what could be called a neighborhood bar. It was literally in a neighborhood and offered a place to simply fraternize. There were no dancing go-go boys to ogle, no dance floor, and not the usual thumping music. It was a place to meet, have a drink, play pool, and talk with friends.

The men loved it as they could now come down from their high, have a drink, and hear themselves think. We'd take over a quiet section of the place, which had several rooms, and discuss everyone's experiences that night. The thank you's I received were genuinely proffered. The men were amazed at what they'd seen, what they had to look forward to, and having had a guided tour within the safety of the Men's Group. They'd had no idea the range of people and venues available to them even existed. In one night, they'd been to a dance bar, drag bar, leather bar, chi-chi girl bar, school boy bar, S&M bar, b-boy bar, silver daddy bar, bear bar, fetish bar, biker bar, lesbian bar, sports bar, and local's bar.

As in any group, certain members gravitated to those with similar values and issues, so they began making plans to visit the bars with each other. They also felt free and emboldened enough to make forays into the gay Hillcrest neighborhood, on their own to check out the businesses, restaurants, and shops.

Much more was at stake than just visiting gay clubs with the intent of attaining a date. This was part of each man's acclimation process, getting used to the stratified community in which they were now being introduced. Aside from the obvious fact that there's something for everyone, there was just the idea of getting used to being in the gay community, which meant that they were out and gay — the gay world recognized them as such. That was one big step.

Next came the thought that somewhere in the hundreds of men frequenting these bars was at least one guy with whom they could meet up, perhaps the man of their dreams — or at least their fantasies.

> "This guy says, 'I'm perfect for you,
> 'cause I'm a cross between a macho man
> and a sensitive man.'
> I said 'Oh, a gay trucker?'"
>
> ~ Judy Tenuta

If you're at this stage, then in order to find and attract that person, all the usual steps and precautions need to be attended to:

> how do you look, how are you dressed, is your breath okay, do you look desperate or inviting, are you at the right type of bar, will anyone look at you, how do you start a conversation with someone you're interested in, what shouldn't you say, do you offer to buy the guy a drink, do you ask him if he wants to dance, how can you tell if someone is interested in you or just looking for a lay, what if you go with a friend and you meet someone you like, is there an unspoken guide to your type approaching different types, do people still wear colored hankies to indicate what they're into, what if you're not getting any bites, should you visit several bars in one night or stick with just one, what do you do if someone offers you drugs,

what if someone invites you home, how do you know this person is safe, how to you bring up the subject of HIV status, what do you say to someone who wants you but they're HIV+, do you know how to have safe sex, what's the current trend in dating and HIV transmission, how do you politely tell someone you're not interested and get your message across, when do you get gruff with someone who won't take "no" for an answer, who do you reach out to if you need help, what if you're interested in someone but not quite ready to go home with them, what if someone wants a threesome or more, how far are you willing to go, are you too old for the dating game, should you use a gay dating service instead, what if friends set you up on a blind date, do you tell your date you're divorced and have kids, do you tell him he's your first date with a man, what if he wants to have unprotected sex, what if all you want is sex and no relationship — and on and on.

Though you will have a zillion questions, you may have to forgo some of them and just get out there and play it by ear. Think about how you'd answer the questions above, but don't let that stop you from exploring. If you need to do research, there's plenty you can find on the Internet and in bookstores, as well as by having candid discussions with other gay people you may know. Check out current and past issues of gay magazines like *The Advocate*, *Frontiers*, *Echelon*, *Instinct*, *Men's Fitness*, *Out*, *Out Traveler*, *Passport*, *POZ*, and *Transformation* for information on a variety of subjects that could answer a lot of questions for you.

Even though you may approach dating heavily armed with facts, figures and data, interfacing with another man you're considering dating or even as husband material is still going to be a bit of a gamble. The number one rule in dating: be yourself. Attempt to be someone other than who you are — something you're already dealing with by coming out as a married man — and you'll not only find yourself dateless, but word will get around in the gay community. You'll be seen not as a Blue Light Special, but a Red Herring.

If you've taken the time to at least think about everything you've read up to this point, then you will most likely begin dating someone and have a pretty good idea *why* you're dating this particular man. If not, then you could end up as Dennis did.

Dennis and Trent, both original members of the Men's Group, decided to break one of the group's cardinal rules:

no dating between group members. Dennis was in his 30's and Trent in his mid-50's.

Dennis was attracted to older men, men who had bodies that looked "lived in" rather than all buffed out. Trent had that older bearing with some silver in his hair, a slight paunch, and composed energy that gave Dennis a feeling of security and solidity.

Knowing they were breaking group rules, Dennis opted to step away from the group so that he could continue dating Trent. Trent continued attending group sessions.

After a few months, the two broke up. Dennis called up wanting to have a private discussion. He was confused and didn't understand why the two had broken up. Being that he was in school working toward a Masters in Counseling Psychology, what helped Dennis gain some clarity was for me to turn the tables on him by having him be the observer.

It didn't take Dennis long to come to the conclusion that what he was looking for was a father surrogate. He'd never resolved the conflicts with his own father and was trying to gain the fatherly love he'd always wanted via a relationship with a father stand-in.

Trent felt that he was being pigeon-holed for a specific role instead of being allowed to be himself. So, the relationship dissolved, leaving Dennis unhappy and confused.

What also provided confusion was whether Dennis was expressing affection to Trent or Dennis's father or both at the same time. It had a kind of weird, incestuous feel to it.

Dennis's next step was to get to the heart of his issues concerning his father, something he knew he'd have to do on his own as his father was a rigid man, unmoving in his beliefs about homosexuality.

Dennis decided to get into therapy to resolve those issues and to address his deep need for his father's love, which he was unconsciously transferring onto any unsuspecting man he was dating.

Working with a therapist to gain a broader perspective can be most illuminating, as it was in Dennis's case. He was so focused on having a relationship that he was acting unconsciously, sort of like being in a trance. All the more reason for each of us to take the time to do our introspective homework. Otherwise, we're hostage to our emotional patterns and will just cycle through relationships like re-runs: different people, same issues, same outcome.

In closing, dating is not the easiest phase to go through, but you'll get the hang of it. One thing you want to be cautious about is the "kid in a candy store" affect. You'll feel like you want to try everything all at once. Be patient. Take your time, you don't need to go on a dating rampage either to satisfy your drive, to prove a point to yourself, prove something to someone else, or even get back at or prove something to your wife or ex-wife. This is not a game or competition. There's no need to compare what you may experience with a man with your former married relationship — only whether both parties are getting their needs met, your heart is engaged, and whether you're being true to yourself.

While you're in the dating process, you'll figure out what works for you and what doesn't and just take it at your own pace. There really is no hurry and there's no such thing as making up for lost time or opportunities. That kind of thinking can get you into the kind of trouble you don't want.

Speaking of trouble, one thing you'll want to be careful about is on-line dating sites, a.k.a. hookup sites, like Grindr, M4M, Manhunt, ManList, Gawker, Men Nation, Manjam, Gay Romeo, Adam 4 Adam, Gaydar, G Cruise, Man Central, Real Jock, Big Muscle Bears, Gay Date, and Squirt. Though the prospect of checking out prospects without actual contact may sound most appealing because it's easy and seemingly safe, you need to be careful of several things — you may already be aware of the fact that people pull all sorts of stunts.

- Some people lie about who they actually are in their personal profiles. They may even go so far as to load someone else's hot picture in order to get bites. The truth, when discovered, can be quite disappointing and frustrating, and some people can get quite angry over it.

- Predators abound and dating sites are a magnet for such people. Be very careful where you decide to meet someone. The best place is in public. Though you don't want to come across with the third-degree, you're actually conducting a sort of interview. Be thorough without coming across like Homeland Security. Plan on several dates before choosing to get intimate with the individual and always inform a friend of your dates, who you're dating, and where you're meeting them. An ounce of precaution is worth the effort!

- Various types of stalkers also trawl on-line dating sites. Not only can a stalker be bothersome, but such people can bring about dangerous situations. If you should get ensnared by such circumstances, report the person to the authorities. The following site can be helpful: www.thesite.org/homelawandmoney/law/victims/dealingwithstalkers

- Some on-line dating users have nefarious agendas, such as a married person looking for an affair or, even worse, someone looking for prospects to rob or attack gay people. Never give out personal information that would allow someone to research you via the Internet and find out where you live or work.

You may suffer some setbacks in the dating process and you may also meet some sterling people with whom you'll want to stay friends. Whatever your experience is, it's all part of a learning process and the more you stay positive and open, the more enjoyment you'll have. Just remember what Wendy Liebman has to say about dating: "I've been on so many blind dates, I should get a free dog."

## *Addicted to Love*

The song by British rocker Robert Palmer does a great job of pointing out the roller coaster aspect of love addiction. To be precise, love addiction is all about the thrill ride over the prospect of love and the rush of being in love — but not necessarily being involved sexually — and the object of one's addiction isn't available physically, mentally, or emotionally. It also means that once the thrill is gone, then the hunt begins anew for another "love" relationship.

What this scenario isn't is love, but instead a whole 'nother animal. The obsessive/compulsive, dependent, and co-dependent facets of it are what put it squarely in the middle of the addiction arena.

Addiction to love is a hard one for people to recognize and work with as it involves perpetual hope, the longing for love, and plenty of high-octane emotionality — akin to what an adrenalin junkie experiences — on the part of the person addicted to love.

The person on the receiving end of all this is usually scared away by the love addict's intensity or they're working the relationship for their own agenda. That agenda could include a person who is also a love addict, a player who's already in a relationship and wants something on the side, a person who likes having power over someone else, or a selfish narcissist who likes being the object of so much attention. The important point here is that neither party is feeling or experiencing real love. Instead, it's a mockup, a caricature, Plato's shadows on the wall of the cave.

> Jerry called me one day, crying, his heart breaking, his life in shambles. He explained that he'd received a restraining order from the police. Surprised, I asked what why.
>
> It seems that Jerry had become obsessed with a guy, Ramon, and couldn't leave him alone. Ramon was straight, but Jerry absolutely knew that they were meant to be together.
>
> Jerry couldn't stop thinking about Ramon and he was constantly fantasizing ways in which they could be together. He spent an inordinate amount of time figuring out how to prove his love to Ramon and even though Ramon had no interest in men romantically or sexually, that it was just a matter of time before he came to his senses and moved in with Jerry.
>
> Though Ramon had continuously spurned Jerry's advances, Jerry had driven over to Ramon's family's home one night and had stood outside yelling and screaming for Ramon to come talk to him, that Jerry loved him with all his heart, and that he'd do anything for him. If Ramon didn't come out, Jerry would kill himself. Amazingly, Jerry wasn't even drunk or on drugs when he'd done this.
>
> The neighbors came out to watch the scene and Ramon's family finally called the police. The outcome was Jerry's having received the restraining order. He was beside himself as he realized he'd gone too far — but he absolutely knew he couldn't live without Ramon. He was sure that Ramon hadn't really meant to call the police, it was all a mistake and it was his family that had actually done it — Ramon would never do anything to hurt him.

What Jerry experienced was a new level of hell: love addiction. No matter what the facts of the situation were, in Jerry's mind, he was in love with Ramon and Ramon just needed to realize that Jerry was the man for him — even though Ramon was 100 percent straight. Jerry had put his whole heart into his "love" for Ramon and despite the fact that Ramon clearly let him know that he wasn't interested, Jerry persisted, blinded by his addiction.

Jerry, caught up in his delusion and fantasies about Ramon, kept upping the stakes by sending him romantic cards, extravagant letters, and flowers and gifts. He poured his heart out in lengthy phone messages and finally took to stalking Ramon, following him all over town. He'd sit in his car out front of Ramon's home night after night hoping to catch sight of him and to also see if Ramon was with someone else.

The irony of Jerry's situation is that he was fully cognizant that he was obsessed with Ramon and that he was enacting the same behaviors as other addicts. Jerry, after receiving the restraining order, realized that he'd just about reached rock bottom. What rock bottom actually looked like, he didn't want to find out. Jerry was in terrible emotional turmoil and pain. It was time he sought help.

Jerry's story is not unusual. We hear about such situations in the newspapers with many ending very badly, as in the movie *Fatal Attraction*. Thankfully, Jerry got into therapy and joined a support group. A couple of years later, he met a wonderful man and they've now been together for over two decades.

There are many reasons why a person becomes a love addict. Do some research to learn more about the "why" and "how" of it. To shed some light on the behavior connected to love addiction, the following survey gives a much clearer understanding of just what's involved with an addiction to love. Written by Susan Peabody, the survey was donated to the group she co-founded, Love Addicts Anonymous. (For more about Susan and her work, visit brightertomorrow.net.)

Susan writes: "If you can answer 'Yes' to more than a few of the following statements, you are probably a love addict. Remember that love addiction comes in many forms, so even if you don't answer yes to all of the questions, you may still be a love addict."

❏ Yes ❏ No 1. You are very needy when it comes to relationships.

❏ Yes ❏ No 2. You fall in love very easily and too quickly.

❏ Yes ❏ No 3. When you fall in love, you can't stop fantasizing — even to do important things. You can't help yourself.

❏ Yes ❏ No 4. Sometimes, when you are lonely and looking for companionship, you lower your standards and settle for less than you want or deserve.

❏ Yes ❏ No 5. When you are in a relationship, you tend to smother your partner.

❏ Yes ❏ No 6. More than once, you have gotten involved with someone who is unable to commit — hoping he or she will change.

❏ Yes ❏ No 7. Once you have bonded with someone, you can't let go.

❏ Yes ❏ No 8. When you are attracted to someone, you will ignore all the warning signs that this person is not good for you.

❏ Yes ❏ No 9. Initial attraction is more important to you than anything else when it comes to falling in love and choosing a partner. Falling in love over time does not appeal to you and is not an option.

❏ Yes ❏ No 10. When you are in love, you trust people who are not trustworthy. The rest of the time you have a hard time trusting people.

❏ Yes ❏ No 11. When a relationship ends, you feel your life is over and more than once you have thought about suicide because of a failed relationship.

❏ Yes ❏ No 12. You take on more than your share of responsibility for the survival of a relationship.

❏ Yes ❏ No 13. Love and relationships are the only things that interest you.

❏ Yes ❏ No 14. In some of your relationships, you were the only one in love.

❏ Yes ❏ No 15. You are overwhelmed with loneliness when you are not in love or in a relationship.

❏ Yes ❏ No 16. You cannot stand being alone. You do not enjoy your own company.

❏ Yes ❏ No 17. More than once, you have gotten involved with the wrong person to avoid being lonely.

❏ Yes ❏ No 18. You are terrified of never finding someone to love.

❏ Yes ❏ No 19. You feel inadequate if you are not in a relationship.

❏ Yes ❏ No 20. You cannot say no when you are in love or if your partner threatens to leave you.

❏ Yes ❏ No 21. You try very hard to be who your partner wants you to be. You will do anything to please him or her — even abandon yourself (sacrifice what you want, need and value).

❏ Yes ❏ No 22. When you are in love, you only see what you want to see. You distort reality to quell anxiety and feed your fantasies.

❏ Yes ❏ No 23. You have a high tolerance for suffering in relationships. You are willing to suffer neglect, depression, loneliness, dishonesty — even abuse — to avoid the pain of separation anxiety (what you feel when you are not with someone you have bonded with).

❏ Yes ❏ No 24. More than once, you have carried a torch for someone and it was agonizing.

❏ Yes ❏ No 25. You love romance. You have had more than one romantic interest at a time even when it involved dishonesty.

❏ Yes ❏ No 26. You have stayed with an abusive person.

❏ Yes ❏ No 27. Fantasies about someone you love, even if he or she is unavailable, are more important to you than meeting someone who is available.

❏ Yes ❏ No 28. You are terrified of being abandoned. Even the slightest rejection feels like abandonment and it makes you feel horrible.

❏ Yes ❏ No 29. You chase after people who have rejected you and try desperately to change their minds.

❏ Yes ❏ No 30. When you are in love, you are overly possessive and jealous.

❏ Yes ❏ No 31. More than once, you have neglected family or friends because of your relationship.

❏ Yes ❏ No 32. You have no impulse control when you are in love.

❑ Yes ❑ No 33. You feel an overwhelming need to check up on someone you are in love with.

❑ Yes ❑ No 34. More than once, you have spied on someone you are in love with.

❑ Yes ❑ No 35. You pursue someone you are in love with even if he or she is with another person.

❑ Yes ❑ No 36. If you are part of a love triangle (three people), you believe all is fair in love and war. You do not walk away.

❑ Yes ❑ No 37. Love is the most important thing in the world to you.

❑ Yes ❑ No 38. Even if you are not in a relationship, you still fantasize about love all the time — either someone you once loved or the perfect person who is going to come into your life someday.

❑ Yes ❑ No 39. As far back as you can remember, you have been preoccupied with love and romantic fantasies.

❑ Yes ❑ No 40. You feel powerless when you fall in love — as if you are in some kind of trance or under a spell. You lose your ability to make wise choices.

Some additional warning signs are provided by The Ranch, a mental health center that provides innovative residential treatment for addictions, compulsive behaviors, and mental health disorders (www.recoveryranch.com):

- Mistaking intense sexual experiences and new romantic excitement for love.

- When in a relationship, being desperate to please and fearful of the other's unhappiness.

- Inability to maintain an intimate relationship once the newness and excitement have worn off.

- When not in a relationship, compulsively using sex and fantasy to fill the loneliness.

- Choosing partners who demand a great deal of attention and caretaking, but who do not meet, or even try to meet, your emotional or physical needs.

- Participating in activities that don't interest you or go against your personal values in order to keep or please a partner.

- Using sex, seduction, and manipulation (guilt/shame) to "hook" or hold on to a partner.

- Using sex or romantic intensity to tolerate difficult experiences or emotions.

- Using anonymous sex, porn, or compulsive masturbation to avoid "needing" someone, thereby avoiding all relationships.

A couple of the men who attended the Married Men's Coming Out group were deeply embedded in an addiction to love. I'd hear a constant running dialogue about their current love interest. For the most part, the object of their "love" was actually unavailable for myriad reasons, yet the group member still pursued the other person because of hope, longing, and the intense emotional appeal of romance.

Once these guys were ensnared in a relationship, all manner of excuses were intoned to assuage the fact that the relationships weren't working out as hoped or planned. The men developed a dependency about the relationship that was really about fear of rejection and loss rather than love. That then devolved into a co-dependent scenario wherein the men would bend over backwards to avoid upsetting the object of their love desire or they'd frantically work to appease the other person when they threatened to leave the relationship.

When the relationship did end, despondency engulfed the men and thoughts of suicide were sometimes entertained. Thankfully, attempts were never made. The pain, frustration, disappointment, anger, and sense of betrayal and abandonment were quite real for these men. They were dealt with compassion, but firmness to stay reality-based. We focused on discovering what in them was driving the all-consuming need to be in a relationship at all costs, sometimes to their detriment.

Like any addiction, it required diligence on their part to catch themselves in the act of reactivating the habitual mental and emotional behaviors of their addiction. New habits were individually designed and exercised to replace debilitating habits. It is a struggle they'll most likely face the rest of their lives. Why? Because the highs are wonderfully high and the flame of hope forever remains lit. Until the individual learns to love themselves first, to be happy living without being in a relationship, to be comfortable with who they are and learn to love another without grasping, the longing remains.

There are people who just love being in love. It feels so-o-o good, life is beautiful and worth living, God's in His heaven and all's right with the world. But then, reality hits, disenchantment sets in, and hurt and anger replace joy. You can literally hear the guy's heart breaking. Yet, let some time pass and someone else will appear on the horizon and our guy will be running headlong into the next big relationship. This time, it's "*The* One!"

We all want to be loved and being in a loving relationship makes life appear so much richer and worthwhile. Our feelings seem so real and genuine: there's someone out there who says they love you, they want to be with you, you have so much in common, you can talk for hours with the stars in your eyes twinkling so brightly you're almost blinded. And, indeed, you are blinded by your own neediness and addiction.

The most challenging thing when you're dealing with an addiction to love is being able to take a step back to gain a better perspective of the situation. Instead, you get sucked into an emotional undertow. You may be ignored, manipulated and abused in the relationship, but can't see that for the stars in your eyes.

What's difficult when the possibility of love presents itself is to ascertain whether the tsunami of feeling you're experiencing is real or not. It feels like love, it looks like love, it sounds like love — but is it?

Reviewing Ms. Peabody's survey — being completely honest with yourself — along with the additional warnings by The Ranch, should allow you to begin pulling aside the veils of illusion. If you determine that you're not addicted to love, great. If you find that you fit the profile, then you may want to seek therapeutic support and/or find a love addict's support group. Being enslaved to an addiction is hell. We each deserve freedom.

Being caught up in the rapture of love is a very heady experience. One very important thing to remember is to never make permanent decisions based on temporary feelings. Give yourself time, let the budding relationship breathe, make sure you have other things going on in your life so that you don't obsess over the individual, be yourself, and don't try to change the other person to be what you want or push them to become something they are not. Very importantly, remember to honor yourself. No person is worth giving your life away.

> "He thought her beautiful,
> believed her impeccably wise;
> dreamed of her, wrote poems to her, which,
> ignoring the subject,
> she corrected in red ink."
>
> ~ Virginia Wolf, *Mrs. Dalloway*

## Chapter 9

# Coming Out in the Gay Community

Les was all of 21 when he joined the Men's Group. He'd been married a few years when he realized that what he really wanted in his life was to be with a man. There was only one thing about his coming out: he was terrified of the gay community.

When Les came in for his intake interview, we eventually came around to his fear of gay people and everything that goes with it. It had taken a lot of courage for him to just come in to the LGBT Community Center. Not that he was afraid of being seen, it was the people who use the Center: gay people. It wasn't that they might be HIV+ or have AIDS, it was gay people themselves — all the weird and strange types that comprise the gay community.

As it was dinnertime and I was getting hungry, I suggested we get something to eat, my treat. Les didn't know this part of town so I suggested Hamburger Mary's. We drove over. At the front gate, I had trouble getting Les to enter the restaurant. His eyes were practically bugging out of his head, he was so frightened. This from a guy who's 6 foot and weighed in at about 230 lbs, a real linebacker type. I pointed to a table near the front door where we could sit in the event he felt the need to bolt.

Sitting down, we were given menus. Les could barely lift his eyes from his menu, he didn't dare look around for fear people would look back at him. Once our orders were taken, I tried to engage Les by getting him to talk further about his situation at home and any experiences he might have had with men.

Then, in through the front door waltzed a drag queen whose volunteer effort in the gay community was to be the cigarette girl with her tray of cigarettes, Tiparillos, and condoms. This was her way of helping reduce the spread of HIV and getting people to be responsible. I knew the person and called her over to our table. Les almost fainted from fright. I introduced him and explained what my drag queen friend was doing. Les could barely get a squeak out and his hands were shaking.

My drag queen friend left to do her rounds, Les and I finished our dinner, and returned to the Center. Les had just survived his introduction to the gay community.

It took Les just one trip to a gay bar with go-go dancers and a dance floor filled with shirtless, buffed men rockin' under the party lights for him to get over his fear. Interesting what eye candy does for people. It took longer for Les to accept a hug from me, the group's facilitator. It took much, much longer for Les to be part of a group hug, which is the way the men's group ended each session. Once Les got into a steady relationship with a man, though, he opened up quickly realizing that hugging another man was non-threatening and was yet another way of creating connection. There really wasn't that much difference between hugging his wife and hugging a man. Essentially, he got over himself.

It takes a while to get used to the gay community. Many men, even though they're coming out, find certain "characters" associated with the gay community difficult to accept. They've been so a part of the heterosexual world that even though they know they want to be identified as gay, being immersed in gay culture is another thing altogether and can be a bit daunting. The good news is that this is an opportune chance to get the idea of being inclusive under your belt. You don't have to like all the types you may come across and you don't have to necessarily fraternize with them, but accept them as being part of the whole? Yes. *You* want to be accepted for who *you* are, right?

## *Beyond Baptism*

Let's say you've gone to your first gay party or gay bar. You've been baptized or born again or however you want to describe yourself. You have now been seen in a gay setting with gay people who are going to automatically assume that you're one of them. You're in. Now what happens?

Actually, not much. The gay world doesn't really care if you're coming or going or that you even exist at this point. What will change that is you deciding to get involved by being a part of gay activities. If you like playing pool, perhaps you can start playing at the bars that have pool tables. If they have a gay pool league, you could join them. The same goes for bowling, softball, tennis, and other sports. There are book clubs, food clubs, computer clubs, swim clubs, baton twirling clubs — all manner of clubs to check into.

Then there are gyms, the theater, the gay men's choir, activist groups (Gay & Lesbian Alliance Against Defamation, The Human Rights Campaign, Reciprocity Foundation for Homeless Gay and Lesbian Youth, etc.), political clubs, the LGBT Community Center, Gay Pride Festival, gay and lesbian historical society, Meals on Wheels, AIDS organizations, recovery groups, Gay Royal Court, Metropolitan Community Church or Unity and other spiritual followings supportive of gays — the activities are endless. It's up to you to go with whatever resonates for you, holds your interest, and/or speaks to your heart.

There is always the option of working in the gay community. The lifestyle you've previously had as a married man may completely not fit with who you want to be now that you're out. Perhaps you know you'll be much happier quitting your place of work and maybe even starting a new career. For some men, that's exactly what they need: a fresh start in all arenas.

> Patrick had a construction firm and a young son he adored. What he wanted, though, was a change of pace.
>
> Very quietly and unbeknownst to the men in the group, he began working on a new business. The next thing we all knew, he was announcing the opening of a new business in the middle of Hillcrest: a European wine bar and bistro.
>
> Turns out that this was something he'd wanted to do for a very long time — and he did it. The place received rave reviews.

Switching jobs and/or careers is a lot to take on in addition to coming out as a married man and all that entails. Search within yourself to understand why you might want to make such a shift. If it's based on stressors in other parts of your life, you may want to hold off for a while until you get your bearings. Turning your entire world upside down might prove to be overwhelming and then additional challenges will appear that could impinge on your health, both mental and emotional. No need to go that route. The desire to get on with your life can be overpowering at times and your patience is going to wear thin, yet there really is no rush. Take your time, give yourself space to think things through thoroughly, and rely on your support team to give you feedback.

Now, besides joining in gay activities, organizations, clubs, et al, being part of the gay community means learning some of the vernacular thrown about. Some of the words and phrases you already know and may dislike, e.g., fag, faggot, fag hag, homo, sissy boy, pansy, girlfriend, Mary, Dorothy, friend of Dorothy, fruit, cupcake, queen, queer, diva, auntie, knob polisher, and bitch. These are just a small sampling of names given homosexuals and used by gays to refer to each other. For a more complete list, visit: http://andrejkoymasky.com/lou/dic/dic00.html and choose "Gay Slang Dictionary." And, no, you don't have to start slinging gay slang so you'll fit in. To be aware of insider language, though, will be helpful so you know whether you're being playfully teased or dissed.

One last thing you'll want to be aware of is important yearly events particular to the gay community. The following is a list of notable LGBT holidays:

**Ally Week** – October
    Begun in 2005
    http://glsen.org/allyweek

**Celebrate Bisexuality Day** – September 23
    Begun in 1999
    www.timeanddate.com/holidays/world/celebrate-bisexuality-day

**Day of Silence** – April
    Begun in 1996 (day varies from year to year)
    www.dayofsilence.org

**LGBT History Month** (UK) – February
    Begun in 2005

**LGBT History Month** (USA) – October
    Begun in 1994

**Harvey Milk Day** – May 22
    Begun in 2010

**International Day Against Homophobia** – May 17
    www.homophobiaday.org/

**International Holocaust Remembrance Day** – January 27
Begun in 2005
https://en.unesco.org/international-days/holocaust-remembrance

**Intersex Awareness Day** – October 26
Begun in 1996
http://isna.org/

**National Coming Out Day** – October 11
Begun in 1988
www.hrc.org/resources/entry/national-coming-out-day

**Pride Month** – June-August
June is celebrated as Pride in honor of the Stonewall Riots, though pride events occur all year round.

**Stonewall Riots Anniversary** – June 27
http://socialistalternative.org/literature/stonewall.html

**Transgender Day of Remembrance** – November 20
Begun in 1999
www.transgenderdor.org/

**World AIDS Day** – December 1
Begun in 1988
https://www.worldaidsday.org/

http://en.wikipedia.org/wiki/List_of_LGBT_holidays

For a list of Gay Pride, AIDS Walks, rodeos, fairs and other events both nationally and internationally, visit any of the following sites:

- http://en.wikipedia.org/wiki/List_of_LGBT_events#United_States
- www.nighttours.com/gaypride/
- www.interpride.org/?
- http://canyonwalkerconnections.com/str8apology/
- https://metrosource.com/list-of-pride-2018-celebrations-around-the-world/
- www.travelgay.com/events/

Another aspect of the gay community we've briefly touched on is the different "types" of gay people you'll find. I've listed a few in earlier chapters and I'm sure you're already aware of what some of those types are. Take a look at Appendix C: List of Gay Archetypes. The list doesn't really qualify as archetypes, but they are distinct types of "characters" you'll find in the gay community. You'll notice that a number seem rather derogatory. If you look at the larger list of universal archetypes in Appendix B, you'll see that there are plenty included that appear to be cynical and mean. Such is the labeling capacity of human beings.

Aside from that, the full spectrum is brought into play so that you can see how people — straight and gay — characterize each other. The next step, obviously and hopefully, is to see people in a better light and drop the habit of labeling one another. It's not only limiting and divisive, it is hurtful and feeds into the negativity permeating the world. Choose to shine, uplift others, and help others shine.

## *Homophobia within the Ranks*

Speaking of negativity, certain gay types don't like other gay types for various reasons. Some of it is left over from antediluvian racial tensions. Some of it, ironically enough, is left over from a cultural stereotype of "real" men versus non macho types. Another involves the more intellectual/sophisticate group looking down their noses at the party boys. Then there are those who want to live life as one continuous outrageous episode and those who want to just be regular guys who many would never guess are gay — and never the twain shall meet. It runs the gamut.

Just as in any community, there is a wide array of personality types ranging from boring to bizarre, from unadorned to excessive, from unpretentious to affected. To disenfranchise or discriminate against anyone is against the law, yet it's done insidiously and quietly under the radar, so to speak. What is it with humans that they are always looking to put something down or make someone or a group a scapegoat just so they can feel good about themselves? Why is being different such a threat to people? Is it that all-pervasive and perverse drive to be atypical yet "normal," different yet the same, individuated yet indistinguishable from the whole? Are people's egos that fragile?

Apparently so, as we see examples of prejudice everywhere: gay men don't like lesbians and vice versa; trannies (transgendered people) are too fringe and incomprehensible; drag queens are way over the top and uncontrollable; leather men are too brutish and Nazi-ish; fetish people are too creepy; bondage people are too dark and scary — let's victimize that person or group by discriminating against them, cut them out, speak disparagingly about them, make fun of them, endorse rude behavior towards them. In effect, this is a type of hate crime minus the physical violence. It's emotional and psychic violence coming from within the gay community towards its own members and borders strongly on homophobia.

I pointed out in an earlier chapter that homophobia does exist in the gay community. It shows itself via what I just covered. What it's all based on is fear. I love this acronym for fear: **F**alse **E**vidence **A**ppearing **R**eal. Granted, there are people we gravitate toward and those we don't for any number of reasons. But to outright dislike, disparage, and shun another person or group simply because they're different than we are is truly sad. It says that we as a culture and society haven't progressed very far. We're still subject to often unreasonable and unrealistic fears.

I'd like to go on record here about the other half of the gay community: lesbians. What an amazing, stalwart, creative, insightful, assertive, compassionate, indomitable, playful, and immensely supportive force. Are they different than gay men? Yes. Are they just as fragile and vulnerable as all human beings? Yes. Are they resilient and activated? Yes. Are they to be feared? No. What they are is an integral component of not just the gay community, but the larger world society. Without them, our lives would be that much drearier, less colorful, less meaningful. They are worthy of all that we have to give from our hearts and minds.

Lesbians are our sisters, mothers, grandmothers, girlfriends, pals, teammates, comrades in arms, warriors, caretakers, and most importantly, dear friends accompanying us on our life journeys. They have been faced with and survived many of the same issues that gay men have, so they are definitely allies in our quest for understanding, acceptance, freedom, and equality. Let them be a part of your life and heart and, conversely, invest your heart and life in theirs.

> "The people I'm furious with
> are the women's liberationists.
> They keep getting up on soapboxes
> and proclaiming women
> are brighter than men.
> That's true, but it should be kept quiet
> or it ruins the whole racket."
>
> ~ Anita Loos, *The New York Times*
> February 10, 1974

Back to discussing men and dealing with fear — one strangely ironic segment of the gay community are those who have never completely come to terms with being homosexual, so they've turned their inner aversion to themselves outwardly into the gay community in the form of homophobia. These people exhibit the 4 C's: they're caustic, cruel, cynical, and corrosive. The sub-text of what they express vituperatively is that they hate themselves. Unable to resolve their self-hate, they eviscerate the gay world, stigmatizing gay people and aspects of the gay community.

> "There is a tendency in the gay community
> to become worse than straight people
> ever could be!"
>
> ~ Michael Lucas

Such people may have gay friends, yet they still hate being gay, the gay lifestyle, and everything the gay world stands for — yet they can't leave it for good. They're gay, they're stuck with who they are, and they're bitter. For a scathing example, watch the film "Boys in the Band." It's painful to watch one specific scene toward the end of the movie in which the self-loathing finally rears its ugly head. Though the movie is dated (1970), the message is clear and devastating even for men today.

Thankfully, we've come a long way, baby. So much has transpired in this country in terms of opening wide the door of acceptability and inclusion. Though there is still a way to go for gay people not being discriminated against and to enjoy the full civil rights enjoyed by other citizens, they can go a long, long way by accepting who they are and realizing that there's nothing wrong with them, only in some people's understanding and perception. The only way to change that throughout society is by being who they are and loving themselves. And that's *your* homework assignment for the rest of your life: be authentic, be real, and love yourself for all that you are.

## *What to do if...*

Being out and about in the gay community is very freeing. You feel unencumbered by doubts and issues and playing hide and seek with who you are. It's a wonderful feeling. Then, while in the gay part of town or a known gay business, you run into someone you either work with or a friend whom you've not come out to yet. Bam — reality hits you in the face. What do you do? What do you say? How do you explain being where you are? Does this mean the other person is gay or lesbian? Do you come out to them right on the spot? Are they going to be safe with your secret until you're comfortable with coming further out of the closet?

If there's one thing that will drain the blood from your face and turn your stomach to jelly, it's this situation — when you least expect it and aren't prepared for it. We all fantasize about this happening and dread the day it manifests. It doesn't happen often, but it might and you need to be prepared to step up to the plate and deal with it effectively and with grace. As discussed in earlier chapters, you want to manage your coming out process as best as possible. In the case of running into someone you know who has no idea that you're gay, how you handle the situation will impact future events.

> Pablo came up to the Men's Group meetings from Tijuana, Mexico as often as he could. A sweet and unassuming young man, he was reticent to talk about himself in front of the entire group, but enjoyed hearing what others had to say about their situations.
>
> I received a call from Pablo one day. He was very upset. It seems that he had decided to visit Hillcrest, the gay neighborhood in San Diego, during daylight hours. He was seen by some men he knew as they drove by in their car. Some of the men were relatives. As soon as they got back to Tijuana, they exposed him to his family, relatives, friends — and his wife.
>
> All hell had broken loose and his family was threatening him with being thrown out of the house and going to their parish Priest to have him excommunicated. What could he do? He'd never even had a chance to explain himself, everyone just assumed that his being in Hillcrest meant he was gay. It never occurred to him to ask his male friends and relatives what they were doing there.

Pablo thought that by being gay in a different city would be enough protection from anyone he knew finding out. He wasn't at that stage in his process where he was ready to come out to his wife and family members. Just as in Chapter 2 where Grady's secret life was exposed via printouts of his Internet chat sessions, Pablo was outed by others before he was ready. Fortunately, or unfortunately, his process was speeded up for him and he had no choice but to deal with the consequences. Pablo attended the group one more time, a year later. He kept silent the entire meeting, but I talked with him afterwards. He wouldn't divulge anything, just that he was okay. We never saw him again after that, so we have no idea how his life has fared since his outing.

So, you never know what circumstances will develop for you, but if you think about how things can happen serendipitously or you support Murphy's Law, do your homework and like a good Boy Scout: Be Prepared. Even though your primary mantra is "be yourself," there is a time and place for everything. Decide whether coming out to the person you've just run into is appropriate at that moment. Think about who they are and where they rate on your trust meter. Consider whether there will be negative ramifications if you come out to them and they're a co-worker, colleague, or client. If you do decide to disclose to them, make sure you get their promise that they'll not divulge this information to anyone else, that this is your process to manage. Ask them to maintain confidentiality and clearly define what that means.

Here's the other thing: What if you're with another gay man and you run into someone you know? Again, it's the same criteria. How you were with this man when you were spotted will determine your answer. If the two of you were just walking along and there was no intimacy involved, you'll answer one way. If you were doing anything that remotely suggested that the two of you are intimately linked, you may have a different answer. It's up to you. It's your life, so you call the shots as you see fit. Remember, people will talk unless you dialogue and set some boundaries.

You may decide to come out, as well as introduce your friend. Well before that happens, though, decide between you how you want that man associated with you: as an acquaintance, friend, co-worker, boyfriend, lover, life partner, or even an ex. Don't accidently expose your relationship for what it is if you're not ready.

To sum up, the gay community is not that much different than any other community: it's made up of people from all walks of life, all trying to thrive in their own ways. You are now becoming a part of that and you can integrate into it as much as you desire. The choice is yours.

# Chapter 10

# The Future

Frederick arrived for his intake interview literally looking like he'd seen a ghost: he was sweating, shaking like a leaf, tears in his eyes, and filled with fear. I'd never seen anything like it before.

Frederick was too terrified to say anything, but through my gently describing the Men's Group, how it functioned, the types of men attending and some of their stories, he began slowly unwinding the coiled spring within him.

It had taken Frederick incredible courage to come to this neighborhood and walk in broad daylight into the Gay Men's and Lesbian Community Center. He was so far removed from anything gay that just the thought of being around it reduced him to abject fear. He could barely talk, his mind numb. Admitting he was gay took almost everything he had in him.

An hour of discussion later, the weight lifted from his being was visible. Still rather scared, he was quite nervous about his future. He didn't want to lose his son, his wife seemed to initially be handling his coming out rather well but had her moments, and he had no idea what was in store for him. Were people going to hate him? Was he going to lose his family and friends? Would he keep his job? How would he survive?

Despite his fear, Frederick began coming to the Men's Group. With their considerable help, camaraderie, gatherings and forays into the gay social world, he began shedding his fear and we found out what a delight he was.

Time passed and Frederick fell in love with a group member, Bernard, who had been one of the original members. Bernard stepped away from the group feeling he'd been in it long enough. The two bought their first home together on, get this, Dorothy Way. (If you don't know, calling a person a "friend of Dorothy" refers to Dorothy in The Wizard of Oz. Judy Garland, who played Dorothy, is a huge gay icon and has had an immense gay following for decades. Thus, two gay men moving to "Dorothy Way" says unequivocally, "Yes, we're gay!")

Frederick has a wonderful relationship with his former wife, who is happily remarried, and his son, who astounded everyone by being a child violin prodigy. In 2009, he was accepted at age 18 into the Berklee College of Music in Boston.

Frederick and Bernard are still together and have moved into their second home. Over the years, they've hosted Married Men's Coming Out Group parties as a reunion for past members to catch up with each other, a means for new members to meet others who've been through the coming out process, and a chance to begin community building and networking.

The man who walked into the Community Center several years earlier is nowhere to be found. Frederick had truly come out and blossomed.

"The future belongs to those who believe in the beauty of their dreams…. The purpose of life, after all, is to live it, to taste experience to the utmost, to reach out eagerly and without fear for newer and richer experiences." Eleanor Roosevelt gave us those memorable words and I use them here as a jumping off point for the married men coming out who are reading these pages.

You dream of being who you truly are at heart, the real you, the authentic and genuine being who has the entire world before you to explore as you — the person you were born to be and express and share and delight in. No matter how frightening the prospect of coming out *appears* to be in your mind, you have the wherewithal to make it through. It is intrinsic to your being to not only survive, but thrive.

Once a married man has come out and gone through the process of claiming and owning his true identity, there is more work to be done. Just as we have all survived the challenges of our lives to live another day, the time comes when we can turn around and proffer a helping hand to those to follow in our footsteps.

The phenomenon of married men coming out is relatively new on the American landscape. Those who have come through the process over the last couple of decades are groundbreakers, pioneers. The leaders they had to emulate were those who forged the modern gay movement back in the 1940s, men and women who fought for civil protections and equality and recognition. And the struggle continues person by person, community by community, legislative bill by legislative bill.

It takes all kinds of people to enact a successful movement, working consistently, patiently, and long term. Those in the vanguard are like the men of the Married Men's Coming Out Group. Terrified as many of them were to acknowledge their true being, they did it in spite of obstacles, in spite of losing people, in spite of society's fear of homosexuality. They became the living embodiment of three things: a pioneer, a role model, and an educator.

I remember when I introduced this idea to the men. Few of them felt that I was speaking about them. They were just ordinary men striving to be themselves and lead a life of self-acceptance, peace, joy, and love. Yes, they'd been through a lot, but they were still too close to their journeys. They didn't see the courage it took them, the stamina, self-reflection, discipline, strength, patience, research, tears, surrender, integrity. They were just doing what they needed to do. Yet, that's what each had become: a pioneer, a role model, and an educator.

There are innumerable and remarkable ways in which people become LGBT pioneers, role models, and educators. They come from every field and background imaginable from Caitlyn Jenner to Michael Sam to politicians, academics, people in the military, church reformers, scientists, etc. It could be your next door neighbor, someone on the opposite side of the world, a veritable unknown to a highly visible personality. In some way, one of these people or even groups can touch your heart and mind that then brings about a shift within you, that lights your candle of expansiveness and illumination. You then have the chance to blossom and in time "pay it forward" by lighting someone else's candle.

## *On Being a Pioneer*

On one level, none of the men realized that this Men's Group was the first of its kind in the US, to anyone's knowledge. In 1992, it was revolutionary: a group to support and facilitate married men coming out? Amazing…unheard of…about time! Would any men show up?

About 12 men launched the original group. And they just kept coming in. Seventy some men out of a population of approximately 3 million in greater San Diego doesn't sound like much, but being the only such group in that city, over 70 men in a seven-year period is a lot. Since then, of course, similar groups have started up all over the country. These men got it all rolling.

The dynamics of support groups are relatively similar. With this group, it began as an issues-based platform, quickly moved on to emotional ramifications, and then solutions, growth, and goals. Issues covered included:

> self-esteem, loneliness, boundaries, attractiveness, age, AIDS, relationships (what they are, dynamics, what a person brings to a relationship (issues/baggage), why want one), lovers, male versus female, gay personality types, lesbians, dislike of gay people and culture, gay pride, homophobia, the media, portrayals of gays in our media, gays in the military, gays and politics, fathers and sons, acceptance/rejection, potential loss (of current identity, sanity, family, friends, jobs, home, property, religion, and community), children, the court system, custody, divorce, finances, personal history, patterns (emotional, mental, behavioral), emotions, personal space, going with the flow, change, Prozac, substance abuse, lifestyles, roles, what it means to be a man in today's society, being a family man (how to deal with children and gayness, children getting married and being invited to the wedding), developing a global (macro) perspective, disclosure, shame, confidentiality, guilt, needs, therapy, trust, paranoia, hate, hate as a family value from the religious right, self-loathing, insecurity, gay bars, where and how to meet people, promiscuity, sexual addiction, sexual practices, bi-sexuality, transvestites and transsexuals, socio-cultural myths and conventions, dating, gay-related clubs and associations, religion and spirituality, and love.

Emotional ramifications is where we spent much of our time. Many of the men were amazed at how emotional they could be in spite of the fact that they'd fallen right into the cultural trap about men being shut off from their emotions. With a number of these men, you would never guess they were gay. They were standard issue, mentally focused, emotionally suppressed guys. With time and caring support from the group, most of the men moved from their heads into their hearts and discovered a whole new side of themselves. Actually, they were getting reacquainted with a side of themselves that had been closed down from an early age. And with the release from their self-made confinements, they found a new level of freedom.

In order to not get sucked into emotional undertows, the group sought out creative, practical, and reasonable solutions to their challenges. They worked on their identity, who they had been and who they were becoming, what they were willing to let go of and what they were taking on. With that, they were then able to develop goals for themselves without becoming rigidly attached to outcomes. Instead, they wanted to remain flexible, something they'd felt they'd not been in their marriages. They didn't want to confine themselves again by re-constituting and transferring the heterosexual paradigm they'd formerly lived with into their new lifestyle. They were breaking free and creating their futures.

Pioneers within their own being, pioneers with each other, and pioneers in the wider community. They had no idea what they'd got themselves involved in or where it would take them, but they bravely took their first fledgling steps on a journey of a thousand miles, lighting the path for those to follow.

## *On Being a Role Model*

The second embodiment is that of role model. Again, many of the men from the group looked askance at me. A role model? Them? That was actually what I charged them with becoming. We don't exactly have a plethora of positive role models for married men who are coming out. What we have instead are scandals, obfuscation, denial, lawsuits, and plenty of lying. There are very few men we can name who have voluntarily come out and done it with respect and integrity.

A host of people have been outed, forcing them to publicly acknowledge that they're gay, but none have done it on their own without prompting or pressure. That's where the guys from the Men's Group came in and why they were and are so important. There are men of all ages who are looking for a man who comes out with dignity and is able to weather the struggles and controversy that can ensue. Here is one such role model:

James Edward "Jim" McGreevey (born August 6, 1957) is an American Democratic politician. He served as the 52nd Governor of New Jersey from January 15, 2002, until November 15, 2004, when he resigned from office. McGreevey coupled the announcement of his decision to resign with a public declaration of his homosexuality and an admission to having an extramarital affair with the man he had appointed homeland security adviser. McGreevey was the first and, to date, the only openly gay state governor in United States history.

McGreevey was criticized for appointing as homeland security adviser Golan Cipel, because he lacked experience or other qualifications for the position. In addition, Cipel could not gain a security clearance from the Federal government, as he was Israeli and not a U.S. citizen. McGreevey had met him in Israel during a trip there in 2000.

According to McGreevey in *The Confession*, *The Record* was the first newspaper to break the news of a relationship between McGreevey and Cipel. McGreevey brought up Cipel's name six weeks into his administration in a February 14, 2002, interview with The Record's editorial board at its offices saying: "We will not skimp on security. We actually brought on a security adviser from the Israel Defense Forces, probably the best in the world."

The interview prompted news investigation into Cipel's background. On February 21, The Record published a profile of Cipel, calling him a "sailor" and a "poet." The article stated, "Democrats close to the administration say McGreevey and Cipel have struck up a close friendship and frequently travel together," prompting McGreevey's own mother to confront him about his sexual orientation. Various media organizations sent reporters to Israel to ask questions about Cipel and his background.

In August 2002 at McGreevey's request, Cipel stepped down from his position as homeland security adviser.

On August 12, 2004, faced with threats from Cipel's lawyer Allen Lowy that Cipel would file a sexual harassment lawsuit against him in Mercer County Court, McGreevey announced at a press conference, "My truth is that I am a gay American." He also said that he had "engaged in an adult consensual affair with another man" (whom his aides immediately named as Cipel), and that he would resign effective November 15, 2004. New Jersey political circles had speculated about McGreevey's sexual orientation and questions about his relationship with Cipel had been alluded to in the media. McGreevey's announcement made him the first openly gay state governor in United States history. The Star-Ledger won the 2005 Pulitzer Prize for Breaking News Reporting for its "coverage of the resignation of New Jersey's governor after he announced he was gay and confessed to adultery with a male lover."

In September 2006, McGreevey published a memoir, written with assistance from ghostwriter David France. The memoir was entitled *The Confession*. McGreevey appeared on The Oprah Winfrey Show on September 19 to discuss and promote the book. It was the start of a two-month promotion of his memoir.

In *The Confession*, McGreevey described the duality of his life before he came out as gay: "As glorious and meaningful as it would have been to have a loving and sound sexual experience with another man, I knew I'd have to undo my happiness step by step as I began chasing my dream of a public career and the kind of 'acceptable' life that went with it. So, instead, I settled for the detached anonymity of bookstores and rest stops — a compromise, but one that was wholly unfulfilling and morally unsatisfactory."

Wikipedia<br>
February 17, 2009<br>
Wikipedia Foundation, Inc.<br>
http://en.wikipedia.org/wiki/Jim_McGreevey

McGreevey's story is what we usually hear about. At least he chose to publicly announce that he's gay before actually being outed by someone. Being in public office, he was surrounded by people who could "spin" the heck out of his story, which was going to be focused on his political aspirations. It's something we'd all do whether we're in the public eye or not. It's called damage control. For the purposes of this book, it's called managing your process. The truth of who you are needs to extend to being honest in all aspects of your life. Yes, you'll be guarded about what you disclose and when, but eventually, the whole you needs to step into the light. Remember your primary mantra: be yourself.

What McGreevey's story provides is an example of how one person dealt with their coming out, the effect it's had on their life and others, and what can be done to shed a positive light on a subject with which thousands of men are dealing. There are positive and negative role models, and we dearly need positive ones that will give men hope and provide a benchmark upon which they can set their sights and goals.

Conversely, those who have come out and established themselves as gay men can turn around and be role models. They've attained the life experience required to share what they've learned and provide insight into the process from first steps onward. Life will go on no matter what and it helps to have guidance and at least one supportive companion along the way. It's very similar to the philosophy in the movie *Pay It Forward*. Married men who have come through the process of coming out were given a gift by those who were there to support them. Now it's time to pay it forward by being the gift itself — a role model for others.

## *On Being an Educator*

We have narrowly defined parameters when it comes to a definition of what a "man" is: he enjoys sports and roughhousing, is left brain (analytical, aggressive doesn't display but a very small range of emotions), isn't "touchy/feely," doesn't cry, isn't into the performing arts, wears only certain colors, must be in control of self and others, it's okay to resort to violence to guard honor or pride, okay to objectify women, okay to play the field even when married (double standard), feels sex between and with two women is great but strictly taboo between two men.

In this new millennium, that's all being challenged. Young people are the ones really changing established role parameters by blurring the lines of what's considered acceptable and how one is defined. Pockets still exist of clear delineation, yet even those are being somewhat modified to reflect shifting cultural interests, fads, and movements. The change is slow to come, but it is inexorably moving through society just as the ocean erodes the shoreline.

One of the components of change involves education. Each of us begins as a student of life and at some point we become the teacher. The dynamic of student and teacher works symbiotically as we move back and forth between them, one moment one, the other moment the other. It is a humbling process that allows us to move beyond ego to a middle point of balance. And, life being the classroom that it is, we're given continuous opportunities to wear both hats interchangeably day to day throughout our lives. As the student, we are given the chance to ask for help and guidance; as the teacher, to be available to offer both. The student becomes the teacher becomes the student becomes the teacher becomes the student in an endless cycle of becoming — a progressive blossoming.

> Russell joined the Men's Group in the late 1990s. He was one of the rougher individuals to join the group. I was concerned that because of his background he might not find the support he was looking for.
>
> Russell had had a tough life. He'd grown up poor and learned to con his way through all sorts of situations using the street smarts he'd acquired. He dropped out of high school when he found illegal means for making a lot of money. He'd been in plenty of fights and had a glass eye, compliments of one brawl he'd been in, a prominent scar running down his forehead, across his eye, and down his cheek. His life involved selling and using drugs, moving items through the black market, and periods of drunken stupor and/or drug haze.
>
> That was then. When friends of his starting dying from AIDS, he realized he needed to clean up his life or he could end up with AIDS, too. He started by enrolling in AA and NA. A year or so into that, he asked to join the Men's Group as he'd come to the conclusion that part of the reason he was so hard on his wife was because he was in denial about who he really is. She, too, was into drugs and the potential of attaining AIDS via needle exchange didn't faze her, but it did Russell. He needed to drastically turn his life around.
>
> A year went by and Russell had stuck to his program and had stayed clean and sober. He'd also attained a divorce. What he was very energized about now was helping other people to clean up their lives. He'd taken a hard look at his life and realized that he was the one who had made the choices that had brought him to his current circumstances. Many of his choices had taken him down a road that led to a dead end — literally. Now his life was so much different. He felt as though he'd been given a second chance. And if he could do it, then others could — and he'd lead by example. He'd educate people.

Not everyone can be as driven as Russell was, but he had a lot at stake. The wonderful thing is that he realizes how life works: you learn, you teach; you take and you give. It's a natural inflow and outflow.

Being an educator doesn't need to be a formal scenario. It can happen at any moment in any situation. It's a matter of just being aware and open to the flow of energy and dynamics between people. If you end up going into a situation thinking you're going to teach people and you're open to learning something in return, that's exactly what will happen. You don't need to have an epiphany, though that may happen now and then. Learning, for the most part, is a very subtle process. The same with educating. Sometimes it's the simplest of expressions that is the most meaningful for those on the learning end. And you don't always know which subject you'll be teaching — or learning — about. It will just happen, for you and with you.

The important factor about education is ensuring that it is flourishing in all arenas. There is a lot of misinformation and ignorance activated in the world, especially when it comes to something like homosexuality. Married men who find themselves at a point where they can no longer stay in their marriages and pretend to be something they're not are craving help. As a person who has conquered the challenges of coming out with the support of others, pay it forward and help those needing a helping hand — be their lifeline to a more authentic life.

> "Our deepest fear is not that we are inadequate.
> Our deepest fear is that we are
> powerful beyond measure.
> It is our light, not our darkness, that most frightens us.
> We ask ourselves, who am I to be brilliant, gorgeous,
> talented, and fabulous?
> Actually, who are you not to be?
> You are a child of God.
> Your playing small doesn't serve the world.
> There's nothing enlightened about shrinking
> so that other people won't feel insecure around you.
> We are all meant to shine, as children do.
> We are born to make manifest
> the glory of God that is within us.
> It's not just in some of us, it's in everyone.
> And as we let our own light shine,
> we unconsciously give other people permission
> to do the same.
> As we are liberated from our own fear,
> our presence automatically liberates others."
>
> ~ Marianne Williamson

## *Becoming a Part of the Global Community*

If there is one thing to be learned through this book, it's that you don't live in a vacuum, but in an intricate and dynamic web of interconnectedness. Everything you think, say, and do ramifies the world around you. You are not only a part of the microcosm, but the macrocosm. You may think that coming out is one small act in a world teeming with activities overwhelming in their scope. What, then, do you matter to the whole? Everything — because the greatest gift you can give anyone is the truest essence of yourself. In a world of illusions and delusions, imagine the gift you have to offer.

The global community isn't just the gay community as it's found around the world. It's the community of all humanity, each of us an integral component of the whole investing all of life with our particular expression of humanness. Ultimately, whether you're gay or straight doesn't really matter except in the context of the actions you take that uplift humanity. Your input, your creativity, your honesty, your authenticity, your investment in life gives hope to those who need a hand up in the world.

What you do from day to day as a man of authenticity will radiate out into the world around you. If you think globally and act locally, you have the capacity to be an agent of change. No matter where you are in the world, people will gravitate to you as they'll recognize the energy signature of an authentic human being. You then have the chance to bring your truth into the clear light of day. No more hiding, no more double life — just honesty.

Don't be afraid to tell your story. It's hard for men to share the stories that show their vulnerability and that express the pain of having had experiences that aren't considered "manly." They don't support the myth that men are supposed to tough it out. How are we to grow beyond our pain if we continue to hold it in and mask it? There truly is no shame to be had except by those afraid of their own feelings. By your sharing, you create a safe place to be human, to express a full range of feelings that are native and essential to being a man. By accessing your full being, you'll discover what it means to be free. You'll be a transformed man.

To quote Gandhi, "Be the change you want to see in the world." Don't wait for someone else to create change, be the change you seek by truly being yourself. Be a trendsetter in that respect and watch the world around you reflect back to you a greater version of you and itself. Be a pioneer, a role model, and an educator. You never know who will benefit from the sharing of your life experience. You may save a life by it. That's how important each of us is in the world.

The web of interconnectedness is always present and activated, so never think that you are an island in a sea of uncaring and over-busy humanity. Rather, and significantly so, you are a beacon. The world needs you and what you have to offer. Become the man you were born to be.

> "A journey of a thousand miles begins with a single step."
> ~ Confucius

> "Whatever you can do or dream, you can begin it. Boldness has genius, power, and magic in it."
> ~ Goethe

# Resources

## Books

- Barbetta, Dr. Francine, *A Pebble in His Shoe: The Diary of a Straight Spouse*. Xlibris, 2008.

- Browder, Brenda Stone, *On the Up and Up: A Survival Guide for Women Living with Men on the Down Low*. Kensington, 2005.

- Buxton, Amity Pierce, *The Other Side of the Closet: The Coming Out Crises for Spouses and Families*, 1st ed. Wiley, 2008.

- Buxton, Amity Pierce and R.L. Pinely, *Unseen-Unheard: Straight Spouses from Trauma to Transformation*. 2nd ed. CCB Publishing, 2013.

- Gochros, Jean S., *When Husbands Come Out of the Closet*. Routledge, 1989.

- Grever, Carol, *My Husband is Gay: A Woman's Guide to Surviving the Crisis*. Crossing Press, 2012.

- Grever, Carol and Deborah Bowman, *When Your Spouse Comes Out: A Straight Mate's Recovery Manual*. Routledge, 2012.

- Kaye, Bonnie M., *Is He Straight: A Checklist for Women Who Wonder*. iUniverse, 2000.

- Kaye, Bonnie M., *Straight Wives: Shattered Lives*. Bonnie Kaye Services, 2007.

- King, J.L., *Coming Up from the Down Low: The Journey to Acceptance, Healing, and Honest Love*. Harmony, 2007.

- Klein, Fritz and Thomas Schwartz, *Bisexual and Gay Husbands: Their Stories, Their Words*. 11th ed. Routledge, 2014.


- Clemons, Rick, *Frankly My Dear, I'm Gay: The Late Bloomers Guide to Coming Out*. Motivational Press, 2016.

- Eichberg, Rob, *Coming Out: An Act of Love: An Inspiring Call to Action for Gay Men, Lesbians, and Those Who Care*. Dutton, 1990.

- Isay, Richard A., *Becoming Gay: The Journey to Self-Acceptance*. Vintage, 2010.

- Kaufman, Gershen and Lev Raphael, *Coming Out of Shame: Transforming Gay and Lesbian Lives*. Main Street Books, 1996.
- Kaye, Bonnie and Doug Dittmer, *Over the Cliff: Gay Husbands in Straight Marriages*. 1st ed. CCB Publishing, 2011.
- Marcus, Eric, *Is it a Choice? Answers to 300 of the Most Frequently Asked Questions about Gay and Lesbian People*. 3rd ed. HarperOne, 2005.
- Marcus, Eric, *What If Someone I Know is Gay? Answers to What It Means to Be Gay and Lesbian*. Simon Pulse, 2007.
- McNaught, Brian, *Now That I'm Out, What Do I Do? Thoughts on Living Deliberately*. 1st ed. St. Martin's Press, 2011.
- McNaught, Brian, *On Being Gay: Thoughts on Family, Faith, and Love*. St. Martin's Griffin, 1989.
- Signorile, Michelangelo, *Outing Yourself: How to Come Out as a Lesbian or Gay to Your Family, Friends, and Co-Workers*. 1st ed. Random House, 2011.

- Achtemeier, Mark, *The Bible's Yes to Same-Sex Marriage: An Evangelical's Change of Heart*. Westminster John Knox Press, 2014.
- Bouldrey, Brian, *Wrestling with the Angel: Faith and Religion in the Lives of Gay Men*. Riverhead Hardcover, 1995.
- Johnson, Toby, *Gay Spirituality: The Role of Gay Identity in the Transformation of Human Consciousness*. Lethe Press, 2004.
- Kurek, Timothy, *The Cross in the Closet*. 3rd ed. Green Bridge Press, 2014.
- Marin, Andrew, *Love is an Orientation: Elevating the Conversation with the Gay Community*. IVP Books, 2009.
- Pearce, C.S., *This We Believe: The Christian Case for Gay Civil Rights*. Pomona Press, 2012.
- Robinson, Gene, *God Believes in Love: Straight Talk about Gay Marriage*. Vintage, 2012.
- Rogers, Jack, *Jesus, The Bible, and Homosexuality, Revised and Expanded Edition: Explode the Myths, Heal the Church*. Westminster John Knox Press, 2010.

- Signorile, Michelangelo, *It's Not Over: Getting Beyond Tolerance, Defeating Homophobia, and Winning True Equality*. Houghton Mifflin Harcourt, 2015.
- Smid, John, *Ex'd Out: How I Fired the Shame Committee*. CreateSpace Independent Publishing Platform, 2012.
- Venn-Brown, Anthony, *A Life of Unlearning: A Preacher's Struggle with His Homosexuality, Church, and Faith*. Personal Success Australia, 2015.
- White, Mel, *Stranger at the Gate: To be Gay and Christian in America*. Simon & Schuster, 2015.
- Wink, Walter, *Homosexuality and Christian Faith: Questions of Conscience for the Churches*. Augsburg Fortress Publishers, 1999.
- Yarhouse, Mark A., *Homosexuality and the Christian: A Guide for Parents, Pastors, and Friends*. Bethany House Publishers, 2010.


- Burda, Joan M., *Estate Planning for Same-Sex Couples*. 2nd ed. American Bar Association, 2013.
- Clifford, Denis and Frederick Hertz, Emily Doskow, *A Legal Guide for Lesbian & Gay Couples*. 17th ed. Nolo, 2014.
- Hertz, Frederick and Emily Doskow, *Making It Legal: A Guide to Same-Sex Marriage, Domestic Partnership & Civil Unions*. 3rd ed. Nolo, 2014.
- Kranz, Rachel and Tim Cusick, *Gay Rights* (Library in a Book). Facts on File, 2005.
- Lustig, Harold L., *4 Steps for Financial Security for Lesbian and Gay Couples: Expert Advice for Reducing Your Tax Burden, Increasing Your Wealth, and Protecting Each Other*. Ballantine Books, 2010.
- Munoz, Jose Esteban, Cruising Utopia: The Then and There of Queer Futurity (Sexual Cultures). New York University Press, 2009.
- Rauch, Jonathan, *Gay Marriage: Why it is Good for Gays, Good for Straights, and Good for America*. Times Books, 2005.
- Schleicher, Dennis J., *Forbidden Love with a Married Man: E-mail Diaries*. AuthorHouse, 2006.
- Sember, Brette McWhorter, *Gay & Lesbian Medical Rights: How to Protect Yourself, Your Partner, and Your Family*. Career Press, 2006.

- Sullivan, Andrew, *Same-Sex Marriage: Pro and Con*. Vintage, 2009.
- Warner, Michael, *The Trouble with Normal: Sex, Politics, and the Ethics of Queer Life*. Harvard University Press, 1999.
- Yoshino, Kenji, *Covering: The Hidden Assault on Our Civil Rights*. Radom House, 2011.
- Bereznai, Steven, *Gay and Single…Forever?: 10 Things Every Gay Guy Looking for Love (and not finding it) Needs to Know*. De Capo Press, 2009.
- Hazel, Dann, *Moving On: The Gay Man's Guide for Coping When a Relationship Ends*. Kensington, 1999.
- Isensee, Rik, *Love Between Men: Enhancing Intimacy and Resolving Conflict in Gay Relationships*. Backinprint.com, 2005.
- Kaminsky, Neil, *When It's Time to Leave Your Lover: A Guide for Gay Men*. Routledge, 2014.
- Kort, Joe, *Ten Smart Things Gay Men Can Do to Improve Their Lives*. Alyson Publications, 2003.
- Marcus, Eric, *The Male Couple's Guide: Finding a Man, Building a Home, Building a Life*. Harper Perennial, 1999.
- Nutter, Chris, *The Way Out: The Gay Man's Guide to Freedom No Matter if You're in Denial, Closeted, Half In, Half Out, Just Out or Been Around the Block*. HCI, 2010.
- Pezzote, Angelo, *Straight Acting: Gay Men, Masculinity and Finding True Love*. Kensington, 2008.
- Price, Patrick, *Husband Hunting Made Easy: And Other Miracles for the Modern Gay Man*. St. Martin's Griffin, 1998.
- Silverstein, Charles, *The Joy of Gay Sex, Revised & Expanded*. 3rd ed. HarperCollins e-books, 2009.
- Singleton, Dave, *The Mandates: 25 Rules for Successful Gay Dating*. Harmony, 2007.
- Sullivan, Jim, *Boyfriend 101: A Gay Guy's Guide to Dating, Romance, and Finding True Love*. Villard, 2003.
- Tessina, Tina, *Gay Relationships for Men and Women: How to Find Them, How to Improve Them, How to Make Them Last*. Tarcher/Penguin, 1989.

- Alvarez, Erick, *Muscle Boys: Gay Gym Culture*. Routledge, 2008.
- Amaechi, John, *Man in the Middle*. 1st ed. ESPN, 2007.
- Fellows, Will, *Farm Boys: Lives of Gay Men from the Rural Midwest*. University of Wisconsin Press, 1998.
- Louganis, Greg, *Breaking the Surface*. Sourcebooks, 2006.
- Simmons, Roy, *Out of Bounds: Coming Out of Sexual Abuse, Addiction, and My Life of Lies in the NFL Closet*. Da Capo Press, 2006.
- Tewkbury, Mark, *Inside Out: Straight Talk from a Gay Jock*. Wiley, 2006.
- Tuaolo, Esera, *Alone in the Trenches: My Life as a Gay Man in the NFL*. Sourcebooks, 2007.
- Warren, Patricia Nell, *The Lavender Locker Room: 3000 Years of Great Athletes Whose Sexual Orientation was Different*. Wildcat Press, 2013.
- Woog, Dan, *Jocks 2: True Stories of America's Gay Male Athletes*. Alyson Books, 2002.


- Adams, Jon Robert, *Male Armor: The Soldier-Hero in Contemporary American Culture*. University of Virginia Press, 2012.
- Lemer, Bronson, *The Last Deployment: How a Gay, Hammer-Swinging Twentysomething Survived a Year in Iraq*. University of Wisconsin Press, 2011.
- McGowan, Jeffrey, *Major USA, Major Conflict: One Gay Man's Life in the Don't-Ask-Don't Tell Military*. Broadway, 2007.
- Pasfield, Scott, *Gay in America*. Welcome Books, 2011.
- Savage, Dan, *It Gets Better: Coming Out, Overcoming Bullying, and Creating a Life Worth Living*. Plume, 2011.
- Seefried, Josh, *Our Time: Breaking the Silence of "Don't Ask, Don't Tell."* Penguin Books, 2011.


- Amani, Khalil, *Hip-Hop Homophobes: Origins & Attitudes Towards Gays and Lesbians in Hip Hop Culture; as Perpetuated by Rappers, Thugs, Athletes, Reggae Rastas & Religionists; Essays on the 3,000 Year Old Polemic Against Homosexuality; A Religious Hoax*. iUniverse, Inc., 2007.

- Bailey, Mark, *Poetry from the Heart*. Amazon Digital Services, Inc., 2011.
- Cash, Thomas F., *Body Image: A Handbook of Science, Practice, and Prevention*. 2nd ed. The Guilford Press, 2012.
- Isensee, Rik, *Reclaiming Your Life: The Gay Man's Guide to Recovery from Abuse, Addictions, and Self-defeating Behavior*. Backprint.com, 2005.
- Lafair, Sylvia, *Don't Bring It to Work: Breaking the Family Patterns that Limit Success*. Jossey-Bass, 2009.
- Shelton, Michael, *Gay Men and Substance Abuse: A Basic Guide for Addicts and Those Who Care for Them*. Hazelden, 2011.
- Wilhelm, James J., *Gay and Lesbian Poetry: An Anthology from Sappho to Michelangelo*. Routledge, 2014.
- Winfeld, Liz, *Straight Talk about Gays in the Workplace: Creating an Inclusive, Productive Environment for Everyone in Your Organization*. Routledge, 2014.


- Barlow, Jack, *Kings are No Trouble. It's the Queens. A Humorous View of Gay Men and What Makes Them Tick*. PublishAmerica, 2010.
- Callahan, Rory, *How Can We Have Sex if You Don't Call? Gay Dating and Other Horrors*. CreateSpace Independent Publishing Platform, 2012.
- Davies, Steven Paul and Simon Callow, *Out at the Movies: A History of Gay Cinema*. Oldcastle Books, 2008.
- Ford, Michael Thomas, *The Little Book of Neuroses: Ongoing Trials of My Queer Life*. Alyson Books, 2001.
- Jordan, Leslie, *My Trip Down the Pink Carpet*. Gallery Books, 2008.
- Kichi, John, *Civil Unrest: Scenes from a Gay Marriage*. Pyga Media, 2012.
- Michaelmas, Joshua, *The Gay Man's Instruction Manual: Advice for a Happier, Healthier, Wealthier, Smarter and Sexier You!* Amazon Digital Services, Inc., 2012.
- Price, Patrick, *Drama Queen: The Gay Man's Guide to an Uncomplicated Life*. St. Martin's Griffin, 2001.

- Rauch, Karen and Jeff Fessler, *When Drag is Not a Car Race: An Irreverent Dictionary of Over 400 Gay and Lesbian Words and Phrases*. Touchstone, 1997.
- Reuter, Donald, *Gaydar: The Ultimate Insider Guide to the Gay Sixth Sense*. Crown Publishers, 2002.
- Riglioso, Raymond, *Gay Men and the New Way Forward*. Mond Press, 2015.
- Rosenberg, Corey, *The Gay Man's Guide to Timeless Manners and Proper Etiquette*. Chelsea Station Editions, 2011.
- Smith, Travis, *Guide for the Modern Bear*. Modern Bear, 2012.
- Stewart, William, *Cassell's Queer Companion: A Dictionary of Lesbian and Gay Life and Culture*. Cassell, 1999.

**Internet**
- List of LGBT centers in the U.S.: www.lgbtcenters.org/Centers/find-a-center.aspx
- LGBTQ Nation: www.facebook.com/lgbtqnation
- Gay and Lesbian Victory Institute – Building successful LGBT leaders: www.victoryinstitute.org/out_officials/view_all
- LGBT and LGBT-Gay Friendly Business Directory: glbtdirectory.com/
- Straight Spouse Network: www.straightspouse.org
- Lambda Legal – Pending Marriage Equality Cases: www.lambdalegal.org/pending-marriage-equality-cases
- Gay Christian Online: www.gaychristianonline.org/index.html
- Christian Gays: www.christiangays.com/index.shtml
- Inclusive Orthodoxy: www.inclusiveorthodoxy.org/
- Married Man coming out blog: www.mytripout.com/
- Soulforce: www.soulforce.org
- Colage – People with a Lesbian, Gay, Bisexual, Transgender or Queer Parent: www.colage.org

- Empty Closet: www.emptycloset.com
- Gay Parent Magazine: www.gayparentmag.com/
- Gay Fathers Association of Seattle: www.gfas.org/
- Guy Dads: guydads.blogspot.com/2006/10/coming-out.html
- PFLAG (Parents, Families, and Friends of Lesbians and Gays: www.pflag.org

- Australasian Married Gays: https://groups.yahoo.com/neo/groups/ozmarriedgays/info
- BMMG (Bi/Gay Married Men's Group): www.socialweb.net/Events/51638.lasso
- Gay Married Men's Association of Washington, D.C.: www.meetup.com/GAy-Married-Mens-Association-GAMMA-of-DC/
- Bi Men Network: www.bimen.org
- Gay Men's Health Concerns: http://menshealth.about.com/od/gayhealth/a/Gay_Concerns.htm
- FS Magazine (the Gay Men's Health Charity): www.gmfa.org.uk/fsmag
- Healthy Gay Lifestyles: http://healthygaylifestyles.com/
- Men's Health Magazine: https://secure.rodale.com/webapp/wcs/stores/servlet/OaeEntryPage?storeId=10057&oae&mktOfferId=HLH60107&keycode=I3EA0D01

- YouTube: Gay Pride www.youtube.com/results?search_query=gay+pride&oq=gay+pride&gs_l=youtube.3..0l10.13090.13589.0.14084.5.4.0.1.1.0.125.420.1j3.4.0...0.0...1ac.1.D9mcakz1Wdk
- YouTube: It Gets Better: www.youtube.com/watch?v=7IcVyvg2Qlo
- (There are many extraordinary, heart-wrenching, and uplifting videos to watch.)

- www.CEOptions.com
- http://en.wikipedia.org/wiki/List_of_LGBT_holidays
- http://gaymarriage.procon.org

## Movies:

- A comprehensive list of movies and TV series that are gay-themed or have gay characters; with plot/story descriptions: www.gaycelluloid.com/
- Netflix: check throughout the various genres

# Appendix A: Gender Identification Options

In February of 2014, Facebook expanded their initial designations of "male" or "female" when users identified themselves in their personal profiles. The list below is not their complete list, but will give you a sense of just where humanity is in terms of self-identification. One person commented in a blog that the list was great, but was still missing the designation she was looking for: human. Ah, well....

1. Agender
2. Androgyne
3. Androgynous
4. Bigender
5. Cis *
6. Cisgender
7. Cis Female
8. Cis Male
9. Cis Man
10. Cis Woman
11. Cisgender Female
12. Cisgender Male
13. Cisgender Man
14. Cisgender Woman
15. Female to Male (FTM)
16. FTM
17. Gender Fluid
18. Gender Nonconforming
19. Gender Questioning
20. Gender Variant
21. Genderqueer
22. Intersex
23. Male to Female (MTF)
24. MTF
25. Neither
26. Neutrois
27. Non-binary
28. Other
29. Pangender
30. Trans
31. Trans*
32. Trans Female
33. Trans* Female
34. Trans Male
35. Trans* Male
36. Trans Man
37. Trans* Man
38. Trans Person
39. Trans* Person
40. Trans Woman
41. Trans* Woman
42. Transfeminine
43. Transgender
44. Transgender Female
45. Transgender Male
46. Transgender Man
47. Transgender Person
48. Transgender Woman
49. Transmasculine
50. Transsexual
51. Transsexual Female
52. Transsexual Male
53. Transsexual Man
54. Transsexual Person
55. Transsexual Woman
56. Two-Spirit

(http://abcnews.go.com/blogs/headlines/2014/02/heres-a-list-of-58-gender-options-for-facebook-users/)

---

* Cisgender has its origin in the Latin-derived prefix cis-, meaning "on this side of," which is an antonym for the Latin-derived prefix trans-, meaning "across from" or "on the other side of." http://en.wikipedia.org/wiki/Cisgender

# Appendix B: Archetypes

Many of these "archetypes" may appear to be nothing but general or second tier personality characteristics or even job descriptions. When considered more deeply, though, they are actually a distinct archetype as they have become — whether consciously or unconsciously recognized — an intrinsic expression of our daily behavior. Oftentimes, the job positions we hold also identify the primary archetype by which we can define ourselves or by which we characterize others. For many of us, we move in and out of a number of archetypes throughout our day with several more prominent than others and finally, one that can be considered our umbrella archetype. It is important to note that we have the ability to change archetypes, especially the one that better resonates with our deepest sense of self: our authentic being.

- Ace
- Actor
- Addict
- Adventurer
- Advisor
- Advocate
- Aesthetic
- Alarmist
- Ambulance Chaser
- Anal Retentive
- Anarchist
- Angel
- Antagonist
- Anthropologist
- Antichrist
- Archeologist
- Architect
- Archivist
- Artist
- Ass Kicker
- Athlete
- Authority
- Average Person
- Bad Boy
- Bachelor
- Barbarian
- Bastard
- Best Friend
- Big Brother
- Big Spender
- Black Sheep
- Body Guard
- Bootlegger
- Boozer
- Boss
- Boy Next Door
- Boy Toy
- Brain
- Breadwinner
- Bum
- Bumbling Professor
- Bumpkin
- Bungler
- Busybody
- Capitalist
- Captain
- Caretaker
- Catalyst
- Celebrity
- Chameleon

- Champion
- Charlatan
- Charmer
- Chaperone
- Cheerleader
- Child
- Class Clown
- Clod
- Coach
- Comic
- Complainer
- Composer
- Con
- Conductor
- Connoisseur
- Conspirator
- Controller
- Counselor
- Coward
- Cowboy
- Critic
- Danseur Noble
- Dare Devil
- Demon
- Devil
- Derelict
- Destroyer
- Devotee
- Dictator
- Dilettante
- Director
- Do-gooder
- Dominatrix
- Doormat
- Drama King
- Dreamer
- Drill Sergeant
- Drunk
- Eccentric
- Ecologist
- Economist
- Educator
- Effete
- Egomaniac

- Engineer
- Entrepreneur
- Escape Artist
- Evangelist
- Everyman
- Executive
- Executioner
- Extremist
- Faddist
- Failure
- Fair-haired Child
- Farmer
- Father
- Fighter
- Firstborn
- Flirt
- Follower
- Fool
- Freeloader
- Fugitive
- Futurist
- Gatekeeper
- Geezer
- Genius
- G.I. Joe
- Giver
- God
- Good Sport
- Gopher
- Gorgon
- Gossip
- Gourmet
- Grandparent
- Grouch/Grump
- Groupie
- Guardian
- Guide
- Guru
- Healer
- Hell Raiser
- He-man
- Hen-pecked
- Hermit
- Hero

- Home Wrecker
- Hotshot
- Huckster
- Humanitarian
- Humble Servant
- Humorist
- Hunter
- Hypochondriac
- Iconoclast
- Idiot
- Illuminator
- Impersonator
- Impresario
- Incompetent
- Industrialist
- Innocent
- Innovator
- Instigator
- Intellectual
- Inventor
- Jack-of-all-trades
- Jerk
- Jock
- Journeyman
- Judge
- Junkie
- Juvenile Delinquent
- Killer
- King
- Knight
- Know-it-all
- Kook
- Lady's man
- Leach
- Leader
- Leatherneck
- Lecher
- Lecturer
- Little Napoleon
- Lobbyist
- Loner
- Lord
- Loser
- Lost One
- Lounge Lizard
- Lover/Casanova
- Lush
- Maestro
- Magician
- Magnate
- Maniac
- Manic
- Manipulator
- Marketer
- Martyr
- Masochist
- Master
- Master Planner
- Mediator
- Meddler
- Mercenary
- Miser
- Misogynist
- Model/Mannequin
- Moderator
- Mogul
- Monitor
- Mover & Shaker
- Mystic
- Nag
- Narcissist
- Native
- Naturalist
- Navigator
- Nazi
- Neanderthal
- Necromancer
- Negotiator
- Nerd
- Nitpicker
- Noble
- Nomad
- Oakie
- Observer
- Ogre
- Opportunist
- Orchestrator
- Organizer

- Orphan
- Outsider
- Outcast
- Pacifist
- Pack Rat
- Pacesetter
- Parent
- Pariah
- Partier
- Patriarch
- Patriot
- Patron
- Patsy
- Peacekeeper
- Performer
- Pervert
- Philanthropist
- Philosopher
- Phobic
- Pimp
- Pioneer
- Pirate
- Planner
- Playboy
- Politician
- Populist
- Pothead
- Pragmatist
- Predator
- Preppie
- Pretender
- Priest
- Prick
- Prince
- Prisoner
- Procrastinator
- Prodigal Child
- Producer
- Professor
- Promoter
- Prophet
- Proselytizer
- Protagonist
- Provocateur
- Psychopath
- Pundit
- Puppet
- Pushover
- Quack
- Rapist
- Rebel
- Recluse
- Renegade
- Renaissance Person
- Reporter
- Rescuer
- Researcher
- Revolutionary
- Ringleader
- Risk Taker
- Rival
- Rocker
- Romantic
- Roustabout
- Rubbernecker
- Ruler
- Sadist
- Sage
- Saint
- Salesman
- Savant
- Savior
- Scapegoat
- Schemer
- Scholar
- Scientist
- Scribe
- Seeker
- Seer
- Segregationist
- Sensationalist
- Sentimentalist
- Shaman
- Shepard
- Slave
- Sleuth
- Slob
- Sneak

- Snob
- Social Architect
- Social Climber
- Spendthrift
- Spiritualist
- Spoiler
- Soldier
- Spy
- Star
- Stoic
- Straight Arrow
- Strategist
- Strong & Silent
- Student
- Sycophant
- Tagalong
- Taker
- Tattler
- Teacher
- Techie
- Tempter
- Therapist
- Thinker
- Tightwad
- Traditionalist
- Traveler
- Trickster
- Troublemaker
- Tyrant
- Underdog
- Universalist
- Untouchable
- Upstart/Usurper
- User
- Vagabond
- Veteran
- Victim
- Villain
- Visionary
- Volunteer
- Voyeur
- Waif
- Wanderer
- Warrior
- Weakling
- Weasel
- Whiner
- Whiz
- Whore
- Widower
- Wild Man
- Wino
- Wrangler
- Yahoo
- Yuppie
- Zealot

For some fun, this website lists the "real" meaning of men's names: www.thegloss.com/fashion/the-meaning-of-mens-names-from-a-to-z/

# Appendix C: Lexicon of Gay Archetypes

- Bear
- Beginner
- Binational Couple
- Bisexual
- Bottom
- Bug chaser
- Butch
- Chaser
- Chicken Delight
- Closet Case
- Cross Dresser
- Cub
- Daddy
- Diva
- Drag King
- Drag Queen
- Drag Top
- Ex-Gay
- Fag
- Fag Hag
- Fag Stag
- Femme
- Fluffer
- Fresh Flesh
- Friend of Dorothy
- FTM (female-to-male)
- Gay
- Gay Curious
- Gift Giver
- Grower
- Heterophobe
- Homophile
- Homophobe
- Homosexual
- Judy
- Leatherman
- Metrosexual
- MTF (male-to-female)
- Newbie
- Otter
- Partner
- Queen
- Queer
- S & M-er
- Second Generation Gay
- Silver Bear
- Silver Daddy
- Size Queen
- Stromo
- Top
- Transphobic
- Transgendered
- Transsexual
- Transvestite
- Trick
- Twink
- Two-Spirit
- Versatile Bottom
- Versatile Top
- Voguer
- Wolf

# About the Author

**David Christel** was bitten by the theatre bug at age 10, which eventually led to his moving to New York City at age 21 to pursue a career in dance. He worked with numerous luminaries in the dance field, as well as in opera, music, television, and theatre. He has appeared on PBS Great Performances, taught at many well-known schools, and traveled extensively throughout Europe and Central, South, and North America.

Upon retiring from dance in 1986, he was hired by a computer-based training company and either worked on or led projects for clients ranging from American Airlines to Halliburton Oil Company, NASA/Lockheed, Northern Telecom, NYNEX, Fireman's Fund, Boeing/McDonald-Douglas, and the Top Gun School when it was still located north of San Diego. David also taught offices in Canada and throughout the U.S. in computer-based training methodology, design, technical writing, and on-line course authoring.

In 1982, he began working with Persons With AIDS (PWAs) in New York and upon moving to San Diego, co-founded the AIDS Response Wholistic Health Program at the LGBT Community Center. He continued working with PWAs and their families, as well as facilitating numerous support and therapy groups and leading seminars in identity building for people in recovery from substance abuse.

David has been an editor, ghost writer, and book coach for over 20 years. He currently lives in Nevada with his partner.

**Other books by David Christel —**

Convergence of Being –
Awakening to the Interconnection of You, Me, and We

Now What?
One Man's Search for a Father

Stimulus Addicted –
America Adrenalizing Out of Control

**Books in the Pipeline —**

The Black Sheep Imperative –
Understanding the Black Sheep in Families
and How They Save Us from Ourselves

Clarissa's Flight
*A children's novel*

A Life of 2 x 4's to the Head –
Wake-up Calls and What to Do About Them

www.ingramcontent.com/pod-product-compliance
Lightning Source LLC
Chambersburg PA
CBHW021402290426
44108CB00010B/349